Approaches to Homer

Approaches to Homer

Edited by Carl A. Rubino and Cynthia W. Shelmerdine

 University of Texas Press, Austin

International Standard Book Number 0-292-70361-9
Library of Congress Catalog Card Number 81-52859
Copyright © 1983 by the University of Texas Press
Printed in the United States of America

First Edition, 1983

Requests for permission to reproduce material from this work
should be sent to Permissions, University of Texas Press, Box
7819, Austin, Texas 78712.

For reasons of economy and speed, this volume has been
printed from camera-ready copy furnished by the editors, who
assume full responsibility for its contents.

Contents

Acknowledgments

The essays collected in this volume had their origins in a symposium and lecture series held during Spring 1979 at The University of Texas at Austin. The editors wish to thank those in the University who gave financial support to the project: the Department of Classics, the Department of Speech Communication, and the College of Humanities, which has since become part of the College of Liberal Arts. We are also grateful to Carl Huffman, whose diligence in proofreading, checking references, and other labors made our responsibilities as editors much easier to bear. Finally, we would like to extend our special gratitude to Pamela Bratteng, whose contributions to this volume, editorial and otherwise, went far beyond her typing skills.

Abbreviations

Abbreviations of the names of classical authors and their works are those of the second edition of the *Oxford Classical Dictionary* (Oxford: Clarendon Press, 1970). Abbreviations of journal titles are those of *L'Année philologique*; titles not abbreviated there are given in full.

Introduction

The title we have given to this book reflects its scope:
the approaches taken to Homer range from the thirteenth-cen-
tury B.C. background of the *Iliad* and *Odyssey* to Homeric
scholarship in the twelfth century of our era, from the nature of the epic hero to the creative genius of the epic
poet. Our contributors approach the poems from a variety of
perspectives, bringing many disciplines and modes of analysis to bear on various problems posed by the texts. In
bringing these essays together here, we do not mean to dis-
count the different and specialized insights that each approach can offer or to reduce those approaches to a common
but superficial ground of uniformity. Rather we hope that
juxtaposing several different points of view will produce a
deeper understanding of Homer than considering any one point
of view in isolation. It is in this sense that we would describe this volume as a true area study, with the whole containing insights beyond the sum of its parts.

This mode of procedure seems especially helpful in approaching Homer, who perhaps more than most ancient authors
requires a certain breadth of focus. Not too many years ago,
in an age more confident of itself and its knowledge of the
ancient world, Homer was called "the Bible of Greece." Today
we are far less confident and a good deal more cautious, but
we still view the Homeric poems as a repository of the as-
tounding variety and complexity of ancient Greek culture, as
the medium of transmission for the civilization that perished
when Mycenae fell, and as a kind of cultural handbook for the
generations that followed their composition. In the *Iliad*
and *Odyssey* we can observe the oral poet's special gift for
linking past, present, and future: he reawakens the vanished

past in the memory of his listeners, and preserves it for the generations to come.

Several of the essays in this volume are concerned with what the Homeric poems tell us about their past. In 1970 Richard Hope Simpson and John F. Lazenby argued that the Catalogue of Ships in the *Iliad* presents a remarkably accurate reflection of the geography of Greece in the Mycenaean period.[1] Hope Simpson's paper reviews the controversy sparked by that work and offers some of his current views on the subject. He admits that Homer was indeed a poet, not a geographer or historian, but a poet who shared with his audience a deep concern for faithful accuracy, since the oral tradition that shaped his poetry was the only means the Greeks had for transmitting information about their past. "For this reason," Hope Simpson concludes, "in the Catalogue the great singer subordinates creativity to memory."

Gregory Nagy begins his paper with a brief discussion of archaeology, comparative linguistics, and the study of oral poetry, the three areas of inquiry that animate his reflections on the death and funeral of Sarpedon as they are described in the *Iliad*. Nagy detects in that description traces of the hero's traditional immortalization in cult, a process that in Sarpedon's case is shifted from the sphere of religion to that of epic poetry itself. Nagy admits that his presentation amounts to a series of questions rather than answers, but he leaves us with one enigmatic certainty: "Homeric epos is a repository of secrets about life and death--secrets that it will never fully reveal."

David Francis presents a detailed examination of the prehistory of the word $\breve{a}t\bar{e}$, finding in the etymology of this elusive term another instance of the Greek penchant for taking a word that originally designated some external,

natural phenomenon and applying it to some aspect of human
psychology and internal existence. Francis' paper succeeds
at the special task of uniting rigorous and very technical
linguistic argumentation with the mainstream of classical
scholarship as represented by such figures as Dodds,
Schadewalt, and Snell.

Mabel Lang's contribution to this volume concerns the relation of the *Iliad* to the poetic tradition that shaped it;
her paper may be said to bring together the past and present
of the poem's subject matter. Lang offers a detailed and
closely argued analysis of the way mythical *paradeigmata*
function in the *Iliad*: she traces a kind of reverberation
in which traditional material influences the shape of the
poem's narrative and that narrative in turn draws on traditional material and shapes it to its own ends. The result
is that "imitation and innovation go hand in hand on a two-
way street." One of the most telling aspects of Lang's
analysis is that, for all its attention to pre-Iliadic
material, it never takes us very far from the *Iliad* itself.
Instead, we are brought to see the poem once again as a repository, a kind of tapestry where past, present, and future
are woven into a single, seamless fabric.

Ann Bergren, like Mabel Lang, is concerned with problems
of narrative in Homer. She finds in the *Odyssey* two temporal patterns that correspond on the narrative level to the
formulaic method known as ring composition: her paper argues that the rhetorical figures of prolepsis and hysteron-
proteron, commonly observed at the level of diction, are also structures of thought that function in the arrangement of
narrative. In making this connection, Bergren invokes the
findings of contemporary narrative theory, especially the
work of Gérard Genette, which deserves to be better known

among classical scholars. Although Bergren's approach may seem strange to a good many classicists, she offers fresh and significant insights into more than one Homeric episode that might have seemed quite familiar or even overworked: for example, the Cyclops tale.

Norman Austin also presents an original reading of that well-known story; but he transfers our attention from the structure of the narrative to the tone in which it is told. That is, of course, the tone adopted by Odysseus himself; and for Austin, as for Bergren, it is no accident that Odysseus is the narrator of this particular story. Austin's elegant discussion is animated by psychoanalytic theory and also, as he is careful to tell us, by his work with two practitioners of optometric visual training. In his view Odysseus' story of his encounter with the Cyclops can be understood only if it is read as a child's fantasy, in which the one-eyed giant emerges as a condensation of parent and sibling, the opposition to the desires of our "little Nobody," and the materialization of his need to be recognized in the big world out there as somebody who counts.

James Redfield takes a more pragmatic approach to the world of Odysseus, as befits that most pragmatic of heroes, whom Redfield defines as "the economic man," someone who "does a kind of cost-benefit analysis of everything, weighing present expenditure against hoped-for utilities." This marks Odysseus as a man of culture, for all cultures that are to survive are dependent upon economic deliberation and must include some people for whom economic questions are paramount. Odysseus' adventures, on the other hand, take place in a world without culture: the dangers and monsters he encounters are characterized by the extremes of the primitive and decadent, by the insufficient accumulation of

goods on the one hand and their excessive consumption on the
other. These two extremes meet only in the real world of
Ithaca, where they are mediated and achieve the cultural
norm, the economic ethic of proper accumulation and consumption. Tensions between self-sufficiency at home and harmony
in the community, between the individual's desire for affluence and the public need to limit that affluence, permeate
the social universe of the *Odyssey*. Redfield suggests that
these tensions reflect the economic concerns of Greece in
the late 8th century B.C., thus giving an historical dimension to his socio-economic analysis.

In 1960, Arthur Adkins, today a colleague of Redfield at
the University of Chicago, published an influential and con-
troversial study of moral values in Homer.[2] Though there
has been much criticism of Adkins' book in the twenty years
since it first appeared, no one has produced an account of
Homeric morality to replace it; furthermore, Adkins has responded to his critics in a series of articles which make no
important concessions. Christopher Rowe sets out to examine
and evaluate some of the major objections to Adkins' position "in order to see how well it has survived." Rowe's
paper provides a useful review of the whole question of morality in Homer, including as it does a discussion of the
view of Dodds, which exerted considerable influence upon
Adkins, as well as a full treatment of Adkins' principal arguments, followed by a discussion of criticisms and his re-
sponses to them. Rowe concludes that in Homeric society the
freedom of the individual to assert his own interests is
limited by the requirement that he respect the claims of
others, but he agrees with Adkins that Homeric values center
on the demands of the individual rather than on the claims
of society.

If the essays of Austin, Bergren, Redfield, and Rowe can be said to treat the Homeric poems from various contemporary perspectives, Gareth Morgan offers us a fascinating glimpse of the fortunes of Homer and Homeric scholarship in twelfth-century Byzantium. His portrait of John Tzetzes and his discussion of Tzetzes' allegorical method of interpreting Homer call to our minds a time long past, when an Homeric education was highly prized by society and when much of Homer's language was still on people's lips. Best of all, we are introduced to the spectacular figure of Tzetzes himself, a kind of Homeric hero in his own right. Though Tzetzes' approach to the Homeric poems and the solutions he offers to the problems they pose violate what we see as good sense and what we define as good taste, Morgan eloquently demonstrates that they nonetheless reveal "a man soaked in Homer, a man revelling in Homer, a man who had occasional curious insights into Homer that can instruct us even in this clever century of ours."

In attempting to present brief summaries of the essays contained in this volume, we have tried to sort out the various ways in which our contributors approach the Homeric poems and the problems they pose. In doing so, however, we have been compelled constantly to recognize that those lines of inquiry often intersect, that the approaches taken frequently complement one another. It has been impossible to produce a neat and clean division of the various methods and disciplines employed, since the contributions to this volume are by no means self-contained and mutually exclusive.

It is unfortunately true that Homeric scholars have too often tended to make their differences in approach and results absolute. Thus difficult Homeric questions that begged for complex answers have acquired misleadingly simple

formulations. One author or several? Oral or written? Tradition or innovation? Bronze age or dark? More recently it
has become accepted that neither alternative alone will suffice, that a correct answer will lie somewhere in between.
Thus the issue has become one of proportion. How much tradition to how much innovation? How much bronze age to how
much dark? The considerable effort required to produce answers to such questions has created in recent Homeric
studies a trend toward extremely specialized forms of analysis. Archaeologists, for example, sift through the poems in
an attempt to isolate strata that correspond to different
periods of history. Social historians, on the other hand,
look at Homeric society as a whole, seeking to identify manners and mores. The obvious difficulty is that the archaeologist and historian often seem to have little common
ground for discussion. What can one say to the other, or
either of them to the linguist or literary critic, who have
quite different concerns and methods?

We hope that this volume will provide an answer to that
question. One of the strongest impressions to emerge from
this collection of essays is that many different approaches
and disciplines can and do enrich each other and work toward
common ends. Thus Gregory Nagy's paper combines comparative
linguistics, archaeology, and the study of oral narrative
poetry. Likewise, Norman Austin makes use, in one way or
another, of all the various approaches that comprise contemporary Homeric studies; his discussion also contributes
something to those disciplines and cannot be dismissed simply as an exercise in some new form of psychoanalytic criticism. Mabel Lang's observations on the relation of traditional *exempla* to the *Iliad*-narrative complement, in their
turn, Austin's analysis of the Homeric technique of

reduplication and inverted perception. Ann Bergren's treatment of the Cyclops story is quite different from Austin's,
but both discussions overlap and combine to produce fruitful
insights into that extremely fertile episode of Odyssean
autobiography. In short, to borrow Mabel Lang's term, there
is much reverberation in this volume, whose essays continually echo and illuminate one another, despite their different
points of departure.

At the beginning of this introduction, we suggested the
need for such a combined approach to Homer, an approach that
would broaden the focus of research. Of course, we do not
claim that the essays contained herein have answered any of
the great Homeric questions mentioned; but it does not seem
foolish to say that they do illustrate how different disciplines can contribute to one another and thus produce significant advances. In the past few years the perception of
this truth has lent great impetus to Homeric studies, where
an increasing number of scholars are no longer content to
search merely for nuggets of linguistic prehistory, historical fact, or archaeological data, but have moved on to consider the Homeric narrative as a whole. We hope that this
volume, with its various academic languages that remain intelligible to one another, its different perspectives that
do not exclude one another, and its lines of inquiry that so
often intersect, will do its part to demonstrate that in
certain extremely important instances fragmentation and dis-
unity are neither inevitable nor insurmountable. To us it
is no accident that the particular instance in this case is
the Homeric text, which has once again manifested its power
as a unifying cultural document. Various and diverse as it
is, it provides an elusive but richly rewarding focus for
the essays that follow; thus the great text that inspires

them all and reconciles them all has once more reaffirmed its position as the alpha and omega of classical studies.

Carl A. Rubino

Cynthia W. Shelmerdine

NOTES

1. R. Hope Simpson & J. F. Lazenby, *The Catalogue of the Ships in Homer's Iliad* (Oxford: Clarendon Press, 1970).
2. A. W. H. Adkins, *Merit and Responsibility: A Study in Greek Values* (Oxford: Clarendon Press, 1960).

Approaches to Homer

Odysseus and the Cyclops: Who Is Who

Norman Austin

In Memoriam: Lawrence Macdonald

Book 9 of Homer's *Odyssey* is full of oddities. Oddities?
Grotesqueries rather. Homer excludes the grotesque, we have
been told. In the encounter between Odysseus and the Cyclops, however, the grotesque is uncensored, indeed revelled
in. The story of the Cyclops is not odd in itself. It is
among the commonest of folktales, its provenance almost ubiq-
uitous.[1] As a folktale it is pleasant entertainment. Isolated from any other context, the story is a rewarding fantasy of the triumph of wit over brawn. It is, as a colleague
has remarked, a version of the closed room story, in which
the hero must engineer his escape with the random materials
lying at hand. As such, it is a very good story. But when
the context for this story is Homer's epic society, we question its moral. Is this really Homer's best paradigm for the
workings of intelligence? Odysseus certainly seems to think
so, to judge by the primary significance he attaches to this
adventure. Unless Homer is jesting at his hero, possibly at
us too, we may well wonder what intelligence must have meant
back then in the Bronze Age.

Page examined in detail several significant structural
anomalies in Homer's Cyclops story. Sensing something disturbing in the story, Page followed analytic procedures in
locating the disturbance in a traditional oral poem's multi-
ple authorship. Yet, despite the structural anomalies, more
numerous even than those Page perceived, the real oddity is
not in the story's structure, but in its tone, more

particularly in the tone of its narrator, coincidentally also
its hero. The adventure sets up a disequilibrium between the
folkloric and the epic. The buffoonery in the story, the or-
giastic revelry, the burlesque phallicism, suggest a satyr
play. We sense an irregular oscillation between Odysseus'
epic journey, and this satyr play which motivates that
journey.

Buffoonery is essential to this peculiar version of the
tale. The Cyclops is a buffoon, and made even more so. But
Odysseus too is a buffoon or, to put the best light on it,
masquerades as one. Buffoonery is an important component in
Odysseus' character in the rest of the poem. Odysseus is
comfortable playing the clown even in his own house, even too
in his reunion with his father. Here, however, the clowning
is disturbing. Tell a child the story of a witty little fellow blinding a grotesque ogre with only one eye, and chances
are the child will fall asleep with pleasant dreams and an
innocent conscience. When Homer tells the tale our conscience
troubles us, if only because neither poet nor hero seems trou-
bled by conscience. No one expects characters in folktales
to be burdened by conscience; generally speaking, the plot is
the vehicle for the conscience.[2] But a hero of epic without
a conscience is a problem, especially when he lauds himself
and is extravagantly lauded by others, including the poet, as
a man of supreme consciousness. Homer seems to have adopted,
rather than adapted, the primitive ethos of the folktale and,
strangely, attributed this primitive ethos to his most sophisticated hero, using the story indeed as proof of the hero's
superior sophistication.

Odysseus, identifying himself to his Phaeacian hosts as he
begins the tale of his wanderings, chooses first to state his
name, Odysseus son of Laertes, a trouble to all humans for

his tricks (9.19-20). Odysseus is forthright in advising his hosts that he is a trickster, and as a trickster something of a troublemaker.[3] His tricks we are prepared to accept, up to a point. What we find harder to commend in the Cyclops story is the trickster-hero's gloating over his own brutality. Rarely in great literature do we encounter a hero so wittily brutal, who at the same time expects our warmest admiration. The glee Odysseus displays in this adventure is surely inappropriate in great heroes, however necessary his actions. It is distinctly childish. He laughs and jokes and smirks, even when the ogre is roaring in pain administered by our elegant comedian.

Here lies the answer to our problem. The Homeric story of the Cyclops is acceptable by virtue of its childishness. The story is explicable, in fact, only if it is a child's fantasy. The grotesque elements, improper in lofty epic, are entirely proper in nursery tales. If this is not a child's fantasy then it is most improper.

Particularly characteristic, the principal signifier even, of the child's fantasy is the size reversal in the story. The principle of size constancy of objects in our visual field we learn slowly and laboriously in our first struggling attempts to gain control of our optical apparatus. It is a peculiar principle indeed, a law of human optics which contradicts the laws of physical optics. A merely physical lens does not record distance, only size change in the image. Bishop Berkeley long ago observed that we do not see distance.[4] Yet our human eyes invent distance, so to speak, learning to interpret size change of the object as a function of distance. Somehow we master, more or less adequately, an equation which computes size differences, which we can see, into distance, which we cannot see.

The mathematics required for this computation brings with it a profound alienation, which most of us as adults are happy to forget. The object in the visual field alters its size in the two-dimensional plane at every instant, unless both it and the observing eye are kept rigidly immobile. Yet we, as observers of the object, translate the alterations, up to a certain point of accommodation, into an invisible third plane called distance, and register the change as a change of a hypothetical location rather than as a real change in the size of the image. We plunder from the visible object its real and present property, that is its visible size, in all its variability, and project what we have plundered onto an unreal (optically speaking) property, namely its distance. The flux visibly inherent in the size of the object we register as a flux in its location, as a perpetual advance and retreat of the object. Forget the trauma as we may, millions of sufferers carry on their persons, as myopia, hyperopia, or astigmatism, the painful symptoms of this alienation. In such pathologies, the sufferer becomes unable to determine accurately either the size or the distance of the object, and is, so to speak, doubly confounded.

So laborious a task is it to maintain the optical illusion of size constancy in the objective world, translating always optical size into the optical illusion of advance and retreat, that we experience a vertigo, sometimes anxiety, but sometimes also a blessed relief, on looking into a magnifying glass or microscope, where the physical property of the lens compels us to forego our learned computations about distance and restores to us an object whose size is disentangled for the moment from distance altogether. Fantasy literature of all kinds performs the same vertiginous or therapeutic function on the psychological level.[5] Children's fairy tales, cartoons,

comic strips, and science fiction, so richly populated with
dwarves and giants, relieve us from computing size change as
an absence gradient. In literature of this sort, so well ex-
emplified by Lewis Carroll's *Alice in Wonderland*, we lapse
again into a world where objects resist the alienation of
their properties required by the mathematics of distance, and
assume their real size, their psychic size. A student of
mine reminded me that in our dreams we frequently violate the
principle of size constancy. Put another way, dream objects
are not required to violate the official principle of size
variability.

Early in our visual adaptations to the world, before we
mastered the computations for registering size as degrees of
presence or absence, the face, even the kindly face, peering
over the bars of the crib where we lay caged in immobility
may well have seemed a mountainous apparition, with one monstrous eye not yet split into two, lurking within a shaggy
cave. The Cyclops tale resonates with the size reversals
proper to a child's fantasy, and the child in us delights in
their extremes. Everything in the story is monstrously magnified or monstrously diminished. The child in us delights
in the huge size of the Cyclops, of his voracious appetite,
his club, his cupidity, his stupidity, in the size of the
boulder stopping the mouth of the cave, of the mountain peaks
the giant hurls after Odysseus' ships, which almost raise a
tidal wave. Even sounds are monstrous: the clatter of the
giant's firewood on the floor of the cave; the giant's bellowing; the cave and mountain bellowing in echo of the giant's
pain; the screaming of the heated wood plunged in the aqueous
humors of the giant's eye. The orgy of cannibalism, the orgy
of drunkenness, the orgy of the surgical operation on the
giant's eye, are all of the same order.

Thoroughgoing magnification requires equivalent diminution
elsewhere. The child in us delights in the terror of the
Lilliputian humans huddling in the giant's cave, so diminutive it needs five of them to wield even a short segment of
the giant's club. The hero, hefty as he is, can escape by
clinging to the belly of a sheep. The child delights too in
the very neatness of the hero's verbal pun, the perfect opposite to the grotesque orgies of the giant's mind and behavior.
A pun is the most diminutive weapon, and Odysseus' pun is
diminuendo taken to the vanishing point.

As a child's fantasy the Cyclops tale is perfectly acceptable. The *Boys' Own Annual* tolerates, demands even, a high
incidence of brutality, an orgy of the gruesome. As boyish
readers we cherish our revulsion at every revolting detail.
The tale is enormously satisfying, sensuous, precise, yet
mysterious, as delirious as a nightmare, and as delicious.
As the child hero of the fantasy, Odysseus is everything such
heroes should be, suave and sassy. But a censor intervenes
as we read. Epic heroes, surely, are not suave and sassy.
If our heroes are Greek, we should discourse on their *aretē*,
on their courage, not their pluck. Is this *aretē*, to mutilate a stupid ogre when one has first befuddled him with wine?
The censor is disgusted at the brutality, at the very deli-
ciousness of the brutality. The child in us is ashamed to be
caught smirking with the hero.

The secret is out. The hero, coincidentally the author,
is a child. The precocious author engages the child in us in
an act of complicity. The child, no less clever as author
than as hero, plots his tale with a subtle intuition for the
adult censor's moral code. It is astonishing how suavely the
child author allays the censor's suspicions, how much restricted material he smuggles past the censor's eye. Even

before we hear of the Cyclops, the author has been careful to enlist the censor's support. Immediately prior to the Cyclops episode we hear the tale of Odysseus' misadventure in Lotus-land, where we are relieved to see manly Odysseus dragging his weaker brothers from their regression to a drug-induced infantile state. This is the kind of hero the adult censor approves as the leader of a band of explorers.

With the near catastrophe safely avoided, the author swings past Lotusland and on to his adventure among the Round Eyes. He wisely postpones describing their fantastic size and appearance until he has satisfied the censor with an observant discourse on their manners. The censor falls for manners every time. Call it anthropology and the censor will approve almost anything.[6] The child author is ready with an excellent piece of anthropological research. The Round Eyes, as he calls them (by a name which should immediately sound some kind of alert), don't practice agriculture, not as adults understand the term. They don't hold legislative assemblies. They don't even live in houses. They are only semi-domesticated. The censor is satisfied. Clearly our author is an adult who puts manners next to godliness. The Round Eyes, don't you see, must be the children, overgrown bullies with a stunted morality.

The child author passes to his description of Goat Island. Once again he finds the occasion convenient for a discourse on the Round Eyes' manners, or lack of them. The island could be cultivated if the Round Eyes were cultivated, which we have just been informed they are not. The Round Eyes don't study economics, engineering, navigation, the life sciences. They are sadly wanting in the manly habits the censor approves. Again the censor is reassured. The author is the adult. His opponents in this adventure must be the vicious and lazy children.

The sly author continues on his way, drawing us at last to
the mouth of the ogre's cave. The author prepares us for our
entry into the cave by first drawing off a goatskin of nearly
lethal wine. Before we enter the cave with him, the author's
elaborate and most convincing discussion of Maron's magical
wine keeps us and the censor safely located in the heroic
world, the world of gods and priests, of chivalrous commitments, of the economics of cultural exchange and manly derring-
do. [7]

Now we are in the cave. And what do we see? Treasures,
of course. Caves, as we well know from our adventure books,
are always filled with treasures. That's what caves are for.
And what's the treasure here? Cheese. Can you believe it?
Cheese, and lambkins, and little kids, all neatly segregated,
and curds and whey. Are we really to imagine our great hero
returning home, hallooing in triumph and brandishing aloft a
great wheel of Gouda cheese? Odysseus' first adventure on
his homeward journey, among the Thracian Cicones, gives the
outline of the conventional piracies of conventional heroes.
The Greek adventurers sack the town of Ismarus, kill all the
male population, and forcibly remove the wine and women for
future pleasures. That's proper men's work. But curds and
whey? Men don't sack a city, or even ransack a cave, for
curds and whey. Reeling at the sight of the treasure, our
hero all but drops his disguises and ruses. This is no epic
hero telling the tale. This is little Tommy Tucker hungry
for his supper.

You can tell it's little Tommy Tucker telling the story
because milk is his obsession. But hungry as he is, he doesn't
quite abandon all his ruses. He's still smart enough to project his obsession on to the ogre, hoping to convince us that
the ogre is the compulsive and the narrator the objective

anthropologist. Remember the wine? That's the narrator's
drink, so he would have us suppose. The elaborate ceremonial
of gift exchange between the narrator and the priest Maron
persuades us of the author's maturity and his manners. The
ogre's drink is milk. And what an obsession it is. The tiny
hero, watching the ogre at work from his dark corner, sees
milk; milk and milking everywhere. The ogre milks the sheep
and goats. The *embryos*, to use the narrator's word for them
(9.245), milk their mothers. Observe the ogre's milking rituals punctiliously performed morning and night. Observe his
scrupulous procedures for dividing up the milk, setting it in
appropriate containers, and, when his tasks are done, drink-
ing his share for supper. Observe too his scrupulous segre-
gation of the young animals into three groups according to
age. No doubt who is the compulsive in this story. It would
be ridiculous to expect decent gift exchanges from this mi-
serly dairy man who hoards his milk and drinks it in soli-
tude--and *unmixed*, as the little hero enviously observes.[8]

Well, at least we know where we are. We're in the cave of
embryos staring with our hero, no longer an embryo himself
but pretty thirsty all the same, at a supply of unadulterated
mother's milk multiplied beyond the belly's wildest fantasy.
But the little hero has been remarkably successful in dis-
guising his own greed as anthropology and persuading us that
the ogre is the addict. With milk practically flooding the
cave, brimming over every available container, through their
lattices and from their teats, with the cave, huge as it is,
jam-packed with nursing mothers and embryos suckling for all
they're worth, and not a single adult male in the whole com-
mune (inside the cave) but one monstrous shepherd, still commentators miss the clues and mistake the hero for a research
scholar instead of seeing him for what he is, another starv-
ing kid homesick for his mother.

Another clue to the author's identity is that he forgets
to introduce a sufficient motive for the ogre's savagery.
The author's preamble on the Round Eyes' deficient manners
and his own ominous forebodings, materializing so aptly into
a goatskin filled with lethal wine, do the trick of course.
What need for a sufficient motive when we have been so effi-
ciently manipulated? Yet the objective evidence seems to be-
lie his thesis that these dairy folk are lawless brutes. Gigantic yes, rustic to be sure, but cannibals? Our Cyclops is
as orderly a shepherd as anyone could wish. Will this oversized shepherd, methodical in his tasks, even tender toward
his animals, turn cannibal just because a little person raids
his dairy for a drink of milk? It's not credible. Yet we
believe it. The ogre is a compulsive; we know compulsives
will stop at nothing. No sharing of this miser's property,
not on your life. The manifest motive for the ogre's spontaneous cannibalism is simply that he is a compulsive; but
his compulsive behavior is, as any detective can see, a projection of the hero's needs. And so we circle around and
find a sufficient motive for the ogre's cannibalism after all,
a latent motive in the little hero's need to discover a
cannibal.

The little urchin, outstaying his need for milk but not
his need to be cannibalized, when sighted at last by the shepherd, remembers his wits enough to introduce a sufficient
provocation for the consequent catastrophe. He boasts of rav-
aging some vast mythical empire, leaving behind him a glorious
wake of carnage. Though an intruder, with time enough in the
cave to enjoy a dinner uninvited and still to escape unscathed,
the urchin yet demands a gift as his prerogative and accompa-
nies his demand with threatening, not to say insulting, allusions to Zeus, the protector God of reverend strangers.

A gift? What gift for heaven's sake? And Zeus. How did
Zeus get into the story? Do urchins ransacking caves for
curds and whey have their gods too? What a strange cave this
is, thickly settled (as they say in Massachusetts) with mothers and their nursing young, where a brazen thief demands special compensation and invokes the Supreme Deity as his authority. Yet we overlook the incongruity. We are so easily enchanted by the rascal, so easily seduced by his reverential
poses, so equally greedy with him, that we forgive him his
thievish ways. We scarcely notice he is a thief, and an agent
provocateur, and with him we shudder at the ogre's blasphemy.[9]

The author, confident of our complicity, continues his tale.
Through his eyes we see the rustic shepherd become a stupid
and savage trickster, a gigantic parody of our own endearing
hero. The oafish shepherd devours human flesh and sprawls
grotesquely among the animals, belching gobbets of human anat-
omy. The cave is awash with human blood. The story doesn't
quite make sense, not if the narrator is a manly hero, but we
believe it. The narrator, feigning the heroic impulse, draws
his sword. But the hero is not an epic hero, not in this episode, not in this cave, and the heroic impulse is stayed.

Necessity drives our hero, deprived of heroics, to retali-
ations less heroic. Swept along, we enjoy his boyish pranks
almost as much as he, perhaps until the moment when he and
his chums poke the olive club into the shepherd's only eye.
The disjunction between folklore and epic, between content
and style, becomes suddenly intolerable. The act of blinding
is a necessary element from the folktale. The plot of the
whole tale revolves, after all, around that point. Homer's
style here is not folkloric, however, but flawlessly epic.
Some daemon, the narrator tells us, breathes courage into the
hero. With the daemonic power surging in him, he plunges the

glowing charcoal into the ogre's eye. He follows the act
with a perceptive description of the process, using images
drawn from the civilized world, that world closed to the
shaggy Cyclops, the world of shipwrights drilling planks and
blacksmiths quenching metal. The act is a nightmare. The
narrator's gloss on the orgy is a study of daily life in civilized communities calculated to hold the attention of text
critics, archaeologists, and ethnographers. Again we are seduced into thinking our hero a manly fellow, virtually a culture hero, a professional, a craftsman, even a surgeon.[10] We
admire good surgery.

The deed done, the hero laughs at his own expertise. His
laugh gives the game away. A good surgeon does not enjoy his
surgery in quite this way. The hero laughs, by his own ad-
mission, at the conceit of his name and his intelligence, his
onoma and his *mētis* (9.413-414). What is this intelligence,
this *mētis* which he shares in common with both Zeus and
Hermes? Surely it is two intelligences: on one side the intelligence of the artist, the creator; and on the other side
the mercurial intelligence of the trickster, the intelligence
which also creates, but creates illusions, the illusion of a
name, the illusion of an anesthetic, the illusion of a surgical operation.[11]

Recognition of the Trickster as the central actor in this
grotesque fable clears the sand thrown in our eyes. Why did
Odysseus blind the Cyclops? Because the Cyclops was a cannibal, the story seems to say, so artfully has the narrator woven his illusions. Not so. Beware the Trickster's ribald
laugh. The Trickster's laugh reveals all the necessities of
the story as a flimsy sham. No necessity, not a single real,
external, necessity motivates the plot of this adventure.
After the Cicones episode, the first of Odysseus' adventures,

and the only one located in objective time-space, the Cyclops
episode is unique in being compelled by no external necessity.
In all the subsequent situations Odysseus finds himself willy-
nilly in some danger from which he must extricate himself.
By contrast, the Cyclops episode stands conspicuously alone,
not motivated by any prior incident, and as itself the over-
arching necessity governing all the subsequent episodes of
the poem.

Odysseus is not stranded by fate on the Cyclops' shore.
He is not driven by hunger, since he has plundered a good
supply of wine from the Cicones and beaches his ship on an
island with fresh water and plentiful game. Odysseus himself
chooses to adventure among the Cyclopes. No necessity intervenes to trap him inside the Cyclops' cave. He chooses, over
his friends' remonstrations, to stay to see and be seen. No
necessity, certainly not the necessity of etiquette, compels
him to demand a gift when he could have removed whatever he
wanted from the cave without making such a demand. After his
escape from the cave, no external necessity requires Odysseus
to undo his witticism and betray his identity. The motiva-
tional necessities in Homer's version of the folktale are all
internal. Internal necessity compels Odysseus to forsake the
security of Goat Island for the dangers on the mainland, to
forage in an obviously inhabited cave, to linger there until
trapped, and once free of the trap to expose himself to the
vengeance of Poseidon. Odysseus invents this particular
adventure. From start to finish the story is a structure designed and signed by Odysseus, as the story of his name and
the proof of his intelligence.

If this episode is the materialization of the dynamism of
Odysseus' psyche, there is, after all, motive enough for the
Cyclops' cannibalism, and for the hero's savage retaliation.

The Cyclops is a phantom, though entirely real for all his
fantastic appearance. The same necessity generating the phantom generates the motive for his blinding. In Freud's language, we see here two wishes fulfilled: the wish to discover a cannibalizing giant, and the wish to mutilate the giant
in revenge. [12] Our narrator, the tiny tot, with his obsession
for milk, prowling in a fantastic cave of embryos, finds his
heart's desire in fantastic abundance, the archetypal treasure trove multiplied a hundredfold.   Alas, he finds his way
to the treasure barred by a fantastic guardian, a grotesque
shaggy ram with one piercing eye.   The tiny tot, fantastic
in his own way, borrows the nearest ramrod he can find, cuts
it down to size, rams it into the Evil Eye, and scoots out
clutching a ram's belly, taking much of the milk supply with
him.   No one since Freud can have any difficulty identifying
the terrifying monster barricading the door to the nursery.

Outside the cave the tiny tot reverts to normal size.   He
becomes the adult, Odysseus sacker of cities.   He sacrifices
the stolen ram, his vehicle of passage, to Zeus, adopting pious procedures to incorporate into the adult, and heroic,
structure, and so to legitimize, this fantastic escapade in
the nursery.

We have, then, a story told by two narrators.   Not two
poets, as Page imagined, but through a single poet two iden-
tities of a single psyche contesting with each other, each
maneuvering to outwit the other.   One narrator is Odysseus,
famed counsellor to the Greek army, the warrior who devastates
great cities and enjoys divine protection, the intrepid ex-
plorer, the perceptive ethnographer.   The other is the little
phantom, the tiny tot masquerading under the phantom name
Outis, Nobody, as his mama and papa call him by his own con-
fession.   One glance from a big person is enough to send this

tiny fellow scuttling into the darkest corner. The one narrator wins honors on the battlefield; the other is the thief
of the milk pail. The one is a professional craftsman; his
phantom a savage little monster. The craftsman makes tools,
and with tools he fashions objects. He objectifies. His ideas
materialize into a world of ships, houses, axes, spears,
bows, and arrows. The savage little monster, well, he hallu-
cinates savage giants, as you would expect. But hallucination
is a form of objectifying too, an earlier stage. Tiny tots
hallucinate giants guarding the milk before they grow up and
go off to lay siege to great cities in foreign lands.

Despite obvious sibling resemblances, the two narrators
don't seem to recognize each other. Each tells the tale as
if it were his alone, even though the other continually interrupts to add a fact or modulate an affect. From the same
material, that common folktale, each works his own version.
When Odysseus, having plundered a cave and mutilated its oc-
cupant, sacrifices stolen goods to Zeus, guardian of guests,
he notes that Zeus declined the sacrifice. Zeus was planning,
says the adult narrator at this point, how he might destroy
Odysseus' ships (9.553-555). What an implication. Zeus, in
his opening speech in the poem, specifically repudiates being
implicated this way in human affairs. How exasperating, he
cries, for the gods to be always projections of human failures
(1.32-34). Here, in the Cyclops tale, and specifically in the
narrator's conclusion, we see the human process of projection
at work in an unequivocal way. Odysseus' scapegoating ritual
and his pious gestures to the god of guests are his ruse to
project the whole savage incident onto some great cosmic Necessity, that arbitrary and inexorable force insatiable for
sleek new victims. What has Zeus of the boomy clouds to do
with this petty thievery from the milk pail? The pious

narrator who brings the tale to its conclusion with his propitiatory rites encourages us to forget the gleeful laugh of
the other narrator, the merry prankster who had no necessity
but his own for stealing into the cave of embryos in search
of cannibalism.

In this single tale told by two authors reduplication is
one of the most conspicuous structural features. Odysseus'
first adventure on his homeward journey dramatizes in brief
this structural device. Returning from Troy, Odysseus puts
in first at Ismarus in Thrace, where he sacks the town and
divides the spoils (9.39-61). Then curiously, while the victorious Greeks sit at their ease over-indulging in their new-
ly acquired booty, the vanquished Cicones split into two sets
of Cicones. Cicones called out to Cicones, reads the Greek
line, the unusual alliteration expressing the essential structure of the episode (9.47). From the mainland another set of
Cicones materializes, more numerous, stronger, and more proficient in cavalry attack than their just defeated kin. Plea-
surable wish fulfillment suddenly swivels into nightmare, as
the Cicones, thought to be safely dead or captive (vv. 40-41),
suddenly flourish as thick as the foliage in spring (v. 51),
now a bloodthirsty horde charging down on horseback on the intoxicated Greeks.

Odysseus is an islander. For an islander the island is a
place of security, the mainland threatening. Odysseus' adventure among the Cicones hints at the island bias which becomes
increasingly apparent and significant as his journey advances.[13]
The contrast in the Cicones episode between easy wish fulfillment and nightmare reversals is the very ground on which the
Cyclops episode is situated. Like Ismarus, the land of the
Cyclopes undergoes mitosis, splitting, now more distinctly
than in the Cicones episode, into mainland and island. The

island, though small and destitute of agriculture, offers an
excellent haven with good anchorage, and adequate food and
water. It is safely uninhabited except for the indigenous
goats. Across the bay lies the mainland, extraordinarily af-
fluent but tenanted, alas, by the fearsome Cyclopes. In this
instance the plot reverses the structure of the Cicones episode. The Cyclops episode begins with island security, from
which Odysseus ventures across to the nightmare on the mainland.

Like the Cicones, the Cyclopes themselves undergo mitosis,
splitting into the solitary Polyphemus on one hand, and on
the other hand the collective Cyclopes, his neighbors. The
mitosis in both instances is similar in that it produces a
particularly vicious form of the species. Mitosis is a regu-
lar feature in mythical collectives. From the centaurs
emerges a single Centaur, Chiron; from the satyrs a single
satyr, Silenus; from the Corybantes a single Corybas. We may
borrow from the Prague School its terms for complementary opposition, *marked* and *unmarked*, to distinguish a solitary hypostasis from the collective. From the collective emerges an
individual marked in a special way. What is being thus marked varies according to the character or context. Chiron has
a character conspicuously at odds with the prevalent character of centaurs. He is sober, self-controlled, and wise,
where they are intemperate and lascivious. Silenus is marked
sometimes as the absolute embodiment of satyric inebriation;
at other times his is a more august role, as Marsyas in
some stories, or as Satyrus, or even as the great enemy himself.[14]

Homer's Cyclopes are wild folk, marked off therefore from
civilized persons, yet in the world of the wild unmarked.
They give no evidence of being bestial. Much about them seems

even attractive. They live peaceably, in enviable harmony
with their environment. Despite Odysseus' slurs, they respond to a fellow Cyclops in pain with genuine social concern.
As a collective they are Nature at large, large incurious
Nature in all its possible significations. Polyphemus, the
marked Cyclops, is the signifier disclosing the latent signif-
icances, the intimidation of Nature's myopia. The Cyclopes
are close to being noble savages, whereas Polyphemus is just
savage. Yet even he is a double, at once a monstrosity of
Nature and a gentle shepherd; on one hand a personification
of Nature in its inhuman, bestial, and predatory aspects; on
the other hand Nature as nurturing parent, not now raw Nature
but Nature merely rude.

Odysseus enters as an extravagant disturbance into this
ecology so delicately poised between the raw and the rude. As
a civilized man, a culture hero, he brings as a gift for his
host wine from Ismarus—a town proverbial for its potent wines
and, in the *Odyssey*, for its nightmares—in Thrace, the home
of Dionysus. Even this wine undergoes mitosis. Odysseus
brings with him, in fact, two discrete wines from Thrace. One
is *vin ordinaire*, plundered from Ismarus. The wine Odysseus
gives the savage is marked wine, marked by extraordinary ci-
vilities requiring sixteen lines in the narrative to give it
its just decorum (9.196-211). This marked wine is not booty,
but a gift from the priest of Apollo, Maron son of Fair-
Flowering, persons whose hieratic names signify hieratic functions. Odysseus receives this wine as the pledge of civilized
behavior between himself and the priest. The wine itself is
especially sacred, kept in a secret place, known only to Maron,
his wife, and one trusty slave woman. It is extraordinarily
potent even for Greek wine which, as we know, was more potent
than wine can be. This sacred wine requires not the usual

dilution of three to one, but twenty to one. This wine has
certainly been *marked* by something; a people versed in the
cultivation and fermentation of the grape would know that no
wine could need that kind of dilution, unless marked by something.

Wine is an essence. The essence of the plant. The essence
of culture, the essence of nature, the essence of contradictions. A product of human agriculture, it remains one of the
most toxic substances in the human pharmocopoeia. Properly
used it is an anodyne. It graces the banquet, as Odysseus
remarks to his Phaeacian hosts as he begins his tale (9.3-11).
Abused, it turns murderous. Intoxication is the mark of the
civilized human; by such arguments Dionysus in his myth-
history devastates Greece as he advances westward from Thrace
to join the Greek gods on their Olympus.

Freud, in his grammar of dreams, places emphasis on the
principle of condensation, by which a single figure (place or
person) consolidates several, even contradictory, values.
Equally significant as a narrative device is mitosis, whereby
contradictory values are ravelled out and distributed abroad
among several figures.[15] The mitosis of Odysseus' Thracian
wine discriminates wine's contradictions. The plundered wine
intoxicates the Greeks after their victory at Ismarus, and in
their intoxication they fall victim to the nightmare Cicones.
Odysseus uses Maron's wine to intoxicate the Cyclops and so
reverse an earlier nightmare. Not that Maron's wine is entirely free from contradictions. The normal exchange of gifts
may lead us to assume that Maron's wine was not intended as an
offensive weapon (that is not wine's function in civilized
communities) but, properly used, to ease Odysseus' voyage
across the great Pontus. Odysseus does not so use it. He administers it instead as a toxin to the Cyclops, whose abuse

of the heavenly draught turns its potency treacherously
against him. Yet surely Odysseus too has abused the properties
of the wine to offer it as a poison disguised as an anodyne.
The gift so misused turns against Odysseus too, the master of
the revels in this tale of essential contradictions. Instead
of easing his passage the abused wine opens up the great Pontus and transforms a conquering warrior into a wanderer. The
rest of Odysseus' hard journey unwinds from that one incident
in the Cyclops' cave. Who's to say who was more intoxicated
that night in the cave, Polyphemus or Odysseus?

With the Cyclopean brains well befuddled by the miraculous
wine, Odysseus befuddles the fellow still further by identifying himself as the little Nobody. But the wine has already
marked the Cyclops as a nobody, a hugely uncivilized nobody
magnified in inverse proportion to the diminutive nobody playing his cup-bearer. Even the Nobody in this tale undergoes
mitosis, splitting into one gigantic apparition and one minia-
ture version, both of them, despite the size difference, looking remarkably alike.

Most interesting is the diminutive Nobody's skill in magnifying the Cyclops into a nobody long before the incident in
the embryonic cave takes place. In approaching the land of
the Cyclopes Odysseus describes them as if they were the Nobodies, not he.[16] The passage in which he describes the land
and its inhabitants, the neighboring island and its non-
inhabitants, and his own approach to this fabulous landscape,
is remarkable for its sustained rhetorical discourse on the
subject of nothing. It would be difficult to find in Homer,
or indeed anywhere else in Greek, a passage of comparable
length so richly sown with negatives as *Od.* 9.106-148. Perhaps only Plato's *Parmenides* can equal it.

The passage divides neatly into three parts: Part I, vv.
106-115, describes the Cyclopes and their mainland ecology.
Part II, vv. 116-141, describes Goat Island and its ecology.
Part III, vv. 142-151, describes Odysseus' arrival by night
at the island. Each of the three parts is in its distinctive
way a paean to the versatility, ingenuity, and ambiguity of
the Greek negative.

In Part I, section 1 (vv. 106-111), Odysseus describes the
Cyclopes entirely by negatives. Even his positive assertions
are recapitulations of statements asserted in the negative.
The Cyclopes have no *themis*; they put their faith in the *undying* gods; they *neither* plant *nor* plough, but everything
grows *unplanted* and *unploughed*, wheat, barley, grape vines,
and the rain from Zeus nourishes their growth.

Many people, asked their impression of the Cyclopean landscape, recall no distinct image. That's the point. It's an
indistinct landscape, yet objectively speaking the place is a
paradise. In fact negatives are a conventional rhetorical
formula for paradise landscapes. Yet you would hardly know
from Odysseus' use of the formula that he had landed in the
Garden of Eden. The blessings of paradise Odysseus adroitly
nullifies with his initial negative: ἀθεμίστων (v. 106).
The Cyclopes are lawless; they do not establish codes; they
do not codify. An uncodified Garden of Eden is an untended
garden, hardly an Eden at all. Odysseus adds another epithet
to shape our perception of this landscape: ὑπερφιάλων (v.
106). Here we detect the first clue to the narrator's method
of magnifying the Cyclopes into nobodies. The Cyclopes are
overgrown, overreaching, oversized, overdetermined. In suggesting at the outset that the Cyclopes are perverse, both
overgrown and uncodified, beyond codes altogether, Odysseus
renders their kind of agriculture, if you can call simply

plucking the fruits of the soil agriculture, somehow contrary
to Nature, though the evidence he cites would state the opposite.

In Part I, section 2 (vv. 112-115) Odysseus turns our attention specifically from the land to its people. Following
the same rhetorical practice as in section 1, he states the
facts in a series of negatives, then recapitulates the negatives in a positive form: the Cyclopes have *no* assemblies,
nor law codes, but live in caves, each codifying for his own
family. This section is rounded off with a final negative
balancing the negative initiating Part I: ἀλέγουσι. The Cyclopes have no concern for each other.

In the ten lines of Part I Odysseus uses nine specific negatives, and in addition ὑπερφιάλων, effectively also a negative by magnification. The concentration of negativity is
even denser than the statistics indicate, since all the positive verbs in the passage are epexegetic of prior negatives.
The Cyclopes are cave dwellers; such is the positive print of
the negative image in their lack of assemblies and codes.
Each Cyclops establishes the codes for his own family; again
a positive print of the negative image of their uncodified
behavior. It is astonishing how the tricky narrator makes
simple assertion of facts, rather splendid facts too, into
negative evaluations. The soil produces food and wine of its
own accord: another piece of circumstantial evidence against
the Cyclopean character. So dense is the negation of this
paradise that even the positive statement in v. 107, that the
Cyclopes put their faith in the undying gods, anywhere else
evidence of an exquisitely harmonious ecology, reads instead
as incriminating evidence of their perversity. The Nature
pole of the Nature/Culture polarity opens up onto its own
poles. We never know whether the Garden of Eden, if found,

will turn out to be paradise or wilderness. Odysseus plays
on this ambivalence, giving us a paradise on one hand, and
with the other hand blurring it into a wilderness. This is a
paradise, if you happen to be a cave man.

Having imagined a paradise and its inhabitants in harmony
with it, Odysseus erases the slates and fantasizes a second
paradise, an island with features compensating for the spe-
cious allure of the mainland. In Part II, where the islander
dreams of paradise a second time, the dreaming technique almost exactly duplicates, down to the repetition of certain
formulas, the technique used in Part I. As before, Odysseus
describes the topography and ecology first, the inhabitants
(in this case the non-inhabitants) second.

In Part II, section 1 (vv. 116-124), Odysseus sets the
scene with his beloved negatives. A fertile island lies outside the harbor, *neither* far away *nor* close by. What does he
mean by that? We might take it the dreamer has found precisely the perfect location for his paradise. On the other hand
a place neither close nor far might be in no location at all.
It is hard to tell. Goats *not to be* numbered, the narrator
continues, inhabit the island. In any other context "not to
be numbered" would mean simply many, but Odysseus' tricks
with the negative make us pause. Not to be numbered: the excess here harks back to the excess in ὑπερφιάλων, and through
that epithet to the excess of paradise on the mainland. Here
however, on the island, excess of goats is no excess. Similar
rhetorical tropes operating on the island produce results contrary to those produced on the mainland. The operative word
for the island ecology is *fertile* (λάχεια, v. 116). The
Cyclopes in their excess are overgrown; the island in its excess is fertile.[17]

Odysseus continues. *No* human foot disturbs the island, *no* hounds press the hunt. The island has *neither* pasture *nor* ploughland. *Unplanted* and *unploughed* (a formula borrowed from the mainland ecology), the island is unhusbanded (lit. bereft of men), but nourishes goats. Yes, a paradise at last. Note the tricks of the dreaming faculty. A series of negatives working on this fertile landscape produces a positive image, whereas a similar run (even some identical formulas) worked on the mainland, where growth runs riot, yields a distinct negative. In the first nine lines of Part II ten negatives assure us the island is a place both fertile and secure.

In Part II, section 2 (vv. 125-130), Odysseus directs us back to the Cyclopes again. Again he is liberal with negatives to describe their character: the Cyclopes have *no* ships; they have *no* builders of ships. Please note that the dreaming faculty has reversed itself. The dreamer has just completed a series of negatives asserting the island's positive attributes, using in the correct way what we may call the Paradise formula, wherein each negative adumbrates a positive quality. Careless readers might assume that the Paradise formula is still functioning in this further adumbration of the Cyclopean character. Is it not a virtue in the Cyclopes to live in ecological harmony, driven by no necessity for territorial expansion? The opposite of course is true. Now we find the Cyclopes incriminated for underachievement. This dream is the dream of an islander. When his dream reveals a landscape destitute of ships and shipwrights, he is dreaming in the Wilderness formula.

Odysseus now recapitulates in the positive form his negative evaluation of the Cyclopes, but with a significant modification. The indicative mood shifts to the optative: the Cyclopes had no shipwrights *who might have belabored* (to

build) ships, *which might have brought to completion* the many
things for which men cross the sea in ships. *They would have
belabored* the island to make it also a good settlement.

The optative is the dreaming mode. Here at last the
dream-work comes through undisguised. The dreamer had inad-
vertently introduced errors into his first dream of paradise.
He had mistakenly located it on the mainland, and had peopled
it with savages barring the dreamer's access. The dreamer
dreams now a corrective paradise, an island properly enough,
located a trifling distance from the first experiment and
free, fortunately, of the defects of the first. Yet something is wrong here too. The very freedom of the island
shifts subtly into a defect. Closer examination reveals its
defect to be precisely what we had thought its principal advantage: it is unpeopled. Even Goat Island, lacking a busy
commerce, is wilderness after all. It would be a paradise if
the Cyclopes but knew it. Surely, we say, it is a paradise
already, just as it is, and a paradise by virtue of being un-
discovered by the Cyclopean apparitions. And besides, we add,
the Cyclopes need no island as their vacation land. They
live in paradise already. Why should the dreamer lapse now
into wishful optatives when the perfect paradise, no, two
paradises, one for himself and one for the Cyclopes, stand
securely situated in the indicative? Why should the Cyclopes
study the optative? What do they need to bring to completion? The dreamer is very confused. Only the dreamer has
needs which need completion. Only the dreamer needs the optative to help him dream one landscape after another.

In his critique of the Cyclopes for their myopic ignorance
of the optative mode, Odysseus twice uses the verb *kamnō* (vv.
126, 130), "to work at, to labor, to belabor, to exhaust,
wear down, wear out someone, something, or oneself." The

word may convey any degree of weariness from simple headache
to terminal illness. Its use in the present context is significant both as a critique of the Cyclopes and as the signifier of the dreamer's method. The Cyclopes do not work.
Odysseus certainly works. He works and works this dream of
paradise. Even when he has worked his paradise, with a nice
equilibration, offshore from the mainland, he fiddles with
its new-found perfections until he renders them imperfect
too. The beauty of the island is its solitude, but solitude,
even fertile solitude, fast comes to seem a desert.

The optative mode carries the dreamer forward into Part
II, section 3 (vv. 131-141). Optatives and indicatives balance each other as Odysseus continues to describe the island
only waiting for someone, say an Odysseus, to prune its perfections into view. The island is not at all bad, the narrator continues; it would bear every kind of fruit. It has
lovely meadows; vines would grow imperishable. The soil is
rich; one could reap a full crop every season. The island
has good anchorage. At this point Odysseus shifts from the
optative back to deploying a series of negatives: *no* need
for moorings here, *neither* for anchor stones *nor* cables.
Then, in the customary fashion, he recapitulates in the positive form, but here substituting the subjunctive for the indicative (vv. 138-139): sailors *could* beach their ships and
rest until the spirit *might* urge them forward and the breezes
breathe on them. The dreaming faculty has again reversed itself. Having turned from the Cyclopes back to topography and
ecology, Odysseus now deploys the Paradise formula in its
correct form again, using negatives to assert positive attributes. Odysseus rounds off his whole extensive description
of Goat Island with an encomium on its fresh water supply
(vv. 140-141). The positive epithet λάχεια , which initiates

Part II, and the positive image of the spring surrounded by, and fertilizing, a poplar grove, fitly frame the island. The fertility both in the initial epithet λάχεια and in the final word of Part II, πεφύασιν, marks the contrast between the island and the excess of the mainland. The island is bountiful; the mainland lushly overproductive.

In the twenty-six lines describing the goat paradise, Odysseus uses negative terms seventeen times. The description of the island is certainly as negative as that of the mainland, but the island is negative with a different charge. The proliferation of negatives, counterbalanced by positives, themselves a subtle interplay of several modes, indicative, optative, and subjunctive, discloses the ambiguous undulations in the dreamer's mind. Goat Island is a paradise, or could be, or should be, or would be . . . The perfections of the mainland the narrator had categorically undermined so as to render them perverse. The Cyclopes do not work their land. They do not exhaust it or themselves. Even dream-work is unknown among the Cyclopes. The vice of the Cyclopes is that they need nothing. They need no ships. They need no extra territory. They need no agriculture. They need no technology. Even dreams they do not need. Certainly they need no visitors from abroad to instruct them in the meaning of need. Monstrous brutes indeed, monstrously myopic, to live ignorant of need. Out of his great need Odysseus fantasizes an alternative paradise, with need now dreamed into its very soil. The island needs. The island needs a man of need.

In Part III (vv. 142-151), Odysseus describes the Greek ships' approach to this confusingly binomial landscape, where negatives are sometimes positive, surfeit sometimes a deficiency, deficiency sometimes a perfection. Again, following his previous practise, Odysseus states the facts mostly in

negatives, and recapitulates with positives. As before, he
looks to topography first, persons second; in this instance,
first the place viewed (more correctly, not viewed), then the
viewers (more correctly, the non-viewers). The approach to
this landscape is as negative as everything else about the
place.

Some god guided us, Odysseus says, through the murky night,
and the island *did not shine forth* to be seen. The fog was
dense, and the moon *did not shine* in the sky, but was muffled
in clouds. *No one* (οὔ τις) caught sight of the island with
his eyes. Does he mean *no one*? Or does he mean only *Outis*,
that famous and phantom voyager, saw this phantom land? In
the syntax of dreams, Freud argued, *either/or* is best translated as *both/and*.[18] More correctly, then, no one saw this
dream land and only Outis the trickster saw it. In Greek it
comes to the same thing, no one and Outis being condensed into one and the same word. The phantom voyager continues: we
did not see the long waves rolling to shore until the ships
were beached. To put it simply: it was night; no one was
seeing that night; there was nothing to be seen. The enter-
prising grammarian narrating this tale, deploying the negative as his pseudonym, cannot be emphatic enough. Twice he
states there was nothing to be seen. Twice he states no one
was seeing.

What a corker. The wanderer, Odysseus at Troy, but at sea
a nobody, blown off course and lost in a storm, wrapped in
invisibility, finds himself beached on an island wrapped in
invisibility. Nobody arrives by night at Nowhere, a nowhere
which bifurcates at once into two Nowheres, an extravagance
of Nowhere.

You know the rest of the story. How Nobody, securely invisible on Goat Island, marveled at the view, sat down to a

gamy dinner washed down with Thracian red. How he stared
across the bay at that other Nowhere and grew quickly dis-
content with the island paradise tailored so precisely to his
needs. How he followed his insatiable eyes across the bay to
the Nomansland neither needed by him nor needing him. How,
needing that unneeded territory, he peopled it with a guardian barricading him from his need, in size and monstrosity
exactly duplicating the extravagance of his need. How the
invisible Nobody sleuthed around Nomansland until his monstrous need was sighted. How, flaunting his need as a provocation, he dealt a cruel punishment to the guardian of the
paradise with zero needs, as if to remedy Nature's deficiency.
Cyclops too will come to know the meaning of need. Cyclops
too will learn to work in darkness, as humans work, in blind
Necessity.

We're back to the milk supply, that abundant, indeed su-
perfluous, liquid in this tale of intoxication. For that
milk the Cyclops must complete his days in dark deprivation.
For his theft of that milk Odysseus must lose every one of
his comrades and all his ships. For this one escapade
Odysseus is indentured to Poseidon, the terrible guardian of
the wine-faced Pontus, for the remainder of his life.

The psychology is obvious. Odysseus' sweet revenge in
this homely fantasy is the act of fantastic envy. Note again
his portrait of the Cyclopes' paradise as Nomansland in the
middle of Nowhere. Odysseus' corrosive envy virtually annihi-
lates the landscape. We have to work hard to recall that the
Cyclopes had any kind of landscape at all, so densely has it
been befogged by the narrator's envy for the land which needs
him not. The sweet rustic harmony is an offense to his eyes.
The shepherd in this pastoral, by the familiar trick we call
transference, pays for the offense with the loss of his
eyesight.

Who is the Cyclops? Bennett Simon has suggested this is
the story of intra-uterine sibling rivalry. Certainly
Odysseus and the Cyclops share many sibling resemblances.
Yet we could as well take the resemblance between them as
that of father and son. The Cyclops, being a phantom, can
certainly be a condensation of both sibling and parent, both
representations simultaneously yet something more than both.
He is the opposition to the little Nobody's need. In the end
he is nothing but the materialization of that need, the projection of the magnitude and ferocity of that need. Little
Nobody's need to weary and be wearied, to see and be seen,
his need to be seen for what he is, his need to be seen for
what he is not, his need to write his need large across the
cosmos, his need to invent inexorable Necessity and landscape
it with apparations of monstrosities and vengeful deities,
with shipwreck, whirlpool, and siren.[19]

NOTES

1. For the relation of Homer's *Cyclopeia* to the common folktale, see especially D. L. Page, *The Homeric Odyssey*
   (Oxford: Clarendon Press, 1955), pp. 1-20, and Justin
   Glenn, "The Polyphemos Folktale and Homer's *Kyklopeia*,"
   TAPhA 102 (1971), 133-181, esp. 177ff. Both studies reveal the individuality of Homer's version, but pass over
   several significant features. I owe special thanks to my
   colleagues Gregory Nagy and Carl Ruck for their many contributions, general and specific, to this present study.
   My thanks too to the several students whose questions and
   suggestions have entered into the body of this paper.
2. The first indication in the *Odyssey* that humans are

endowed with, and expected to exercise, conscience occurs
in Zeus' speech at 1.32ff., where Zeus meditates on the
self-destructiveness of Aegisthus who, disregarding all
warnings, went "beyond his allotment" (ὑπὲρ μόρον).

3. Henry Morrison, in an unpublished seminar paper comparing
Odysseus with the American Indian Trickster, has added
much to, and clarified, my own reading of the *Odyssey*.

4. George Berkeley, *An Essay Towards a New Theory of Vision*,
§2. A strong impulse for this present study has been my
work with two gifted persons practising Optometric Visual
Training, Emily Lyons and Lawrence W. Macdonald, O.D. It
is a pleasure to acknowledge here their extensive contributions to this paper. In recognition of my great debt
to his inspiration and work, I dedicate the paper to the
memory of Dr. Macdonald, lately taken from us by an untimely death.

5. Though it has been commonly noted that Odysseus on his return home ventures far out on the sea of fantasy, little
work has been done to analyze the poem according to the
rules appropriate to fantasy literature. Treatment of
the *Cyclopeia* along these lines has been almost negli-
gible, for all the interest the story has generated.

6. For two modern studies which have fallen for the anthropological bait, see Norman Austin, *Archery at the Dark of
the Moon* (Berkeley and Los Angeles: University of
California Press, 1975), pp. 143-149, and Geoffrey S.
Kirk, *Myth: Its Meaning and Functions in Ancient and
Other Cultures* (Berkeley and Los Angeles: University of
California Press, 1970), pp. 162-171. The episode certainly warrants anthropological analysis, doubtless representing the fascination of the Greeks in the colonial
period with other cultures, with degrees of culture, and

with possible sites for exploration and settlement. The
trickster-narrator, however, greatly complicates the task
of such analysts.

7. With the exception perhaps of Odysseus' punning name,
   Maron's wine is the most significant element in Homer's
   version of the tale.

8. For the significance of the milk and the suckling young
   in the cave, see Bennett Simon, "The Hero as an Only
   Child: An Unconscious Fantasy Structuring Homer's
   Odyssey," *International Journal of Psycho-Analysis* 55
   (1974), 555-562. The scene in the cave is a Dionysiac
   orgy; the milk and the wine are the two materials through
   which the Dionysiac transubstantiation takes effect. Cf.
   E. R. Dodds' edition of Euripides' *Bacchae* (Oxford:
   Clarendon Press, 1960), at lines 704-711.

9. Any anthropological analysis of the *Cyclopeia*, structuralist or otherwise, which ignores the person of the central actor in the episode must do injustice both to the
   story and to its particular shaping of the concepts of
   barbarism and civilization. The trickster-hero violates
   every code of civilized behavior, as nowhere else in the
   Odyssey, and does so before the Cyclops demonstrates any
   deviant behavior.

10. In some versions of the tale the ogre suffers from an
    ailment of his eye, which the little trickster offers to
    heal with the application of a salve. In Homer's version
    the medicinal idea is submerged, remaining ever present
    as a significant latent structure, visible first in
    Maron's wine, that marvelous therapeutic, and surfacing
    again in the simile of a metalworker quenching (φαρμάσσων,
    9.393) metal in cold water. Odysseus' pharmaceutical skill

also plays a significant part elsewhere in the *Odyssey*.

11. In Homeric diction only Hermes shares with Odysseus his most frequent epithet, *polymētis* (*Hymn to Hermes* 319); Zeus is the one deity who possesses *mētis*.

12. Freud offers many invaluable insights into the syntax both of dreams and equally of other kinds of fantasy. The essential core of his theory is that dreams represent symbolically the fulfillment of a wish. The wish is in turn distorted by the agency of the censor, with the resultant dream representing the fulfillment of at least two, often contrary, wishes. See *The Interpretation of Dreams*, tr. J. Strachey (New York: Basic Books, 1955), ch. IV, on distortion in dreams, and *passim*.

13. L. H. Jeffery, *Archaic Greece: The City States, c. 700-500 B.C.* (New York: St. Martin's Press, 1976), pp. 50-51, notes the islander's bias in the *Odyssey*, reflecting the influence of the Greek colonial movement in the poem. Kirk (above, note 6), p. 165, notes that the island is "a colonist's ideal landfall, and its affectionate description reproduces a kind of wish-fulfillment dream"; he goes on to say that it "represents nature . . . not as savage and repellent, but as waiting to be developed by culture."

14. See Joseph Fontenrose, *Python: A Study of Delphic Myth and Its Origins* (Berkeley and Los Angeles: University of California Press, 1959), pp. 384-385. Kirk, pp. 162-171, also discusses the relationship of the collective Centaurs and Cyclopes to their individualized hypostasis, Chiron or Polyphemus. He finds his own attempt to perceive a systematic correlation between Polyphemus and his tribe frustrated because opposed elements are not "precisely mediated" but are combined "into a fantastic

amalgam" expressing the ambiguities inherent in the concepts of nature and culture. Nature and culture, the
large concepts of structuralist anthropology, are rather
blunt instruments for penetrating the mysteries of the
devious *Cyclopeia*. The opposition in linguistics between
marked and *unmarked* can probably carry analysis farther.

15. Repetition is, of course, a major principle in Freud's
    theory of obsession. Many of the instances of mitosis in
    Homer's *Cyclopeia* could fit well enough in Freud's scheme
    of obsessional repetition.

16. Cf. Carl Jung on the relationship between the negative
    and the monstrous, in *Alchemical Studies* (tr. R. F. C.
    Hull) = *Collected Works of C. J. Jung*, vol. 13 (Princeton:
    Princeton University Press, 1967), p. 342: "The general
    rule is that the more negative the conscious attitude is,
    and the more it resists, devalues, and is afraid, the
    more repulsive, aggressive, and frightening is the face
    which the dissociated content assumes."

17. It is incorrect to describe the island as "barren," as
    Kirk does. It is uncultivated, altogether a different
    thing from barren. The Greek specifically states that
    the island was fertile; fertile if you see it with the
    eyes of Odysseus, fertile in potential projections.

18. *Interpretation of Dreams*, pp. 351-353.

19. The *Cyclopeia* is a rich case-history for some of Jacques
    Lacan's essential ideas, derived from his interpretation
    of Freud, on the place of desire in the human psyche. In
    Ecrits: A Selection, tr. A. Sheridan (New York: Norton,
    1977), p. 103, he writes: "These are the games of occul-
    tation which Freud, in a flash of genius, revealed to us
    so that we might recognize in them that the moment in
    which desire becomes human is also that in which the

child is born into language." That moment is represented in the *Cyclopeia* when the child-narrator names himself to the ogre as Nobody, in the act of naming discovering the negative, the first term in any language, not necessarily the first word, but the first articulation which is the beginning of language.

Odyssean Temporality: Many (Re)Turns

Ann L. T. Bergren

> The wisdom of the text is
> self-destructive (art is true
> but truth kills itself), but
> this self-destruction is in-
> finitely displaced in a series
> of successive rhetorical re-
> versals which, by the endless
> repetition of the same figure,
> keep it suspended between
> truth and the death of truth.
>
> Paul de Man[1]

I. ODYSSEUS' POEM AND NARRATOLOGY

It would be hard to find a recent study of the *Odyssey* that
fails to observe its concentration upon poetic craft: in
the characters of Demodocus and Phemius, in its markedly
artificial narrative exposition, and, above all, in the
casting of its hero as the poet of the four central books.[1]
But for all our attention to what one critic has called the
"aedo-centrism" of the epic, we have not fully appreciated
Odysseus' poetic craft.[2] It is common to point to the two
similes that liken Odysseus to a bard (Alcinous' comparison
in the middle of Book 11 and its echo as Odysseus strings
his bow)[3] and to observe how a hero/poet attributes a kind
of heroism to the bard; but beyond that, Odysseus' bardic
role in Books 9-12 has not been explored. Making him tell
his own story seems to be mainly a simile to aid exposition,
another "trope" for the polytropic hero, but not something

to take literally.[4] And, of course, it is a simile, but one
that is more extended than we have seen: to adopt
Quintilian's terminology, this *tropos* becomes a *figura*.[5]

Why have we failed to realize the full extent of
Odysseus' poetic role in Books 9-12? The answer, I think,
lies in the fact that we have read the text naively. To be
specific, we have read it without taking notice of its temporality. Despite several reminders, we tend to forget as
we read that Odysseus is telling a tale in the present about
events in the past. We forget this temporal relation or at
least miss its implications, because we read without sufficient awareness of how narrative works. Reading this text
without "narratological competence" is like trying to interpret a poem in Greek before we know the language well. If
we do not know something can be done, we will overlook it or
mistake it. In this case, we have overlooked the temporal
structure of Odysseus' tale and have missed the rhetoric of
Odyssean temporality. What, then, is this narratology and
what does it reveal in Odysseus' poem?

For its synthesis of previous work, for the range, precision, and integrity of its own system, and for the inter-
pretive subtlety it fosters, I have found the narratological
model of Gérard Genette to be the most valuable.[6] Building
on the work of Russian formalists, French structuralists,
and Anglo-American critics of the novel, Genette formulates
in his book *Narrative Discourse* what may be called an "anat-
omy" of narrative practice and applies it to Proust's *A la
Recherche du temps perdu*. I cannot summarize the whole model here, but I would like to sketch its basic concepts and
how they contribute to the analysis of temporality. First
of all, Genette distinguishes three levels of narrative:

story, the content or events narrated, e.g., the

adventures of Odysseus from the fall of Troy to his arrival at Calypso's island;

narrative, the oral or written text in which the *story* is
narrated, e.g., the text of the *Odyssey*;

narrating, the instance or event of telling the story,
e.g., Odysseus' narrating of his adventures for the
Phaeacians or a poet's narrating of the *Odyssey*.[7]

The ultimate goal of Genette's entire project is to eluci-
date the variety of relations among these three levels. He
categorizes these relations in terms borrowed from the grammar of verbs, supporting his choice with the fact that any
narrative is essentially an elaboration of a verbal form,
an expansion of a verb:[8] *tense*, for the temporal relations
between narrative and story; *mood*, for the forms and degrees
of "dramatization" or *mimēsis* of something in the story vs.
the "telling" or *diēgēsis* of it in the story or narrative;[9]
and *voice*, for the ways that the narrating event is implied
in the narrative. It is the first of these categories, that
of "tense," that directly concerns the temporal patterns of
a text.

The first object in Genette's analysis of "tense" is the
order of events: he compares the order of events in the narrative with the order of the same events in the story, in
order to determine their differences or what he terms their
"anachronies."[10] He finds variations on two basic patterns:
retrospection or "analepsis," a present, narrative evocation
of what is past in the story and then a return to the narrative present; and anticipation or "prolepsis," a present,
narrative forecast of what is future in the story and then a
return to the narrative present. Here are the two schema-
tized:

analepsis: narrative present--story past--narrative

present;

prolepsis: narrative present--story future--narrative
present.

Having determined these anachronies, Genette also measures
their "reach" and "extent," i.e., how far the text goes beyond the present and how long the past or future event lasts.

These two anachronies, analepsis and prolepsis, comprise
the temporal patterns of the *Odyssey*. For, like its hero,
the temporality of the epic is polytropic, made up of many
tropoi or *nostoi* of time, to use Homeric terms: "many
(re)turns" from the past and the future to the present.
Just as in the story Odysseus leaves Ithaca, fights at Troy,
and returns home, with many landings, departures and new
landings on the way, so the narrative repeatedly departs
from the present time to the past or future in the story and
returns to the narrative present again. Both the action and
the temporal form of the poem share the structure of
(re)turn. Ancient Homeric criticism recognized the present-
past-present pattern and described it as "Homeric *hysteron-
proteron*" or, at the opening of the epic, as "beginning *in
medias res*."[11] In terms of twentieth-century research into
the techniques of oral poetry, these present-past-present
and present-future-present deployments would constitute a
variety--a chronological variety--of "ring composition," for
the text always repeats its point of departure. But traditional Homeric scholarship has not connected these two virtual clichés of epic style, temporal reversal and circumstructure. It is only the narratological formulation of
anachrony that illustrates their common property of formal
return.

To summarize: in narratological terms the temporal patterns of the *Odyssey* are anachronies between narrative and

story, either analeptic recollections or proleptic prophecies; moreover, these formal patterns share with the action
of the poem a common structure, the structure of (re)turn.
And, as Parts II and III of this paper will show when we
turn to the poetry of the hero, we find the same temporality
and the same analogical relation between form and content.
Odysseus' tale is made up of many temporal (re)turns and
many actions which share the structure of the *tropos*. Its
overall character as a thematic and formal *nostos* is revealed by Alcinous' bard simile. And then, in individual
episodes, we see Odysseus as poet exploiting narrative
anachrony in order to prove the tropic character of his
challengers and his corresponding capacity to turn, return,
change, and exchange: first, with Polyphemus, the challenge
is *dolos/logos*, *mētis*, and the *xenia* of *onomata*; second,
with Teiresias, *nostos* and *nous* vs. *thymos*; and finally,
with the Cattle of the Sun, memory and the *xenia* of food.
Odysseus' tale thus embodies his *polytropia*. Both on the
large scale and in smaller parts, it demonstrates the form
and action of (re)turn. Thus composed, the account is not a
rhetorically neutral reminiscence. This poem of *nostos* aims
to define and to win *nostos*. no matter what the risk. And,
in the end, the hero's poem will win *nostos*, but at the risk
of revealing too well the nature of (re)turn.

II.   ODYSSEUS' *POLYTROPIA*

Alcinous' Simile: The Form and the Content of *Nostos*
The temporality of Odysseus' narrative is founded upon the
chronological structure of the *Odyssey* as a whole, the
structure that itself is built upon asking the hero's name.
At the end of Book 8 when Alcinous asks Odysseus to identify

himself, his request sets up a long recollection in the story that transforms the entire epic into a large-scale analepsis, a *hysteron-proteron* in which the present situation
in Ithaca, Ogygia, and Phaeacia comes before the past. The
diēgēsis of the story between the departure from Troy and
the start of the epic is thus also a *mimēsis*, an imitation
of the self-identification demanded by *xenia*. In exchange
for what he has already received and for his coming passage
home, Odysseus must give his name and then, like a poet, recall the events that "make" the name. In return for his return home, he must give his return from Troy to Phaeacia:
for *nostos*, *nostos*.

Accordingly, Odysseus shapes his narrative in the manner
of its frame, in the form, that is, of temporal return. He
starts in the present by stating his name in full.

Now first I will tell you my name, so that all of you
   may know me, and I hereafter, escaping the day without
   pity,
be your friend and guest, though the home where I live
   is far away from you.
I am Odysseus son of Laertes, known before all men
   for the study of crafty designs (δόλοισιν)[12] and my
   fame (κλέος) goes up to the heavens.   (9.16-20)

After completing his name with a description of his homeland
(21-36), he moves from the present to the past. To substantiate his claim to a *kleos* that reaches heaven, he will, he
says, recite his *nostos* (37-38). He begins with its earliest
point, the departure from Troy, and proceeds back to the
present at Phaeacia (9.39-11.453).[13] Formally, therefore,
his narrative is a present-past-present circumstructure.
This form is connected with the content of Odysseus' *kleos/
nostos* by Alcinous himself.

To keep the audience from forgetting that Odysseus is the
poet of Books 9-12, the poet of the *Odyssey* weaves into
Odysseus' tale another chronological ring from past to present to past and, in the space thus formed, presents a scene
of commentary upon the hero's tale. In the middle of the
journey to Hades described in Book 11, the text returns from
the story to Odysseus' narrating: "But I could not tell
over the whole number of them nor name all / the women I saw
who were the wives and daughters of heroes, / for before that
the divine night would give out." (328-330).[14] Rather than
ending a tale, such magnifications of the subject coupled
with a personal disclaimer usually fan the audience's interest and good will.[15] That is the effect here, for the
Phaeacians are enchanted (333-334), and Alcinous begs him to
continue:

> Odysseus, we as we look upon you do not imagine
> that you are a deceptive or thievish man, the sort
>   that the black earth
> breeds in great numbers, people who wander widely,
>   making up
> lying stories, from which no one could learn anything.
>   There is
> upon you a *morphē* of words and in you sound intelli-
>   gence (φρένες ἐσθλαί),
> and expertly, as a singer would do, you have told the
>   story
> of the dismal sorrows befallen yourself and all of
>   the Argives.   (363-369)

Odysseus' account of his *nostos* is like a skillful poet's in
its internal intelligence (ἔνι δὲ φρένες ἐσθλαί) and in the
external shape or structure of its narration (ἔπι μὲν μορφὴ
ἐπέων).[16] For here *morphē*, while not excluding from its

reference the "shapeliness" of individual phrases, does not mean the "comeliness" but more precisely the over-all "form" of the tale, its analeptic arrangement.[17] Why should an expert poet use this *hysteron-proteron* form for a *nostos* that displays intelligence?

By this point in its development, Odysseus' tale has shown why first-person analepsis with the prolepses it permits is the right form for imitating and narrating the intelligence behind his many returns. As *mimēsis*, Odysseus' recollection, because it returns from present to past to present, is a virtual *nostos* of the mind, while as *diēgēsis*, it traces the same pattern of *nostos* in its cycles of departure and return, death and rebirth.[18] Just as the hero returns from the dead in Hades, so the narrator's memory resurrects the past from the realm of the forgotten.[19] But by now it is also clear that mental and physical return are not just formally parallel but causally connected. In the Polyphemus and Teiresias episodes, Odysseus the narrator has used anachrony to show Odysseus the hero learning what *nostos* requires: crafty *xenia*, especially the exchange of names and food, "crafted" through remembering the dictates of the prophetic *nous*.[20] And later, in the encounter with the Cattle of the Sun, he will direct the same temporality toward proving that he has met these conditions of *nostos* and that the gods thus will his return.

Polyphemus: *logos* (re-)turned as/into *dolos*

Because it is the longest episode that centers upon the hero's action, the Polyphemus story offers the widest scope for the anachronies of first-person recollection, for the interplay between Odysseus as narrator and Odysseus as hero, between what he saw or foresaw then and what he sees now.

As poet, Odysseus exploits this potential, but by neglecting
the factor of analepsis with its double point of view critics have often simplified or mistaken his complex meaning.
Over the central issue of the name they have split into two
camps: those who approve the withholding but not the giving
of the proper name, and those who criticize the *Outis*-trick
but defend the later revelation.[21] The positions are not
wholly exclusive, however. From the narratological perspective, the defense vs. the criticism of revealing the name
corresponds, as we shall see, to the hero's vs. the narrator's point of view and thus reflects the anachronic structure of the text. As for the *Outis*-trick, no assessment can
be complete without considering the element of disguise
throughout the epic and even in relation to the *Iliad*, but·
in this episode both hero and narrator are delighted with
this *logos/dolos*.[22] Indeed, as narrator Odysseus uses
anachrony to show what happens when such crafty manipulation
of name-exchange is relaxed: the trick returns as and turns
into the trickster.

From the start of the episode the narrator employs prolepsis within the over-all analepsis to evaluate the hero's
actions. In 9.187ff. the narrator describes in advance the
creatures that, as hero, he has just determined to test
(172-176). This description does not, as Page contends,
"mislead" the audience by implying that the hero "already
knows" the Cyclopes' character so that the taking of the
Ismarian wine will not seem unmotivated.[23] It is perfectly
clear that Odysseus is not claiming to be able to observe
from the ship the customs (note the frequentatives in 184
and 189) of those in the cave. In Genette's terms, Page is
confusing the story with the narrative, and in doing so he
misses the narrative craft at work here. The narrator's

foreshadowing makes the audience able to anticipate what is
coming and to applaud what Odysseus does next, that is, to
foresee (not "already know") as hero what the narrator has
just established as fact. For it is now that Odysseus describes the fabulous wine (196-213) and explains why he took
it along: his *thymos* had seen (ὀἵσατο)--perhaps upon sight-
ing the island with its huge, headland cave (181-183)--the
Cyclopes' savagery (213-215).[24] This demonstration of fore-
sight is complimentary to the hero, but it also sharpens the
critical edge of the narrator's next prolepsis. After relating how his companions begged him just to take some food
and escape, Odysseus adds: "but I would not listen to them,
it would have been better their way, / not until I could see
him, see if he would give me guest-presents (ξείνια)" (228-
229). If he can anticipate the Cyclops' character, he
should be all the more able to heed his companions' warning.
Now, as narrator, he says that would have been better, but
then, as hero, he was determined to pit the skills of culture against nature's rude force, to extract the recognition
of *xenia* even from a monster.

Odysseus still sees the contest in these terms. He uses
two narrative techniques, the simile and the pun, to stamp
his former weapons as cultural products. He likens his olive beam to tools of civilized crafts (one of which, ship-
building, the Cyclopes specifically lack, 9.125-130): he
and his men twist the beam as others drill a ship plank with
a brace-and-bit (383-388), and its point sizzles in the
Cyclops' eye like a hot axe or plane in tempering water
(391-394). The olive beam blinds him, but escape from the
beast ultimately depends upon the cultural tool *par
excellence*, speech.

Odysseus wins the contest of speech as weapon because he

can turn *logos* into *dolos*, or so the narrator implies by
glossing the *Outis/ou tis* trick with a pun on *mētis* and *mē
tis*.[25] After recalling the other Cyclopes' answer to
Polyphemus' call for help,

If alone as you are nobody (μή τις) uses violence on
you,

why, there is no avoiding the sickness sent by great
Zeus;

so you had better pray to your father, the lord
Poseidon.   (410-412)

Odysseus adds his own reaction,

So they spoke as they went away, and the heart within
me

laughed over how my name and my perfect trick of intelligence (μῆτις) had fooled him.   (413-414)

By including this pun (and reinforcing it in line 422,
where he repeats the word *mētis* in the same metrical position), the narrator registers his continued pride in what it
implies: Odysseus is "master-troper": he can turn a thing
into the same but different thing.[26] Odysseus can assimi-
late *mētis* and *mē tis*, just as his *mētis* made the Cyclopes
say *mē tis*, and just as his *Outis/dolos* made Polyphemus say
in his call for help, Οὖτίς με κτείνει δόλῳ (408). By thus
repeating Odysseus' *Outis*, even as he calls it a *dolos*,
Polyphemus turns it against himself. The speech/trick of
the "master-(re-)turner" is that Polyphemus must (re-)turn
his speech as/into a trick. Whose speech? Not "Nobody's."
It is the speech of Polyphemus that turns against Polyphemus,
as long as his is the only "proper" name of the two. With
another proper name to say, however, the direction of
Polyphemus' speech will be turned.

In the second round of name-exchange, the narrator's view

diverges again from the hero's. With emphasis on the *thymos*
that overruled his comrades' arguments (an emphasis that
comes clear in the Tiresias episode), Odysseus recalls his
boast to the giant:

> So they spoke, but could not persuade the great
> *thymos* in me,
> but once again in the anger of my *thymos* I cried to
> him:
> "Cyclops, if any mortal man ever asks you who it was
> that inflicted upon your eye this shameful blinding,
> tell him that you were blinded by Odysseus, sacker of
> cities.
> Laertes is his father, and he makes his home in
> Ithaca."   (500-505)

By giving the true, powerful version of his name, Odysseus
activates the powerful version of his adversary's name.
"Polyphemus" means "he of the many *phēmai*," but the compound
may be either active or passive and the sense of *phēmē* either the unmarked "speech" or the marked "speech about the
future, prophecy or curse."[27] Context alone regulates the
polysemy, and in this context Polyphemus now means "he of
the many prophecies or curses," for Odysseus has (re-)turned
to him and against himself the power of speech, the "divine"
power--expressed by the optative mood--to cause what it
says. Polyphemus can now, with two optatives (ὀψὲ κακῶς
ἔλθοι and εὕροι πήματα, 534-535), curse "Odysseus sacker of
cities." The validity of the prophecy is proleptically confirmed by the narrator, when, after describing the hero's
sacrifice to Zeus of the ram he rode to safety, he adds:

> but he was not moved by my offerings,
> but still was pondering on a way how all my strong-
> benched

ships should be destroyed and all my eager companions.

(553-555)

By exploiting the double focus of first-person recollection through prolepsis, simile, and pun, the poet Odysseus
shows what he now knows about the exchange of names. If
your host proves as uncivilized as you expected by inverting
the code of *xenia* (asking your identity before feeding you,
making a meal of instead of for his guests), escape lies in
complementary inversions of the conventions (giving wine to
your host, who drinks it alone, and giving "No-Name" as your
name).[28] If your host is huge but brainless, you may blind
him with the tricks of intellect and the tools of culture.
But, if your host is savage, you must restrain all desire to
gain more from him than escape. To extort personal credit
for victory requires giving your name, thereby restoring the
creature's sight and cancelling the intellectual advantage
you won with your *logos/dolos*. Only culture can accord
kleos. When *xenia* is inverted, *nostos* requires "*polytropia*," the continual, controlled (re-)turning of *logos* as/
into *dolos*, despite the claims of *thymos*.[29] What made this
(re-)vision of the encounter clear to Odysseus was the
prophecy of Teiresias.

Teiresias: The Full Circle of Prolepsis
At the end of Book 10, Circe tells Odysseus what he must do
to return home:

Son of Laertes and seed of Zeus, resourceful Odysseus,
you shall no longer stay in my house when none of you
    wish to;
but first there is another journey you must accomplish
and reach the house of Hades and of revered Persephone,
there to consult as oracle (χρησομένους) the soul of
    Teiresias the Theban,

to whom alone Persephone has granted intelligence
(νόον)
even after death, but the rest of them are flittering
shadows.   (488-495)
Here we meet two paradoxes, each with the same bearing on
nostos and *nous*. To return to life Odysseus must suffer a
kind of death. The way home from Hades can be learned only
from one who can see while blind, whose soul alone among the
shades possesses oracular intelligence. In its formal and
thematic relation to the rest of Odysseus' poem, Teiresias'
prophecy displays this power to return.

    At the heart of Odysseus' recollection lies the prophecy
of Teiresias. The two narrations are complementary in their
anachronic structures. Odysseus' tale is analeptic, tracing
an arc from present to past to present, while Teiresias'
vision stretches from present to future to present. In the
order of the text the hero's account frames the prophet's.
Here is the composite:

    HERO: Present - Past   ↑   Past - Present
    PROPHET: Present-Future-Present
In this double anachronic *morphē,* a circle toward the future
interrupts, opposes and complements a circle toward the
past. When the content, too, is considered, the construction emerges in its reach and extent as an emblem of the
hero's many returns.

    Odysseus' recollection puts in the center of the *Odyssey*
all of his *nostos* that precedes the epic. His analepsis
reaches back to his first stop after leaving Troy, extends
through nine more cycles of coming and going, and ends where
the poem begins, with the hero enthralled by Calypso.[30]
Teiresias' prophecy bisects this recollection of the past
with a vision of Odysseus' future *nostoi*. Through these

anachronies the line of the text imitates the circles of departure and return that make up heroic experience. For the
two parts of Teiresias' prophecy sweep forward, the first
reaching to the end of the epic and the second beyond the
end, round again and back to the center of the poem in Hades.

Teiresias first explains what *nostos* in the second half
of the *Odyssey* will require.

Glorious Odysseus, what you are after is sweet homecoming (νόστος),
but the god will make it hard for you. I think you
 will not
escape the Shaker of the Earth, who holds a grudge
 against you
in his heart, and because you blinded his dear son,
 hates you.
But even so and still you might come back, after much
 suffering,
if you can restrain your own *thymos*, and contain your
 companions',
at that time when you first put in your well-made
 vessel
at the island Thrinakia, escaping the sea's blue
 water,
and there discover pasturing the cattle and fat sheep
of Helios, who sees all things, and listens to all
 things.
Then, if you keep your mind on homecoming, and leave
 these unharmed,
you might all make your way to Ithaka, after much
 suffering;
but if you do harm them, then I testify to your destruction.   (11.100-112)

Nostos demands restraint of *thymos* in accord with what the
prophetic *nous* can see will determine your goal. Teiresias
sees that Odysseus must restrain his hunger to eat the
Cattle of the Sun. If he wants a day of homecoming, he must
preserve *xenia* with the bringer of all days.[31] If he wants
to expel the guests who eat their host's food by force, he
must leave the herds of his host unscathed. With the ability to make the body serve the devisings of the mind, one man
can defeat many.

Teiresias, however, does not stop where the poem ends,
with the defeat of the suitors. The reach and extent of his
prophecy include the future beyond the epic, just as
Odysseus' tale embraces its past.

But after you have killed these suitors in your own
   palace,
either by treachery, or openly with the sharp bronze,
then you must take up your well-shaped oar and go on a
   journey
until you come where there are men living who know
   nothing
of the sea, and who eat food that is not mixed with
   salt, who never
have known ships whose cheeks are painted purple, who
   never
have known well-shaped oars, which act for ships as
   wings do.
And I will tell you a very clear proof, and you cannot
   miss it.
When, as you walk, some other wayfarer happens to meet
   you,
and says you carry a winnow-fan on your bright
   shoulder,

then you must plant your well-shaped oar in the
   ground, and render
ceremonious sacrifice to the lord Poseidon,
one ram and one bull, and a mounter of sows, a boar
   pig,
and make your way home again and render holy
   hecatombs
to the immortal gods who hold the wide heaven, all
of them in order. Death will come to you from the
   sea, in
some altogether unwarlike way, and it will end you
in the ebbing time of a sleek old age. Your people
about you will be prosperous. All this is true that
   I tell you.   (119-137)

In this final return of the hero, the *Odyssey* itself circles
around to reconnect with itself, for Teiresias' vision ends
where a "gentle death from the sea" will bring Odysseus back
to where he and the poem stand now.[32] Odysseus will leave
home, sail the sea, and travel inland with an oar until he
reaches those who have never tasted salt and who interpret
the *sēma* of the oar as a winnowing-fan. There he will plant
this instrument of both commerce at sea and cultivation of
the land, and by this act at last resolve his conflict with
Poseidon, the element through which all *nostoi* occur, all
returns from contests on Athena's soil. In Teiresias' proleptic perspective all these oppositions--commerce and agriculture, sea and land, alien and native, life and death--
dissolve in the "still small point" at the turning of the
epic in Hades.

The Cattle of the Sun: The *Hysteron-Proteron* of Memory

Odysseus does not end his tale without attempting to validate Teiresias' grand prophecy. Here there is none of the
uncertainty that closes the *katabasis* of the *Aeneid*, no
shade from the ivory gate. Odysseus is unambivalent in his
desire for conveyance by his hosts, and his elaborate pre-
cautions and strenuous efforts since arriving at Phaeacia
imply that their response cannot be taken for granted. But
just as another tale by Odysseus will wangle a mantle from
Eumaeus and another by Penelope will elicit gifts from the
suitors, so this story may win passage from the Phaeacians
if it persuades them of two things, that Teiresias' prophecy
is true and that Odysseus can meet its demands.[33] To prove
himself and corroborate Teiresias, Odysseus again applies
the rhetorical force of prolepsis.

In Book 12 Odysseus as narrator risks the tedium of repetition in order to establish a pattern of proleptic admoni-
tion and subsequent response. After rehearsing in full
Circe's forecast of the coming trials (37-141), he then describes how he survived them all by remembering her instructions and acting upon them.[34] By this sequence he demonstrates the "death" of the man who indulged his *thymos* by
boasting to Polyphemus and his "rebirth" as one who can fulfill Teiresias' conditions for homecoming: to remember a
prophecy and to restrain his *thymos* accordingly. Conversely, his success in the trials ratifies these conditions.

Besides Odysseus' own behavior, the fate of his crew confirms Teiresias' *logos* of *nostos*. At every point Odysseus
repeats to them Circe's directions. Encountering the Sirens,
all remember and obey, and no one is lost. Next, preparing
for Scylla and Charybdis, Odysseus tries to encourage his
men by reminding them of their escape from the Cyclops.

Dear friends, surely we are not unlearned in evils.
This is no greater evil now than it was when the
    Cyclops
had us cooped in his hollow cave by force and
    violence,
but even there, by my courage and counsel and my
    intelligence,
we escaped away. I think that all this will be
    remembered
some day too. Then do as I say, let us all be won
    over.   (208–213)

Besides remembering past success, they are to look into the
future to the point where present peril becomes remembered
escape. The men should project upon the future their recollection of the past. Again they respond, and the losses are
kept to the predicted minimum (108–110, 222–250).

On Helius' island, however, the outcome is different. At
the outset Odysseus recalls the warnings of Teiresias and
Circe and conveys them to the crew, but this time to no
avail.[35] They steal the god's cattle and a shipwreck results. Through prolepsis, Odysseus makes this calamity the
rhetorical climax of his tale. He repeats the premonition
of disaster he had as soon as the crew rejected his plea:

And then indeed I recognized that the god was devising
    evils.   (295)

This anticipation of divine vengeance soon blossoms into the
words of the gods themselves. Helius threatens, in effect,
to eliminate all days:

                                                Unless
these are made to give me just recompense for my
    cattle,
I will go down to Hades' and give my light to the dead
    men.   (382–383)

In ignoring Teiresias' prophecy, the shipmates have committed
a crime tantamount to turning the cosmos inside out, to put-
ting the source of life in the place of death.[36]   Zeus promises to restore the natural order:

> Helios, shine on as you do, among the immortals
> and mortal men, all over the grain-giving earth. For
>   my part
> I will strike these men's fast ship midway on the open
> wine-blue sea with a shining bolt and dash it to
>   pieces.   (385-388)

This prediction defines the shipwreck, before Odysseus re-
counts it, as confirmation by the world's undying realities
of Teiresias' ontology of *nostos*. The shipwreck derives
Teiresias' prophecy and Odysseus' homecoming from the righ-
teousness of Zeus. Who now could doubt the truth of the
prophecy or Odysseus' right to fulfill it? Who would refuse
the hero's return?

III. THE ECONOMY OF *NOSTOS*

In the world of the *Odyssey* poetry is exchanged. Sometimes
the process is cast as part of *xenia*, an exchange of "gifts."
And sometimes it is explicitly "economic" with the parties
clearly identified as producer and consumer and the recompense set beforehand.[37]   A poet is one of the *dēmiourgoi*, a
professional who makes his living by trading his stories for
shelter, clothes, food or conveyance.[38]   In either version,
the exchange proves that poetry has "economic value." A tale
is rewarded, if it tells the truth or what the listeners want
the truth to be.[39]   Conversely, a poem's worth in the eyes of
the listeners is measured by what it elicits, what it "makes."
In these terms, the response to Odysseus' tale proves it a
masterwork.

Like a good audience, the Phaeacians in Book 8 indicate
beforehand what they want to hear. Although they have already offered gifts and expressed their willingness to escort
Odysseus home, their *pompē* still requires his self-identifying
tale. Alcinous asks his name and country so that the ships
may know where to take him (8.550-563), and even specifies
the guiding theme for the rest of the story, the degree of
xenia among the peoples he has met (572-576). Coupled with
this request, however, is Alcinous' recollection of his father's gloomy prophecy: how Poseidon will one day wreck a
returning ship and obliterate the Phaeacians for conveying
men home safely (564-571). Along with his request for a poem
in return for *nostos* goes the king's awareness of what *nostos*
may cost. The real "economic" challenge here for Odysseus is
clear. Although this is only *xenia*--for the hero is only
"like" a bard, his tale must nonetheless persuade his audience
to give him *nostos* at a mortal risk. The impact of Odysseus'
remembered prophecy must counteract the prophecy that Alcinous
remembers. And, at the end of his story, the truth of
Teiresias' prophecy seems unassailable. The Phaeacians act
at once to take their guest home.

And the final cost in this exchange of *nostos*? Now we find
something like the poignance and ambiguity that end *Aeneid* 6.
In Book 13, immediately after the Phaeacians leave Odysseus
on Ithaca, the text confirms that this was the return antici-
pated by Alcinous. Like Zeus and Helius before the shipwreck,
Zeus and Poseidon debate the Phaeacians' fate. Poseidon declares his intention to turn their ship to stone and to bury
their city beneath a mountain (146-152). Zeus replies:

Good brother, here is the way it seems to my mind best
    to do. When all the people are watching her from the
    city
as she comes in, then turn her into a rock that looks

like

a fast ship, close off shore, so that all people may
wonder

at her. And cover their city with a great mountain.

(154-158)[40]

And what does Poseidon do? We never learn. In what John
Peradotto calls a "prophecy degree zero,"[41] the outcome here
is left uncertain, as indeterminable as Teiresias' prophecy
of Odysseus' death. This uncertainty raises questions that
challenge the ontology upon which the truthfulness of
Odysseus' tale is based. Can a divinely ordained homecoming
necessitate the divinely ordained destruction of those that
accomplish it? If the two prophecies seem to conflict, was
one of them a fiction? Neither is confirmed in the text.
Can any prophecy or recollection be trusted as true? As with
the *Outis*-trick, the problem requires analysis of the whole
epic. What is true, in any case, is that the prophecy of
Teiresias is coupled with another that opens the question of
prophetic truth, just as Odysseus' recollection in Books 9-12
is matched in 13-24 by his explicitly false "memories" of
Crete, two apparent instances of *alēthea* followed by *pseudea
homoia etumoisin*.[42]

In admitting these questioning counterparts, the text
makes its final disclosure on the nature of *nostos*. It ac-
knowledges the inherent instability of return. It now implies that if Odysseus can turn from controlled *logos/dolos*
to indulgence of *thymos* and back to controlled *thymos*, he can
turn back again.[43] There can be no final return of time, for
the truth of the past or future always eludes its only veri-
fication, occurrence in a present that never returns. The
truth of memory or prophecy can be only a verisimilitude,
achieved by the similarity between temporal and causal relations.[44] In admitting the radical uncertainty of anachrony,

Odyssean temporality takes its own risk in the economy of
nostos. In order to disclose the nature of the poetic
"trope," it risks (re-)turning as an *Outis*-trick against the
rhetorical mastery of its hero/poet.

NOTES

In this paper I have cited the Greek text of T. W. Allen,
Homeri Opera III-IV, 2nd ed. (Oxford: Clarendon Press,
1917 and 1919) and adapted the translation of R. Lattimore,
The Odyssey of Homer (New York: Harper and Row, 1965).

1. The most recent and full account of this aspect of the
   Odyssey is D. Stewart, *The Disguised Guest, Rank, Role,
   and Identity in the Odyssey* (Lewisburg: Bucknell University Press, 1976), pp. 146-195.

2. The term belongs to F. Frontisi-Ducroux, "Homère et le
   temps retrouvé," *Critique* 32 (1976), 538-548, a review of
   Gérard Genette, "Discours du récit," in *Figures* III (Paris:
   Editions du Seuil, 1972), pp. 67-282, translated by Jane
   E. Lewin as *Narrative Discourse: An Essay in Method*
   (Ithaca: Cornell University Press, 1980). This review
   points the way for my essay by illustrating the three nar-
   rative levels with the case of Odysseus as bard.

3. The similes are at 11.366-369 and 21.406-409.

4. For the implications of Odysseus' epithet, *polytropos*, (in
   place of his proper name) in Book 1.1 of the *Odyssey*: (1)
   its attribution to the hero of "manyness" (the repetition
   of the same or the similar (i.e., the "disguised" same),
   the constant economic accumulation and loss, and perpetual
   arriving and leaving) and the efforts of the text to direct this "manyness" toward a fulfillment in conclusive

victory, (2) its possible reference to the text itself as tropological or rhetorical, and (3) its illustration of the excessive or supplementary property of language to "trope on" (multiply) its literal meaning, and how such *polytropia* precludes a single, "proper" name with its attendant *kleos*, see Pietro Pucci, "The Proem of the *Odyssey*," forthcoming in "Text and Contexts: Papers in Honor of Jean-Pierre Vernant," *Arethusa* (1981). While different in range, methodology, and emphasis from my essay, Pucci's demonstration of the "logic of the supplement" in Odysseus' *polytropia* complements and corroborates my analysis of the "tropic" structure of both temporal form and critical action in the poem. Underlying both papers, moreover, is acceptance of Jacques Derrida's analysis of repetition, best delineated, perhaps, in "Signature, Event, Context," *Glyph* 1 (1977), 172-197.

5. On the one-word or two-word *tropos* vs. the extended *figura*, see, e.g., Quintilian 9.2.44-46, 9.1.1-9.

6. See above, note 2.

7. Genette, *Narrative Discourse*, pp. 25-29. Genette's French terms are perhaps clearer than the translations: *histoire* = story, *récit* = narrative, *narration* = narrating.

8. Genette, *Narrative Discourse*, pp. 30-32.

9. This distinction comes from *Republic* 392c-395, where Plato condemns narration through deceptive *mimēsis*, in which the poet speaks as someone else, in favor of *haplē diēgēsis*, narration pure and simple in which the poet always speaks in his own voice. The two narrative forms correspond to "mood" defined by Genette (*Narrative Discourse*, p. 161) as the "name given to the different forms of the verb that are used to affirm more or less the thing in question, and to express . . . the different points of view from which the life or the action is looked at."

10. Genette, *Narrative Discourse*, pp. 35-48.

11. In antiquity *hysteron-proteron* was felt to be so peculiarly Homeric that the figure was regularly termed
hysteron-proteron Homerikos, and illustrated by the order
of *Odyssey* 1-12. See S. Bassett, "῞Υστερον πρότερον
'Ομηρικῶς," *HSPh* 31 (1920), 39. In this article Bassett
argues that the term originally meant not just a simple
inversion of natural order (e.g., *gameonti te geinomenoi
te*), but complete A-B-A or A-B-B-A sequences. When the
units are those of time, however, there is no difference
between these "ring-compositions" and chronological inversions, since the text always returns to its original position: *hysteron-proteron-hysteron*, "later"-"earlier"-
"later," present-past-present.

12. The full significance of this term as part of Odysseus'
name we will realize later in the episode with Polyphemus
and again at the close of this tale for the Phaeacians.

13. Last of all Odysseus mentions the sojourn with Calypso,
but he does not elaborate, since, as he explains, that is
the story he told (*mythologeuein*) last night (12.450-453).
Compare Genette, *Narrative Discourse*, p. 64, on how attach-
ing an analepsis to the primary narrative can give the appearance of "overlapping, unless the narrator has the skill
to extract from this awkwardness a sort of playful charm."
Note the narrative effect of making Odysseus recount his
departure from Calypso separately (7.240-297), before his
grand narration of the *nostos* that ends with that separa-
tion. The end of Odysseus' story recalls both his earlier
account in Book 7 to Arete and the poet's account of the
same action in Book 5 and at the start of the epic in
Book 1: the end curves back to the three "same but different" points at which the *Odyssey* as the story of

Odysseus' *nostos* begins. Compare Genette, pp. 45-46, on
how the repeated analepses at the start of Proust's
Recherche attempt by "propitiatory *mimēsis*" to "exorcize"
the difficulty of any beginning. As the "repeated starts"
of *Odyssey* 5 and 13 testify, this effort to control the
difficulty of beginning by imitating it belongs to the
earliest stage of western narrative.

14. Frontisi-Ducroux, 541-542, observes how this return
    to Odysseus' narrating and the comments of Arete and
    Alcinous stress the double role of Odysseus as hero and
    bard. We should also note that the return of Odysseus'
    narrating is echoed by a return to the poet's narrating:
    "So he spoke, and all of them stayed stricken to silence, /
    held in thrall (κηληθμῷ) by the story all through the
    shadowy chambers" (11.333-334). Besides this reconver-
    gence of the two narrating events, the use of the term
    kēlēthmos, "magic charm of song," marks Odysseus as poet.
    See W. B. Stanford, *The Odyssey of Homer I*, 2nd ed.
    (London: Macmillan, 1959), ad loc.

15. Compare the disclaimers of Nestor (3.113-117), Helen
    (4.240-242), Odysseus (14.193-198, note 463-467 as well)
    and the similar gesture in the *Iliad* at the start of the
    Catalogue of Ships (2.488-492).

16. See Stanford, ad loc.: "Note the antithesis between the
    outward form (ἔπι = ἔπεστι) and inner meaning (ἔνι =
    ἔνεισι)." The word *phrenes* is not connected grammati-
    cally with *epeōn*, but in this context it can refer only to
    the intelligence of Odysseus in the narrative of and by
    himself. Hence Stanford is correct to gloss ἔνι δὲ
    φρένες ἐσθλαί as the "inner meaning" of Odysseus' self-
    defining tale.

17. For *morphē* as "shapeliness of phrase," see Stanford, ad
    loc. Note that if H. Koller, "Epos," *Glotta* 50 (1972),
    16-24, is correct in claiming that in epic diction *epos*
    designates an hexameter verse, then the plural, *epea*,
    would denote an aggregate of such verses, that is, an epic
    narrative, and *morphē epeōn* here should be translated as
    "the form of an epic narration."

18. The formal and thematic relation between return and in-
    telligence in the *Odyssey* coheres with the etymology of
    nous offered by Douglas Frame in *The Myth of Return in Early
    Greek Epic* (New Haven: Yale University Press, 1978). On
    the basis of evidence in the Homeric epics and the *Rig-
    Veda*, and from parallels in other Indo-European languages,
    Frame argues that both *nostos* and *nous* are deverbative sub-
    stantives of the same root, **nes*. According to his deri-
    vation, *nostos* and *nous* make up an unmarked/marked pair of
    nouns: *nostos*, the more general term, means a return from
    darkness, death, forgetfulness or sleep to light, life,
    consciousness, and home, while *nous*, restricted to mental
    activity, denotes what may be termed a *nostos* of the mind.

    Throughout his book, Frame notes with regret that only
    vestiges of the proposed connection between *nous* and
    nostos are found in the language of the Nekyia. Homeric
    diction regularly indicates awareness of etymological con-
    nection by the so-called *figura etymologica*, and it is
    true that in Odysseus' "poem" there is no such figure at
    the level of diction for *nous* and *nostos*. This absence
    may be due to the fact that the thematic relation of *nous*
    and *nostos* here amounts to just such an etymological mark.
    The connection between *nous* and *nostos* may be so deeply
    embedded in the tradition that Odysseus' story is by it-
    self an etymological figure, and word-play between the two

is unnecessary. An inverse relation between lexical and
thematic marks of etymology may be a convention of Homeric
poetics. The instances of *figura etymologica* should be
studied to test this possibility. If such a convention
could be established, we would be able to use contextual
data with greater precision in the effort to choose among
the competing etymological possibilities offered by morphology and phonology alone.

19. As Plato will later maintain in terms of *anamnēsis*, the
return of the past to the present in the *Odyssey* is the
homecoming of the mind. It is self-constituting, "self-
poetic."

20. Note in the Polyphemus and Cattle of the Sun episodes the
parallel inversion of the motifs of eating and speech: in
the first, the issue for Odysseus and his crew is what to
say, while for Polyphemus it is what to eat; in the second,
the crew's improper eating is signified by the equally
"improper" *phōnē* of the meat (12.396).

21. Most representative of those who defend revealing the
name is George E. Dimock, Jr., "The Name of Odysseus,"
Hudson Review 9 (1956), 52-70. Dimock's reading is informed by the tenets of ego-psychology and its foundation
in Existentialist philosphy. For Odysseus, to enter
Polyphemus' cave and there to name himself Nobody is to
return to the womb and pre-birth anonymity. Both the
blinding of the giant and the exclamation of his name are
necessary for rebirth: "This cry of defiance is thought
to be foolish of the wily Odysseus, no less by his crew
than by the critics, but it is in reality, like the boar
hunt, a case of deliberate self-exposure for the purpose
of being somebody rather than nobody. . . . To pass from
the darkness of the cave into the light, to pass from

being "nobody" to having a name, is to be born. But to
be born is to cast one's name in the teeth of a hostile
universe" (55-56). For Dimock the blinding and the
true naming are not separable but are both necessary if
Odysseus is not to remain a nobody in the womb.

In direct opposition to this reading is the ethnographic
approach of C. S. Brown, "Odysseus and Polyphemus: The
Name and the Curse," *CompLit* 18 (1966), 193-202. Invoking
the 1857 *Die Sage von Polyphem* of Wilhelm Grimm and citing
the studies of Hackman, Radermacher, Frazer, Carpenter,
and Page, Brown attempts to demonstrate that the Polyphemus episode exemplifies a folktale common in Europe and
Asia and that the concealment and revelation of the name,
along with Polyphemus' curse, must be understood as an instance of "name taboo" or belief in "the power of the name"
common in ancient societies. Brown documents "the belief
that the personal name is a vital part of the self, that
it is dangerous for anyone to know it and to reveal it puts
one in the power of the other," in order to show how by
giving his name Odysseus "makes it possible for Polyphemus
to lay a curse upon him" (196). From this comparative,
ethnographic perspective, the concealment of the name is
not a psychological regression, but a mature, self-
preserving restraint, while its revelation is the opposite,
just as "Nobody" is the opposite of the proper name (rather than the alternate, but not incorrect, answer, "Myself,"
which appears in all the versions of the folktale except
the Homeric). The risk to Odysseus' selfhood thus lies in
his improper naming, rather than in his proper non-name.
22. With regard to the *Outis*-trick, N. Austin, "Name Magic in
the *Odyssey*," *CSCA* 5 (1972), 1-19, accepts Brown's demonstration of the power of the name, but shares the values

of Dimock. Austin shows how this false naming or non-
naming is one in a series of strategic concealments of
real identity either through language or physical disguise
(at Troy as beggar and in the Horse, at Scheria, and at
Ithaca). These concealments amount, in his view, to self-
negations that "undercut" the identity and achievements of
the "superhero" (15-16). In a pun on Odysseus' pun
that is worthy of the hero himself, Austin writes,
"Odysseus *polymetis*, when he is exercising his *Metis*, then
is he invariably *Outis*. His mask is his Metis; the face
it displays to the world is Outis" (16). From my perspective, however, with its roots in structuralist anthropology, narratology, and theory of meaning by analogous
oppositions, it remains a question whether in the ideology
of the *Odyssey* itself these manipulations of the *nom
propre* undermine the hero or whether, on the contrary,
they precisely define the polytropic heroism of the master
of *dolos*, the lure of false appearance (see the usages at
8.276 of Hephaestus' net, 8.494 of the Trojan Horse,
12.252 of bait, 19.137 of Penelope's weaving, Hes. *Th*. 589
and *Op*. 83 of Pandora, and *Od*. 9.19-20, where Odysseus attributes to all his *doloi* the *kleos* he is about to recount). It is at least true that within the text Odysseus
never suffers from or fails to achieve victory from "im-
personating *Outis*," except in the episode with Polyphemus,
when he gives up control of the role and the rate of recognition. Indeed, the successful "structure of revelation"
constructed by Odysseus at Scheria and Ithaca (Austin,
17), his successful working of the magic, trickster-like
power of visibility and invisibility, identity and disguise, is discernible by its contrast with the earlier
failure.

23. D. L. Page, *The Homeric Odyssey* (Oxford: Clarendon Press,
    1955), p. 19, note 14.

24. The emphasis on the *thymos* here initiates, as we shall
    see, a careful and critical usage of the term in the Poly-
    phemus and Teiresias episodes by which Odysseus both dis-
    plays and evaluates the two sides of his character: the
    defensive, preservative ingenuity we see now and the ag-
    gressive, excessive passion which will nearly destroy him
    later and which Teiresias will declare he must curb in or-
    der to reach home.

25. This pun has often been noticed: e.g., Eustathius, ad
    loc.; Stanford, ad loc; A. Podlecki, "Guest-Gifts and No-
    bodies," *Phoenix* 15 (1961), 130, note 11; Frame (above, note
    18), p. 71; Austin (above, note 22); and W. B. Stanford,
    *Ambiguity in Greek Literature: Studies in Theory and Prac-
    tice* (New York and London: Johnson Reprint Corporation,
    1972 [1939]), p. 105:   "This is the only place in Homer
    where ambiguity and paronomasia motivate a whole episode.
    Technically, it is possibly the cleverest use in all
    Greek.   The symmetry of οὖτις - οὔ τις - μή τις - μῆτις
    and the echo in οὐτιδανός anticipate the most ingenious
    constructions of the sophists."

26. See Austin (above, note 22), 13:   "Odysseus derives
    almost excessive pleasure from outwitting Polyphemos with
    his punning pseudonym *Outis*, No-Man.   It is a good pun be-
    cause a double pun in Greek.   Polyphemos, when blinded,
    wails that Οὖτις is killing him and his neighbors reply
    with the alternative negative μῆτις, thus unwittingly pun-
    ning on μῆτις, intelligence, the suffix of Odysseus' de-
    structive epithet *polymetis*.   Odysseus, hearing their ex-
    change on *Outis* and *Metis* as the cause of Polyphemos' pain,
    laughs that his name and his wit (*onoma* and *metis*) have

deceived them." We should note, however, that it is
Odysseus as narrator, and not the neighboring Cyclopes,
who is ultimately responsible for the pun; both hero and
poet are laughing.

27. In hexameter diction *phēmē* means either an unmarked
"speech," whether report, rumor, or reputation (e.g., *Il.*
10.207, *Od.* 6.273, 16.75 = 19.527, 24.201, Hes. *Op.* 760-
764, fr. 176 MW, and *Od.* 15.468, the place of speech by
the *dēmos*) or a marked "speech about the future," a prophecy or curse. The marked *phēmē* itself may either be
simply predictive (e.g., *Epigrams* 4.10, an autobiographical
epigram, supposedly by Homer, in which the Smyrnaeans ignore what is foretold in his *phēmē aoidēs*) or may aspire
by the optative mood to the "divine" power of causing what
it expresses. In this latter category of word as deed belong the usage at *Od.* 2.35, insofar as it refers to
Aegyptius' wish that Zeus accomplish the aim of whoever
has called the assembly, and at 20.100-101 where Odysseus
prays to Zeus for the appearance of a *teras* and for someone to *phasthai phēmēn*, if the gods truly will his return;
the *phēmē* (so termed, 105) comes from a miller woman in the
form of a wish that the suitors feast today for the last
time in Odysseus' house (116-119) and is glossed in 120 as
a *klēdōn*, omen.

The two usages in epic of the adjective *polyphemos* reflect the diathetic and semantic ambiguity of the compound:
the *agora* of *Od.* 2.150 and the *aoidos* of 22.376 could be
either "much speaking" or "much spoken of" and either
"much prophesying or cursing" or "much prophesied or
cursed." The semantics and morphology of the word permit
four meanings, but exclude none.

28. Compare the earlier instances of *xenia* in the *Odyssey* in which the guest is asked for his name only after and in return for what he has received: 1.119-176, 3.22-71, 4.37-64, and 7.133-239. Note also Odysseus' account of his stay at Aeolus' island, where hospitality is followed by questioning and story-telling: 10.14-16. From Aeolus as from the Phaeacians, Odysseus receives the *hodos* and the *pompē* he requests in return for his recitation: 10.17-18.

29. When Polyphemus first asks his name (before offering food), Odysseus identifies his men as troops of Agamemnon, whose *kleos* for sacking Troy is "now the greatest under heaven" (9.263-266). Later, when he gives his name to Polyphemus, he continues this identification with earlier martial glory by calling himself *ptoliporthios* (9.504), an epithet that the Cyclops repeats in his curse (530) and that is used in the *Odyssey* only of Odysseus. But in 9.19-20, when he gives his name to Alcinous, he shows the effects of the encounters with Polyphemus and Teiresias by claiming *kleos* for all his *doloi*.

30. The ten arrivals are: the Cicones, the Lotus Eaters, the Cyclopes, Aeolus twice, the Laestrygonians, Circe twice, Hades, and the island of the Sun.

31. On a connection between *nostos* and the cult of the Sun underlying the *Odyssey*, see Frame (above, note 18), pp. 28-33.

32. It is no wonder that generations of readers have found the end of the *Odyssey* to be somehow not an "ending," for Odysseus' *nostos* ends only here, in the center of the poem. That is the point of Teiresias' prophecy and of the epic as a whole. On the tradition of dispute about the end of the *Odyssey*, see D. Wender, *The Last Scenes of the Odyssey*

(Leiden: Brill, 1978) and J. H. Finley, Jr., *Homer's
Odyssey* (Cambridge, Mass.:   Harvard University Press, 1978),
Appendices I and II.
33. See 14.459-517 and 18.250-283.
34. In preparing to encounter Scylla (12.226f.) Odysseus
seems to have deviated from perfect adherence to Circe's
instructions.   When the goddess directs him to lose six
men to Scylla rather than confront Charybdis, Odysseus
asks if he cannot somehow fight off Scylla to save the six
men (108-114).   Circe answers: "It is best to run away
from her. / For if you arm for battle beside her rock and
waste time / here, I fear she will make another outrush and
catch you / with all her heads, and snatch away once more
the same number / of men.   Drive by hard as you can, but
invoke Krataiïs. / She is the mother of Skylla and bore
this mischief for mortals, / and she will stay her from
making another sally against you." (120-126).   Upon approaching Scylla, however, Odysseus "forgets" this advice,
arms himself, and stands at the prow, looking intently for
the monster's attack (226-231).   The sight of Charybdis
then diverts his attention, while Scylla takes the six men
from behind his back (244-250).   Contrary to what Circe
"feared," Odysseus does not suffer any further losses (perhaps because he only arms himself and does not "waste time"
by stopping to fight).   Whether or not he forestalls a second attack by invoking Scylla's mother is not clear, for
Odysseus ends his narration of the episode with the sight
of the six being captured, the "most pitiful scene" of all
his sufferings, and turns at once to the landing at Thrina-
cia (258-262).   That Circe herself, in telling him to invoke Crataeis, gave him a "weapon" by which to escape the
consequences of arming himself does suggest, however, that

this limited retention of martial spirit does not contra-
dict divine injunction.

35. Note how Odysseus' periphrasis at 12.266-268 links the
    thymos and remembering: ἔπος ἔμπεσε θυμῷ / μαντῆος ἀλαοῦ
    Θηβαίου Τειρεσίαο / Κίρκης τ' Αἰαίης.

36. On the eating of the cattle as a violation of religious,
    social and alimentary codes, see J.-P. Vernant, "Les
    Troupeaux du soleil et la table du soleil," *REG* 85 (1972),
    xiv-xvii: through their confusion of hunting and sacri-
    fice, domestic and wild animals, and their use of leaves
    instead of grain and water instead of wine, the crew per-
    form a perverted sacrifice, as the crawling skins and the
    bellowing meat, both raw and cooked, attest.

37. As recompense for the *kleos* he sings, the professional po-
    et receives material sustenance and a good *kleos* for him-
    self that will increase the "market value" of his songs.
    Phemius is paid with shelter and food, but is forced to ac-
    cept the transaction (1.154). Demodocus receives similar
    support, along with a choice cut of meat from Odysseus and
    a promise to spread his fame in return for singing the
    "Wooden Horse" (8.477-498). The wandering beggar, Odys-
    seus, tries to ply the same trade without the advantage of
    a permanent position, when he offers his stories in return
    for clothing from Eumaeus (14.459-517) and Penelope (17.
    549-550), and his promise to spread the suitors' *kleos* in
    return for food (17.418).

38. See 17.382-385.

39. See J. Svenbro, *La Parole et le marbre: Aux Origines de
    la poétique grecque.* (University of Lund Diss., 1976)
    pp. 11-45.

40. Reading, with the manuscripts, μέγα, rather than the
    Alexandrian μή.

41. J. Peradotto, "Prophecy Degree Zero: Tiresias and the
    End of the *Odyssey*," forthcoming in *Oralità, cultura, let-
    teratura, discorso* (Rome). This study provides a compre-
    hensive morphology of prophecy in the *Odyssey*.

42. See Hesiod, *Theogony* 27–28.

43. Readers of Paul de Man's analysis of Nietzsche's rhetoric
    of tropes in *Allegories of Reading* (New Haven: Yale Uni-
    versity Press, 1979), pp. 103–118, will recognize in this
    theme of the *Odyssey* an allegory of the philosopher's view
    of figures. As de Man puts it (p. 113), "All rhetorical
    structures, whether we call them metaphor, metonymy, chi-
    asmus, metalepsis, hypallagus, or whatever, are based on
    substitutive reversals, and it seems unlikely that one
    more such reversal over and above the ones that have al-
    ready taken place would suffice to restore things to their
    proper order. One more 'turn' or trope added to a series
    of earlier reversals will not stop the turn towards error."

44. Compare de Man, p. 108, paraphrasing Nietzsche: "Logical
    priority is uncritically deduced from a contingent tempo-
    rality."

Virtue, Folly, and Greek Etymology

E. D. Francis

In her essay, "The Gates of Horn and Ivory," Anne Amory
questions the value of invoking etymology as a means of
Homeric exegesis. "As a general principle," she writes, "I
prefer in determining the meaning of words to follow Homer's
usage, whenever that is clear and consistent, rather than
etymological speculations."[1] Amory's attitude will strike a
responsive chord in classicists who view with suspicion any
attempt to account for the development of Greek vocabulary
by recourse to linguistic reconstruction, whether comparative or historical. Indeed this kind of exercise is widely
regarded as little more than a shell-game played by a cyni-
cal and unscrupulous brood of latter-day sophists. Through
their *legerdemain* of sound-laws and grammatical change, they
prey upon the unwary and naive, authenticating their assertions by claims of privileged access to the pantheon of
Indo-European languages. If straight-thinking philologists
have now become too sophisticated to fall victim to such
esoteric *magi*, they may also occasionally deceive themselves
by a willingness to dismiss practitioners of etymology as
mere "scheming jugglers" and "tricky quacks."

I therefore hope this essay will among other things al-
lay suspicions that the methods of comparative grammar represent no reasonable advance beyond the linguistic unrule of
Plato's *Cratylus* and what Paul Friedländer has called its
"medley of merry pranks."[2] To that end I shall discuss the
etymology of two Greek words, *aretē* and *átē*, and judge the
extent to which their linguistic prehistory reflects in
both valid and illuminating ways upon our understanding of

the development of Greek ethical and psychological vocabulary. In doing so I shall attempt to justify the view that
usage and etymology can at times be considered mutually compatible fields of study rather than remain segregated as the
lexicological counterpart of Dives and Lazarus.

I. ETYMOLOGY AND FOLK-ETYMOLOGY

Since arguments about etymology and usage have often become
as polarized as C. P. Snow's Two Cultures, I begin with a
short protreptic about "etymology." To an historical linguist the etymology of a word accounts for the derivational
ancestry of its form and meaning, characteristically, but
not necessarily, in prehistoric terms. Formal developments
are in general much easier both to reconstruct and to justify by rigorous method than are changes in meaning, and speculation about semantic developments is most rife and least
trusted in those periods from which corroborative textual
evidence is lacking.

A familiar example from English will illustrate this
point. The verb "bless" continues Old English *blœdsian*
which in turn derives as a factitive from the noun *blodan*,
'blood'. The original sense of *blœdsian* was 'make bloody',
hence 'sprinkle [an object] with blood', thereby hallowing
it. The radically changed meaning of the word in Modern
English has been influenced by its early use in Christian
contexts as the translation of Latin *benedicere* and Greek
eulogein. Let us suppose that etymologists did not have at
their disposal a textual tradition whose evidence thoroughly
documents the semantic developments involved. The formal
properties of the explanation would remain unexceptionable,
but without an unambiguous record of cultural and textual
evidence, many might regard the necessary semantic

reconstruction as just another instance of etymological al-
chemy. For example, this lack of verifiable, documentary
proof may have contributed to the reluctance on many scholars' part to accept, even in Emile Benveniste's revision,
Manu Leumann's suggestion that the Greek phrase *hórkon
ómnumi* originally specified the ritual act of grasping a
staff as the physical token of swearing an oath.[3] Though
some have objected to Leumann's analysis on formal grounds,
it is the semantic issue which most critics have called into
question.

The semantic history of any word may obviously be affected by a variety of factors, not least by other words in its
connotative field and words which simply resemble it in
sound. In associations of this kind, etymological factors
are completely neutralized. Thus the English noun "bliss,"
etymologically derived from the adjective "blithe," has
aspired to intimations of paradise through its phonetic
similarity to the verb "bless." Words which are poorly understood may be explained, so to speak, by being remodeled
into more readily comprehensible forms. This process is
especially familiar in, but not restricted to, the case of
proper names. For example, Gnaw Bone on Indiana State Route
40 was originally named Narbonne by its nineteenth century
French settlers. We customarily describe cases such as
"bliss" and "Gnaw Bone" as examples of folk etymology.

Concerning folk etymology, two crucial points immediately
need to be made. In the first place, the operation of *folk
etymology* must be clearly distinguished from what I have
called *etymology* in that its strict domain is not one of
historical explanation, but a sub-set of synchronic usage,
regardless of etymological considerations. My second point
is that folk etymology in no way constitutes an inferior

subject for research. On the contrary, close attention to the evidence of folk etymology, in the absence of native speakers, allows us to judge something of the resonating quality of Greek and Latin and the associative potential of their vocabulary. To take a well-known example, we do not need to make a judgement about the actual etymology of the Greek word for "Muse" in order to argue the incontestable claim that the Greek poetic tradition explicitly associated it with the root of the verb *mémnēmai*, 'remember', and the noun *mnēmosúnē*, 'memory'.

Folk etymological associations sometimes belong to the sphere of mythopoeic explanation. Thus the connection between the etymologically unrelated pair of Greek words *lãas*, 'stone', and *laós*, 'people', resounds in Pindar's telling of the myth of Deucalion and Pyrrha at *Olympian* 9.41-46 (esp. 45-46: . . . ἄτερ δ' εὐνᾶς ὁμόδαμον / κτισσάσθαν λίθινον γόνον· / λαοὶ δ' ὀνύμασθεν).[4] "Speaking names" also belong to this kind of inquiry even though some speak more enigmatically than others. The name of Aphrodite provides a notorious instance, the explicit scrutiny of which is at least as old as Hesiod (cf. *Theogony* 154-210, esp. 195-200). Aeschylus' bravura cadenzas on proper names are well-known: Apollo the destroyer (*Agamemnon* 1080-1082), Helen the hellion (*id*. 681-692, esp. 687-690), and the righteous event whereby Xerxes' "persepolitan" army (*Persians* 65) is itself annihilated (διαπεπόρθηται, *id*. 714). Such gaming is, of course, already Homeric and has long been the subject of investigation. By way of further illustration, however, I offer three short examples, each different in kind: the first suggests the potential significance of a proper name, the second, the transformation of an important epithet, and the third, a play upon etymologically unrelated words (cf. *lãas* / *laós*).

(i)   I begin with Elpenor. As Henry Hayman once commented, "the contrast between the witless drunkard sleeping off
his fumes above, and the sage chief receiving instructions
for the fearful voyage below, is finely imagined."[5] Elpenor,
however, may have a more important role to play than that of
just another feckless member of Odysseus' ship of fools.
When we consider Homeric practice towards Odysseus' companions elsewhere in the *apologoi*, the fact that Elpenor emerges, albeit briefly, as a distinct personality is itself remarkable.[6]   Moreover, his "speaking name" (*elpís* + *anér*)
marks him as a "man of aspiration," not yet of performance;
unlike Odysseus, he has given nobody any "trouble." By his
name as well as by his circumstances, Elpenor serves as a
foil to Odysseus, an impression reflected in the language of
his vignette:

᾽Ελπήνωρ δέ τις ἔσκε νεώτατος, οὔτε τι λίην
ἄλκιμος ἐν πολέμῳ οὔτε φρεσὶν ᾖσιν ἀρηρώς.

(*Od.* 10.552-553)

Each of Elpenor's three traits inverts the character of
his leader. He is the youngest (νεώτατος) of Odysseus'
companions--it is unnecessary to require that Odysseus literally be described as the oldest of the group--none too
adept in battle (οὔτε τι λίην / ἄλκιμος ἐν πολέμῳ) nor capable ("together") in his *phrenes* (οὔτε φρεσὶν ᾖσιν ἀρηρώς).
In these last two characteristics Elpenor is in evident
counterpoint to Odysseus. Furthermore, Elpenor not only
precedes Odysseus in freefall to the Undergloom, but is the
first character to preoccupy Odysseus' attention both on his
entry to the Land of the Dead (*Od.* 11.51-83) and his return
to Aeaea (12.8-15). To the extent that "the Iliadic tradition requires Achilles to prefigure his dead self by staying
alive, and the real ritual of a real funeral is reserved by

the narrative for his surrogate Patroklos," the death of
Elpenor, as Odysseus' *Doppelgänger*, may likewise provide in
small an Odyssean counterpart to this more grandly articulated relationship.[7]

(ii) My second example comes from Scheria, whose native
sons openly resent the advent of Odysseus the outsider.
Euryalus, in particular, vents his defensive scorn against
the stranger. Odysseus responds with a self-description
(*Od.* 8.166-185) which Euryalus, νόον δ' ἀποφώλιος (8.177),
like that other suitor, Antinous, is unable to comprehend:
"in looks a man may be a shade . . . and yet a master of
speech so crowned with beauty . . . he can command assemblies. When he comes to town, the crowds gather I
am no stranger to contests, as you fancy . . . [but] now
pain has cramped me. . . ."[8] Appearances may deceive, but
Odysseus' words reveal: πολλὰ γὰρ ἔτλην (182), "I am
Odysseus *polútlas*," the man of Troy (ἀνδρῶν τε πτολέμους
. . . πείρων), and the man attempting *nóstos* (ἀλεγεινά τε
κύματα πείρων, 183). This same characterization, coupled
with an echo of the opening lines of the *Odyssey*, occurs
again to close the first half of the poem at 13.90-91, and
soon afterwards constitutes one of the "truths" of Odysseus'
"Cretan tale" to the disguised Athena (13.264). The epithet
polútlas[9] is used exclusively of Odysseus in both the *Iliad*
(5 times) and *Odyssey* (37 times; cf. *talasíphrōn*, 11 times
in the *Odyssey*). If its transformation at *Od.* 8.182 is, as
I suggest, self-conscious, then this conclusion finds further support in the view that there exists some particular
"relevance to character in the distinctive epithets, those
reserved largely or entirely for one man."[10]

In addressing the Phaeacian youths Odysseus continues his
subtle indiscretion when, a few verses later, after his

triumph in the discus contest (8.186-198), he declares his
prowess at Troy as an archer (215-228, esp. 221-222). While
his words reflect the general self-assertiveness of Homer's
heroes, they also provide a clear instance of the pleasure
Odysseus takes in celebrating his role as an Iliadic hero.
Compare, for example, his use of *ptolipórthion* as he bla-
tantly announces his identity to Polyphemus (*Od.* 9.504-
505).[11] By thus asserting his Iliadic *kléos* he brings upon
himself the son of Poseidon's curse and thereby motivates
his Odyssean *kléos* (cf. 9.530).

(iii) An obvious contrast between the Phaeacians and
their Cyclopean kin resides in their totally different views
of the *agorá* as a social institution and the ethical reflection of these views in their personalities. The point is
familiar from Alcaeus: in lamenting his exile, the poet
provides a nice instance of definition by opposites, a pattern summarized in the Latin *exemplum* of *lucus a non lucendo*:

ὁ τάλαις ἔγω
ζώω μοῖραν ἔχων ἀγροϊωτίκαν
ἰμέρρων ἀγόρας ἄκουσαι
καρυζομένας ὦγεσιλαΐδα
καὶ βόλλας.

(*fr.* 130.16-20 Lobel-Page)

For Alcaeus alone *en ágrois*, there is no *agorá*. This *schema
etymologicum* had already been employed by Homer in both the
Iliad and the *Odyssey*. In Agamemnon's celebrated aetiology
of Ate, Ate not only is herself *ágrios* and thus "out of
order," but she likewise "made me [Agamemnon] *ágrios*," un-
fit to take part "*ein agorêi*" (*Il.* 19.87-88). Just as the
inhabitants of Goat Island are, appropriately enough,
ágriai, so too, for the Cyclopes, οὔτ' ἀγοραὶ βουληφόροι
οὔτε θέμιστες . . . οὐδ' ἀλλήλων ἀλέγουσι (*Od.* 9.112-115).

The same *schema* is repeated at *Od.* 9.171-175 where Odysseus calls an *agorá* to declare his intention to ascertain whether those who dwell across the bay are, among other things, *agrioi oudè díkaioi*. Alcaeus' *kaì bóllas* also seems to continue a traditional formula (cf. ἀγοραὶ βουληφόροι, *Od.* 9.112).

In the remainder of this essay we shall see other examples of so-called "etymological figures" of the *krētēra kerassámenos*-type. Antinous, as he blindly warns Odysseus of the consequences of uncouth behavior on the part of a guest, thus displays an extended derivational paradigm of the root of *átē*:

ὁ δὲ φρεσὶν ᾗσιν ἀασθεὶς
ἤϊεν ἣν ἄτην ὀχέων ἀεσίφρονι θυμῷ.

(*Od.* 21.301-302)

Eustathius in fact identified the phrase ἄτη, ἣ πάντας ἀᾶται (*Il.* 19.91) as a *trópos etumologías*, and the popular and poetic association of *átē* (contracted from *awátē* following the loss of intervocalic digamma) with etymologically unrelated words like *apátē* and *atasthalíē* had a substantial impact on its semantic development.[12] In Hesiod's *Theogony*, for example, Apate is named as Ate's aunt (223-230) and the words are associated in the context of adultery (cf. Alcaeus, *fr.* 283.5 Lobel-Page; Ibycus, *fr.* 282.10 Page).

These remarks provide a context from which we can now proceed to an account of *aretē* and *átē*. I have already noted that in linguistic reconstruction formal, grammatical relationships are usually easier to judge than semantic ones. Moreover, glossing can have the dangerous effect of leading to anachronistic confusion. As a point of method I shall therefore begin with formal considerations and refrain from testing their semantic consequences until hypotheses

regarding the grammatical relationships involved have been
clearly established.

II. *ARETḖ*

Aretḗ and *átē* are comparable not only in terms of their descriptive formation--both nouns are derived by means of the
feminine suffix *-tā́*--but also in their importance to our
understanding of the development of Greek culture. The record of modern scholarship, however, leads one to doubt that
their usage is clear and consistent, or that their etymologies are the subject of general agreement. The etymology
of *aretḗ*, for example, is usually explained in one of two
ways, either as a derivative of the root of the verb *aréskō*
or as a secondary formation from the stem of the comparative
adjective *areíōn*, associated descriptively with the positive
agathós.[13]

Each of these accounts is, however, open to serious question. No one will deny that the productive nature of the
grammatical process according to which nouns can be derived
from verbal roots by the addition of the suffix *-to-*, feminine *-tā́*, is well established (cf. *thánatos* : *-éthane*;
kámatos : *ékame*; *genetḗ* : *egéneto*; *teletḗ* :
etéles(s)e; *áētē* : *áēmi*, etc.). To propose that such a
relationship similarly obtains between *aréskō* and *aretḗ* may
therefore seem, in principle, plausible enough. On the
other hand, many scholars, among them Werner Jaeger,[14] reject this derivation on semantic grounds. The semantic gap
between the Homeric usage of *arésai* (aorist infinitive),
'appease'--the present *aréskō* is unattested before the fifth
century B.C.--and that of *aretḗ* is indeed formidable. Alternatively, to derive *aretḗ* from *areíōn*, though perhaps
more acceptable from a semantic standpoint, remains

grammatically unattractive due to the absence of any productive analogical model.

To argue that *aretḗ* is not directly derived from either *aréskō* or *areíōn* does not, however, rule out the possibility that all three words are in fact etymologically related, and it will be worthwhile to investigate briefly the origins of *aréskō* and *areíōn*. In Indo-European languages, the neuter *s*-stems, like stems in *-to-/-tā*, form a class of nouns characteristically derived from verbal roots: in Greek, for example, both *genetḗ* and *génos* are thus derived from the root reflected in the aorist third person singular *egéneto*. From a formal standpoint, the relationship expressed by the type *genetḗ / génos* can be paralleled by that of *aretḗ / áros*. Hesychius indeed cites a form *áros* which he glosses as *óphelos*, 'profit, advantage', and Aeschylus may have used the word in this sense at *Suppliants* 885-886.[15] Despite the rarity of its textual attestation, *áros* (stem form, *are[s]-*), as H. Seiler has plausibly observed,[16] may well provide the indirect source of the comparative *areíōn* in the sense of 'more advantageous', hence, 'better' (cf. its close synonym *kreíssōn*, superlative *krátistos*, built from the root attested in *krátos*, full grade *krétos*, 'power': *kreíssōn* thus originally meant 'more powerful'). The aorist *arésai*, 'appease' may also be derived from the noun *áros* (cf. the denominative formation of the type *telés[s]ai* beside *télos*) with the corollary semantic assumption that the gesture of "conciliation, appeasement, atonement" implied by *arésai* was at first expressed in some material form (cf. *aressámenoi*, 'having made restitution, compensation' at *Od.* 22.55). In terms of such a *quid pro quo*, the verb *arésai* can readily be seen as a denominative derived (like *areíōn*, with somewhat euphemistic implications) from *áros* in the sense of a

"profit" or "benefit" considered as a return for a loss.
Aréskō and *areíōn* may thus be interpreted as etymologically
related to *aretḗ* even if they do not constitute its derivational source.

Let us now investigate the possibility that a formal relationship of the type *genetḗ* (: *génos*) : *egéneto* offers a paradigm by which we may understand the origin of
aretḗ. We have just seen that a corresponding neuter *s*-stem
áros may be attested in Greek, both directly and as the derivational source of *areíōn* and *arésko*. If we now seek an
aorist which corresponds formally to *aretḗ* as *egéneto* corresponds to *genetḗ*, then we find *éreto* (ps. *árnumai*). This
verb occurs frequently in Homer in the sense of 'gain,
achieve, obtain'. Its typical complements include *níkē*,
'victory' and such semantically congeneric terms as *timḗ*,
eûkhos, *kléos*, and *kûdos*--words denoting honor and reputation achieved in a warrior society through *níkē*--as well as
terms of material gain, for example *misthós*, 'wages', and
also prizes from competitions, both military and athletic.[17]
Thus, at the Funeral Games of Patroclus, Antilochus won
(ἀρόμην, *Il.* 23.592) Achilles' stake of a six-year-old un-
broken mare, only to be called upon to relinquish this token
of prestige to Menelaus. So too, in the raids upon Eetion
and Tenedos, Achilles himself had won (ἄρετ') the sweet harp
he plucks in the *Iliad* (9.185 ff., esp. 188), and Nestor,
his softly-braided barmaid, Hecamede (*Il.* 11.624-625).

In other Indo-European languages, the verb in question is
characteristically attested as an active formation,[18] but in
Greek *árnumai* is *medium tantum* and appropriately so, because
in every case its complement is something one gains for oneself. The meaning of *áros* as *óphelos* can readily be understood in such terms, and from a formal standpoint the

relationship of both *áros* and *areté* to *éreto* parallels in a
straightforward manner that of *génos* and *geneté* to *egéneto*,
but what are the semantic consequences of regarding *areté* as
derived from the same root as *árnumai*?

Perhaps I can best introduce my response by invoking Bruno
Snell: "When Homer says that a man is good, *agathos*, he does
not mean thereby that he is morally unobjectionable, much
less good-hearted, but rather that he is useful, proficient,
and capable of vigorous action. *We also speak of a good warrior or a good instrument*"[19] (my italics). Snell continues:

> The words for virtue and good, *arete* and *agathos*, are at
> first by no means clearly distinguished from the area of
> profit . . . . *arete*, virtue, does not denote a moral
> property but nobility, achievement, success and reputa-
> tion . . . . *arete* is the objective which the early nobles
> attach to achievement and success . . . . Well into the
> classical period, those who compete for *arete* are remuner-
> ated with glory and honour.[20]

In these terms, *areté* represents an exactly appropriate complement to the verb *árnumai* as I have described its usage.
Just as the abstract noun *geneté*, 'birth' corresponds in form
and meaning to *genésthai*, 'come into being', so *areté*, in the
sense of 'achievement', corresponds to *arésthai*, 'achieve'.
This 'achievement' can be either material or ethical, just as
in Homeric terms the complements of *árnumai* etc. may be thoroughly palpable, like a harp or Hecamede, or more intangible,
if no less real (e.g., *timé*, *kléos*, *kûdos*). Indeed it is
likely that, as in the case of *aréskō*, the sense of material
reward had historical priority over the "ethical" reading of
areté. In other words, a hero's success and therefore the
honor in which he is held were first expressed by the quality
of his material achievements in specified fields of endeavor,
not least in war, for, as Moses Finley has observed, "there

could be no honour without public proclamation, and there
could be no publicity without the evidence of a trophy."[21]
Thus the ready association of *aretḗ* with words like *areíōn*
and *áristos*, and indeed with Ares, both extended and specialized its connotations.[22]

I close this account of *aretḗ* with further evidence to illustrate the etymology I have proposed. In the history of
language it is commonly observed that derivatives may continue to reflect a chronologically more archaic meaning of
the term from which they are derived, long after the reference of the basic term itself has changed. I shall refer to
this point again in my discussion of *thumós*. For the moment,
however, I wish to consider the contract verb derived from
aretḗ, namely, *aretáō*, commonly glossed as 'succeed, pros-
per'. In Demodocus' Song of Ares and Aphrodite the gods
gather to gaze at Hephaestus' handiwork and remark to one
another as follows: οὐκ ἀρετᾷ κακὰ ἔργα (*Od.* 8.329). While
the juxtaposition of *aretâi* and *kaká* may imply the antithesis
of *aretḗ* and *kakotḗs*, the underlying message is clear:
"*kakà érga* yield no gain." One might as well say: οὐδὲν
ἤρετο κακὰ ἔργα.[23]

Such in fact seems to be the sense of the contrast between
kakotḗs and *aretḗ* drawn by Hesiod in his account of the supe-
riority of work over idleness (*Works and Days* 286-316). As
M. L. West remarks in his commentary on verses 287-292,
"κακότης and ἀρετή are not 'vice' and 'virtue' but inferior
and superior standing in society, determined principally by
material prosperity."[24] At verse 313, Hesiod continues:
πλούτῳ δ' ἀρετὴ καὶ κῦδος ὀπηδεῖ. Note that Hesiod collo-
cates *aretḗ*, plausibly taken in the sense of 'achievement',
hence 'standing', with *kûdos*; compare the phrase *kûdos*
arésthai (note 17). *Aretḗ* thus replaces the Homeric use
of *timḗ* as in ἐκ δὲ Διὸς τιμὴ καὶ κῦδος ὀπηδεῖ (*Il.*

17.251). Hesiod's usage is already foreshadowed in Alcinous'
address to Odysseus at *Odyssey* 8.236-240. Whether we are to
understand from this Phaeacian episode that no one in their
right mind would ever impugn Odysseus' "prowess" (so
Fitzgerald) or his "achievement," we can see in such passages as these the kind of potentially transitional contexts
which Benveniste has judged so crucial in the explanation of
semantic change.[25] Finally, even if early Greek poetry offers no example of *aretḕn arésthai* as a *figura etymologica*,
we may note the close association which Pindar draws between
aretḗ and *arésthai* in his celebrated commentary upon *phuá* in
Olympian 9:

τὸ δὲ φυᾷ κράτιστον ἅπαν· πολλοὶ δὲ διδακταῖς
ἀνθρώπων <u>ἀρεταῖς</u> κλέος
ὤρουσαν <u>ἀρέσθαι</u>.

(100-102)

With regard to *aretḗ*, we are surely entitled to conclude not
only that "usage" and "etymology" confirm each other, but
that etymology can significantly enhance our understanding
of the semantic development of this important term.

III. *ÁTḖ*

If, according to Frisk, the etymology of *aretḗ* was "not entirely clear," that of *átē*, *aáō*, and *aáatos*, in the words of
Homer's first modern lexicologist, Philipp Buttmann, provides "striking testimony to the confusion of ancient and
modern grammarians alike."[26] More recently, R. D. Dawe has
despaired of any etymological solution,[27] and neither Frisk
nor Chantraine encourages greater confidence.[28] Early attempts to relate *átē* to words meaning 'blow' (in the sense
of 'strike') remain unconvincing, at least on linguistic
grounds, and are now generally doubted or rejected.[29]

Dawe summarizes the semantic issue as follows: the most important point "is whether the meaning *Schaden* (damage or harm) is the primary one, which can then give us the meaning *Verblendung* (mental blindness) when it is applied specifically to the mental processes,"[30] or *vice versa*. In the *Lexikon des frühgriechischen Epos (s.v. átē)* H.-J. Mette, like Dawe, decides in favor of *Schaden*, but Hansjakob Seiler, in the same *Lexikon (s.v. aáō)* and previously in Albert Debrunner's *Festschrift*,[31] follows the tradition of E. R. Dodds[32] by regarding *Verblendung* as primary. Commenting on Euripides' *Hippolytus*, W. S. Barrett prefers "to regard the two uses as parallel,"[33] while Stallmach concludes his dissertation on *átē* with a page-long portmanteau definition in which he seems to lean hesitatingly towards *Schaden*.[34] The conceptual importance of *átē* and *áasa* etc. in the Homeric poems—not to mention the post-Homeric tradition—remains unquestioned. Under such circumstances, the prehistory of these forms deserves reconsideration, not only in order to clarify the dilemma posed by Dawe concerning the relative priority of their Homeric usage, but especially with regard to the ways in which their etymology may reflect upon developing patterns of Greek thought.

Since all linguistic reconstruction necessarily requires an argument from partial silence, the plausibility of any etymological solution depends in large measure upon the evidence which supports it or, to make the same point somewhat differently, on the extent to which the non-attestation of grammatical or semantic links in the chain of argument diminishes its effectiveness. Due to the incomplete nature of the evidence available to a student of Ancient Greek, some etymological hypotheses remain more tentative and hence less persuasive than others. For these reasons the etymology of

átē I am about to propose may appear to some to be less conclusive than the relatively straightforward account of *aretḗ*
presented in the previous section. Nevertheless, the grammatical and semantic hypotheses involved are, in my judgement, both plausible in themselves and also recognizable in
terms of other developments in Greek language and culture.
As in the case of *aretḗ*, I begin by discussing the formal
properties of *átē* and its corresponding verb. I then suggest, again as a result of formal argument, an etymological
source for the words in question and, after a brief discussion of other related forms (e.g., *áatos*), I conclude by
evaluating the semantic implications of the developments I
have proposed.

The spondaic form, *átē*, represents the outcome of an
earlier, uncontracted form *a(w)átē* (rhyming with *apátē* to
which *átē* may owe its paroxytone accent). From a formal
standpoint, the noun *átē/awátē* can most plausibly be derived
from the verbal root attested in the sigmatic aorist, *áasa*
etc., according to patterns of the type, *teletḗ* :
etéles(s)a. A disyllabic form of the root *a(w)a-* is usual
in the Homeric verb and metrically implicit in the distribution of the noun,[35] while the form with digamma preserved is
found in certain Aeolic and Doric dialects.[36]

Since *átē* can best be interpreted as a derivative of the
aorist *áasa* etc. I shall first examine the Homeric distribution of the verb. With the exception of the thematicized
present *aãtai* in the formula ἄτη, ἢ πάντας ἀᾶται (*Il.* 19.91,
repeated at 129)--its contract formation is patently secondary,[37] the early occurrence of this verb is restricted to
aorist formations, active, middle, and passive.[38] This restriction to the aorist may be highly significant for the
following reason: in terms at least of an early stage of

Indo-European morphology, we can reconstruct a formal correspondence according to which roots with "durative" meaning
formed athematic root presents and characterized (usually
sigmatic) aorists while, conversely, semantically "telic" or
"punctual" roots formed athematic aorists and characterized
presents.[39] Not all athematic root formations form corresponding characterized ones (for example, no aorist is built
from the root present, es-tí, 'is'). On the other hand, a
characterized formation (e.g., an s-aorist) reasonably pre-
supposes a corresponding form from which it has been derived.
Thus, if the present-aorist paradigm of áasa / aasámēn were
complete and inherited from Proto-Indo-European (or at least
continued an inherited pattern), we might theoretically expect Greek to have inherited, for example, an athematic root
present beside the attested sigmatic aorist, áasa / aasámēn.
I therefore submit that the Greek verb á(w)ēsi (3 sg.),
'blows', directly comparable in form and meaning with
Sanskrit váti, may fulfill the formal requirements of such a
correspondence. With the exception of the compound form
kataéssato in Alcaeus,[40] no aorist form of the verb á(w)ēmi
occurs elsewhere in Greek and the silence of other Indo-
European languages suggests that the s-aorist áasa / aasámēn
may be a Greek innovation. Nevertheless, there are potential
objections to an etymological association of áēmi and áasa
on both grammatical and semantic grounds, and I shall discuss
each in its turn.

In the first place, the difference between the root shapes
a(w)ē- and a(w)ă- is by no means a matter of course. Since
the Greek s-aorist characteristically developed as a full-
grade formation (e.g., édeikse) with its inherited ablaut-
distinctions neutralized, we might expect to find, corresponding to a present áēmi, aorist forms of the type (act.)

*á(w)ēsa and (mid.) a(w)ēsámēn (as in Alcaeus' kataéssato).
The s-aorist áasa thus does not continue the expected full-
grade formation from the root of áēmi, and its apparent
zero-grade is not only inappropriate to the formation in
question, but should be a(w)e-, not a(w)a-.[41] Moreover, unlike áēmi, áasa is transitive. It is not enough to speculate that áasa may have developed as a secondary formation
with the function of specializing the "psychological" reference of a(w)a- (as opposed to the primarily physical reference of the root-shape a(w)ē-, 'blows'), without also attempting to account for the mechanism by which this development might have taken place.

   These difficulties may be resolved by reconstructing an
ē-aorist formation from the root of áēmi. The ē-aorist, inherited as a stative before developing in Greek as a passive
formation, remained a productive formation before being
ousted by the thē-aorist (cf. ephánēn beside ephánthēn). I
therefore suggest that the root shape a(w)a- and its derivation as a sigmatic aorist developed from such a formation
(i.e., *a(w)ĕnai, 'be blown') on the morphological and semantic parallel of the type damás(s)ai : damĕnai (originally,
'be tame'). This suggestion necessarily remains tentative
since no aorist *a(w)ĕnai is actually attested. On the other hand, the early elimination of such a form may be reasonably explained on the grounds that the finite forms of the
paradigm would have been identical to those of the imperfect
active, while the infinitive was homonymous with the corresponding present active formation. It is not unusual to
find paradigms replaced in order to relieve homonymy, and
such may have been the case with an aorist passive *a(w)ĕnai.
Moreover, postulation of an original *a(w)ĕnai is in keeping
with the fact "that ate must originally have described

something done to someone, not something of which he is himself the originator."[42]   The model I have proposed also has the benefit of accounting for the transitivity of áasa, which formed the derivational basis of the attested aorist passive, aasthênai; once again we may note the parallel relationship exhibited in the paradigm of damás(s)ai : damasthênai.

While the formal implications of associating áasa with áēmi may be addressed by the hypothesis I have just outlined, the semantic consequences of such an etymology demand clarification.   Μῦθος δ' οὐκ ἐμός, ἀλλ' ἑτέρων.   Already an Ambrosian scholiast has commented on aesiphrosúnēisi at Odyssey 15.470 as follows: ἀπὸ τοῦ "ἄω" τὸ πνέω.   In his Kritisches griechisches Wörterbuch of 1797, Johann Gottlob Schneider continued this tradition by explaining aesiphrōn in terms of aénai, 'blow', an expedient which Buttmann harshly repudiates: "Anyone who examines the original passages must feel how forced [this derivation] is."[43]   Not so Anton Göbel, who is, to my knowledge, the only scholar to have pursued the connection.[44]   He did so, however, to no avail, for as Wilhelm Havers reports, "Göbel's etymological combinations were soon rendered obsolete"[45] in favor of frankly indefensible arguments connecting átē with roots meaning 'strike, wound' (cf. note 29).

Beside an inherited athematic root present like *a(w)ēnai with durative meaning (e.g., 'blow'), we would expect the sigmatic aorist to express a compatible, but "punctual" or "telic" sense.   I therefore suggest that the attested usage of áasa etc. can be derived from a meaning such as 'blast' (i.e., 'blow off balance, off course, suddenly or potentially causing one's ruin').   We may find a paraphrase of this idea in Athena's memorable action when she "caused the

suitors' thought to wander off course (παρέπλαγξεν δὲ
νόημα)" (Od. 20.346).⁴⁶ Moreover, consider the fate of
Agastrophus at Iliad 11.338-342 as he wanders off, stunned,
to die. The fatal offense of Patroclus involves a parallel,
if extended, example of the same type. Immediately following the translation of Sarpedon's corpse to Lycia at Iliad
16.683, Patroclus, in disregard of Achilles' mandate, urges
his team into the Trojan fray, καὶ μέγ' ἀάσθη / νήπιος (Il.
16.685-686).⁴⁷ A hundred or so verses later Apollo strikes
Patroclus' helmet (16.793) and, to assure the hero's doom,
the god again intervenes at 16.804. The effect of his átē
at the beginning of his disobedience has finally caught up
with Patroclus (τὸν δ' ἄτη φρένας εἷλε, 16.805) and, as he
stands ταφών (806), Euphorbus spears him, vulnerable, from
behind. This passage is frequently cited to support the
claim that any etymology of átē must involve a root which
means 'strike', but unless we exclude metaphor from the
antecedents of Homeric diction, I cannot see this requirement as a necessary one.⁴⁸

It is therefore my contention that the meaning of the
verbal noun átē is directly derived from "punctual" uses of
the aorist, of the kind I have just described. I do not require that a strictly "concrete" interpretation of áasa,
'blast' and átē should be imposed on all (or any) of the
Homeric contexts in which the words occur; indeed it would
be impossible and as a point of method improper to insist on
such uniformity. Nevertheless, the etymology I propose may
indeed afford a semantically plausible starting-point for
the attested use and development of átē and I shall presently outline the semantic changes involved. Many readers,
however, may be legitimately concerned to know whether these
ideas have any chance of getting off the linguist's

drawing-board. Two questions are probably foremost in the
minds of those who remain sceptical about the pertinence,
let alone the merit, of etymological analysis: first, can
any textual evidence be advanced to support these suggestions, and second, is the style of semantic development required by my proposal totally isolated, or, on the contrary,
is it congruent with other developments in Greek? I believe
that positive answers exist to both questions.

Let us begin with a use of *áēmi*, 'blow', but not without
first noting that the words *thumós* and *phrénes* frequently
characterize the contexts in which *átē* etc. is attested.[49]
Lattimore translates *Iliad* 21.385-386 from the Battle of the
Gods as follows: "But upon the other gods descended the
wearisome burden / of hatred, and the wind of their fury
blew from division" (. . . δίχα δέ σφιν ἐνὶ φρεσὶ θυμὸς
ἄητο).[50] In this passage, note the collocation of *áēto*,
'blew' with *thumós* and *phrénes*, the middle voice of *sphìn*
áēto, and the adverb *díkha* responding to *éris* in the previous verse, marking Olympus at odds within itself. The passage suggests that the Homeric *thumós* and not merely external phenomena could be affected by gale-force winds, and
also provides tentative support for the thesis that the
"psychological" usage of the root meaning 'blow' developed
in the medio-passive. At any rate I think A. C. Moorhouse[51]
is mistaken in taking Homer's *thumós* *áēto* to refer to 'doubt
and fear' instead of 'angry dissension' (cf. *éris* in the
previous line). The force of nature implicit in *áēto* (cf.
the use of *aémenos* at *Od.* 6.131 and derivatives like *aétē*,
aéllē) distinguishes this metaphor from such phrases as
δίχα θυμὸς ὀρώρεται (*Od.* 19.524) and δίχα θυμὸς ἐνὶ φρεσὶ
μερμηρίζει (*Od.* 16.73) which may well have contributed to
Apollonius' reinterpretation of the phrase *thumós* *áētai* in

terms of anxiety, not wrath (*Argon.* 3.688). The adjective *áēton* in the phrase *thársos áēton*, 'vehement (?) *thársos*' should probably be associated with *áēmi* rather than with the lexicographers' glosses *áētoi* = *akórestoi*, *áplēstoi*, etc., as Moorhouse apparently prefers,[52] since Ares is plainly alluding to the passage which includes *thumòs áēto*.[53]

In the *Odyssey* (4.500-501) Proteus describes Poseidon's rescue of Ajax, son of Oileus, on the promontory of Gyrae. Despite Athena's hatred, Ajax lived on, but "in great *átē* (καὶ μέγ' ἀάσθη)," he yelled that the gods' will and the sea were beaten (502-504). Poseidon in wrath responded by severing the promontory with his trident "so the vast ocean had its will with Aias, drunk in the end on salt spume as he drowned" (Fitzgerald). Just as in the case of Patroclus' doom, *átē* frames the narrative (503 and 509), while Homer, in the second occurrence of *még' aásthē*, seems to become his own sardonic glossographer: "was Ajax ever blasted!" Thus again, at the opening of *Odyssey* 10, Aeolus had first set the favorable zephyr to blow Odysseus home (προέηκεν ἀῆναι, 25), but once his sailors had unleashed the other winds, Odysseus and his crew are driven back to Aeole κακῇ ἀνέμοιο θυέλλῃ (54; cf. 47-48). Πῶς ἦλθες, 'Οδυσσεῦ; In response to Aeolus' query (64), Odysseus seems to skip a step of his explanation: "it was my friends and wretched sleep that blasted me back, blew me off course" (ἄασάν μ' ἕταροί τε κακοὶ πρὸς τοῖσί τε ὕπνος / σχέτλιος, 68-69):[54] the *kakos daímon* Aeolus had suggested in verse 64 is *átē*. A further association between *átē* and stormwinds can be observed in their similar effect upon mortals. Thus, in the *Odyssey*, when Poseidon returning from the Ethiopians unleashes in wrath the *aellai pantoîōn anémōn* upon Odysseus (*Od.* 5.291-296), Odysseus' limbs collapse (καὶ τότ' 'Οδυσσῆος λύτο

γούνατα καὶ φίλον ἦτορ, 297). So too, for Patroclus at
Iliad 16.805, τὸν δ' ἄτη φρένας εἷλε, λύθεν δ' ὑπὸ φαίδιμα
γυῖα.

The devastating effect of winds is a matter of common experience. I have just cited the effect of their combined
onslaught upon Odysseus at *Odyssey* 5.291-297 (cf. 368-370).
Indeed, one readily recalls the pervasive quality of storm
similes throughout Homer,[55] the violence of all winds, especially Boreas, in Hesiod's *Works and Days* (e.g., 504ff.;
cf. 621, 645, 675)--compare his personification of *aéllē*,
'whirlwind' as the Harpy Aello at *Theogony* 267, their role
in Hippocrates' aetiology of the *Sacred Disease* (16, 21),
the emotional chaos they can cause in Sappho (*fr.* 47 Lobel-
Page) and Ibycus (*fr.* 286.8ff. Page), and the "third wind"
of Pindar's *Nemean* 7.17-18.[56] The first strophe of
Sophocles' *Átē*-ode (*Antigone* 582ff.) is replete with the
language of storm. Zeus, as Lord of Storm, is, at least in
the *Iliad*, not only victim but also sponsor of *átē* in men.
Zeus shares the capacity of *átē* to take away one's *phrénes*
(cf. *Il.* 6.234, 19.137), and the connection of *átē* and Zeus
as storm-god can be seen again in Solon's famous simile of
the "spring gale" (13.11-25 West) representing Zeus' *tísis*
for those ὕβριος ἔργα (16) of mortals which guarantee their
ἄτη (13).[57] Finally, note Hesiod's use of *átē* at *Works and
Days* 231, apparently to refer to the "spoilage of crops,"[58]
perhaps from meteorological causes. I also take the redactional confusion of *aasi-* and *aesi-* (as in *aesíphrōn*) to be
part of the evidence which indicates that the Greeks themselves may have perceived a connection between *átē* and
áēmi.[59]

And now a brief note on *áatos*, a word which Wilhelm
Schulze once characterized as *vocabulum plane obscurum*.[60]

Regardless of its etymology, the apparent hiatus following the initial *alpha* is problematic for any interpretation of the word. Moorhouse has correctly questioned Seiler's suggestion that *aáskhetos* and *aáatos* are susceptible of similar explanations.[61] On the other hand, I doubt whether Moorhouse is also correct in separating *aáatos* from *átē*,[62] from which, on morphological grounds, the adjective can be readily derived as a negative compound meaning 'unsusceptible to *átē*'. Such an interpretation is entirely in keeping with its only Iliadic use, as an epithet qualifying the river Styx: ἄγρει νῦν μοι ὄμοσσον ἀάατον Στυγὸς ὕδωρ (*Il.* 14.271). The reason why Hypnos demanded that Hera provide such a guarantee is not far to seek, since in *Iliad* 19 the *átē* of Zeus is a direct consequence of Hera's *dólos* and *apátē*. Indeed, apart from the significant occasion on which Helen so characterizes Aphrodite (*Il.* 3.405), the epithet *dolophronéousa*, along with *dolophrosúnē*, occurs in the *Iliad* only in the *Diòs Apátē* (14.197, 300, 329) and the *Diòs Átē* (19.97, 106, 112), each time with reference to Hera. In the passage in question (*Il.* 14.231ff.) Hera is seeking an alliance with Hypnos to persuade him to inveigle Zeus with sleep. Hypnos, on the basis of previous experience, is plainly hesitant (242-262) and wants firm assurance that he will not be tricked of his prize by Hera's *dolophrosúnē* (or, like Zeus in *Iliad* 19, become a victim of *átē*). He thus asks for a guarantee that will itself be "not subject to *átē*," *aáatos*.[63]

Dawe has remarked on the "particularly striking . . . fact that [*átē*] is never used to refer to the conduct of the suitors in the *Odyssey*."[64] On the other hand, while this statement is in a literal sense accurate, *átē* certainly plays a part in the Hybris-Nemesis theme as it is developed

in the Contest of the Bow. For example, $át\bar{e}$ is present both
in Antinous' use of the epithet $á\acute{a}atos$ to introduce the
Contest (*Od.* 21.91) and in his characterization of the
Centaur's behavior at the Lapith Wedding as potentially applicable to Odysseus himself (*Od.* 21.288ff., esp. 295-296).
These points deserve review. As I have just mentioned, when
he proposes the Contest at *Odyssey* 21.89ff., Antinous asserts that the trial will be μνηστήρεσσιν ἄεθλον ἀάατον.[65]
In response, Odysseus, about to kill him at *Odyssey* 22.5ff.,
cries out: "this $áethlos$ $á\acute{a}atos$ is indeed at an end." In
the center of this scene, between the proposal of the
Contest and its fatal *denouement*, Antinous turns the parable
of the drunken centaur at the Lapith Wedding (21.288-310)
against Odysseus. The speech, with its five instances of
the language of $át\bar{e}$ (296-297; 301-302), reflects upon
Antinous' own behavior as a loutish guest at Odysseus'
court.[66] By his abusive threats to Odysseus and his desire
to intrude upon the marriage of the household in which he is
a guest, Antinous comes close to replicating Eurytion's out-
rageous violence. Moreover, Eurytion first brought harm
upon himself because he was "heavy with wine" (οἰνοβαρείων,
21.304). How appropriate then that Antinous be shot at the
moment of raising the goblet to his lips and that his dying
act, an involuntary reflex, is to kick over a table at the
feast (22.8-20). It was, of course, Antinous who had proposed a contest "without $at\bar{e}$ for the suitors." At the beginning of Book 22, Odysseus is about to wreak vengeance
upon the suitors for what Solon might call their "$h\acute{u}brios$
$\acute{e}rga$." By his retort at 22.5 (οὗτος μὲν δὴ ἄεθλος ἀάατος
ἐκτετέλεσται), Odysseus repudiates Antinous' failure to see
how the proposition of the contest--and indeed the suitors'
conduct in his house--was, from the start, instilled with

átē. Surely there is irony in Odysseus' words: not only have the suitors "deluded" themselves, but Antinous' conceit of a "harmless" contest has brought them to the brink of catastrophe.[67]

Let us now return to Dawe's question regarding the relative chronology of *Schaden* and *Verblendung* as glosses of *átē*. Since *átē* is a verbal noun, Dawe's question may best be considered in terms of the corresponding aorist formation from which it derives. The dilemma can be rephrased as follows: was the connotation of *áasa* / *aasámēn* / *áasthēn* originally *physical* or *psychological*? Though certainty in this matter is beyond reach, it seems to me likely that the new *s*-aorist paradigm would have been developed in order to express the secondary, psychological reference of the root originally meaning 'blow'. At any rate, the Homeric evidence suggests that this aorist formation was from the first used in a highly restricted context since, in Homer, the complements of the active *áasa* and the subjects of all middle and passive forms refer either to individuals or to their *thumós* or *phrénes*. I therefore suggest that the stem form *awa-s-* and hence the root shape *awa-* (as opposed to *awē-*) was specialized to denote the metaphorical effect of a sudden blast of wind *upon human beings* (and, in particular, upon their emotions), as a result of which a person could be "blown off balance" and thereby diverted from a normal course of action. The co-occurrence of *áasa* etc. with such terms as *thumós* and *phrenes* reflects the development of the paradigm in this psychological sense (cf. *thumòs áēto*, and the metaphor implicit in παρέπλαγξεν . . . νόημα, *Od.* 20.346).[68] (Compare the more general sense of subjection to an external force implied by the use of *edámassa* etc., a paradigm which I have suggested may have influenced significantly the development of *áasa*).

In Greek thought, the consequences of any digression from
a determined norm were potentially damaging. Excessive behavior constituted an aspect of such digression and, already
in Homer, we find instances of *áasa* etc. associated with actions which, by transgressing proper limits, occasioned catastrophe.[69] If someone's senses can be blown away by a
metaphorical assault of the wind, then wine, as an instrument of excess, can have a similar effect, as Antinous
preached (*Od*. 21.288ff.) and Elpenor acknowledged (*Od*.
11.61). It is not hard to see how the *effect* of such psychological confusion could be thoroughly catastrophic, as
Elpenor and Antinous both learned. It was in such contexts
that *áasa* came to designate the *harm* that could result from
immoderate or ill-judged action. Compare, for example, the
similar use of *áas(e)* and *bláptei* in the following passages
from the Lapith Wedding: οἶνος . . . ὅς τε καὶ ἄλλους /
βλάπτει (*Od*. 21.293-294) and οἶνος καὶ Κένταυρον . . . /
ἄασ(ε) (295-296), whence ὁ δ' ἐπεὶ φρένας ἄασεν οἴνῳ . . .
(297).[70] Nevertheless, even in such contexts, at least in
the archaic period, *áasa* frequently continued to be associated with some term of mental derangement (e.g.,
mainómenos, *Od*. 21.298).

To return to *átē*, I propose an evolution along the following lines: (i) the noun is never attested in the meaning
'blast of wind'--this fact is scarcely surprising since, as
I have argued, the root shape *a(w)e-* was clearly generalized
in this function;[71] (ii) the psychological use of *átē* (cf.
Verblendung) reflected the specialized use of the root shape
a(w)a- in the corresponding aorist formation; (iii) when
áasa etc. became a partial synonym of *éblapse*--that is, when
it referred to the *effect* of an individual's impaired per-
formance--*átē* likewise came to designate 'harm, ruin,

catastrophe' (cf. *Schaden*), and uses (ii) and (iii) continued to interact throughout the Classical period. From a semantic standpoint this etymology of *átē* therefore shares something with the observations of earlier scholars to the extent that *átē* is defined as the consequence of a sudden "blow." Others, however, have attributed that "blow" to some personal agency (e.g., a fist or a weapon) while I would derive it from a force of nature. The typical delay between an assault of *átē* and a victim's perception of its effect renders the experience akin to that of *apátē*. Whether stunned by a blow (e.g., Agastrophus, Patroclus) or in an intoxicated daze (e.g., Elpenor, Eurytion), if the victim regains any awareness of his circumstances, it has become too late for him to set his life back "on course": "blown beyond" the boundary within which he can exercise control, he confronts his inexorable *némesis*. Even Zeus in *Iliad* 19, though he can punish Ate by hurling her from Olympus, cannot change the course of events initiated while he was under her influence.

In conclusion I want briefly to attempt to justify the more general, conceptual aspect of my proposal. To the extent that they illustrate the process by which the reference of externally perceptible phenomena can be internalized and thus become a part of a developing psychological vocabulary, words like Greek *pneûma* and Latin *animus*, cognate with Greek *ánemos*, 'wind', provide partial counterparts for the semantic development I have reconstructed for the root *awa-*. E. L. Harrison has well observed that "the key to an understanding of Homeric mental terminology is to be found in Homeric man's physical reactions to his environment."[72] On the level of Homeric society, we may find an analogy to this process in Norman Austin's account of the court of Aeolus.[73]

I have already cited the prominence of storm similes in
Homer which are used to mirror the violence of emotions as
well as of war. As Austin has observed of Homeric similes:

> The most pertinent feature of similes is that they almost
> always relate human appearance, human attributes, or hu-
> man action to the world of nature . . . . They see the
> patterns in external phenomena--the action of wind on
> waves, on leaves, or forest fires . . . and draw man's
> life and activity into the orbit of these natural
> events.[74]

Austin goes on to cite Hermann Fränkel's observation that
similes "are Homer's method for expressing complex and invisible relations through visual images";[75] in these similes,
he remarks, "the human world receives its pattern from that
already established in the natural world."[76] Man is a mi-
crocosm by analogy with the coherent system of Homer's external world,[77] and I therefore wish to close this discussion of *átē* by mentioning another crucial entity in that mi-
crocosm, man's *thumós*.

Despite the hesitation of some lexicologists, not least
Chantraine,[78] I remain convinced by arguments that Greek
thumós is cognate with the widely attested Indo-European
word for smoke (cf. Latin *fumus*).[79] *Thumós*, according to
this view, derives from the root of the verb attested in
Greek as *thúō* which, in Benveniste's words, "properly means
'to produce smoke'."[80] He compares *theîon*, the Greek word
for 'sulphur'. That *thumós* indeed originally connoted
'smoke' is, in my judgment, confirmed within Greek itself by
the denominative verb *thumiáō* and its derivatives.[81] From a
semantic standpoint, the etymology is plausibly reflected in
the well-known behavior of the Homeric *thumós* at death as it
rises from the body of the dead hero. The verb *thúō*, 'rush',
could however be used to refer to "hasty" judgment and

behavior, for example: ἦ γὰρ ὅ γ᾽ ὀλοιῇσι φρεσὶ θύει (*Il.* 1.342). Under the influence of a folk etymological associa- tion with such uses of *thúō*, 'rush', the reference of *thumós* was subsequently extended to the semantic range we find at- tested in the Homeric poems.

What is my point? In developing a rudimentary, psycho- logical lexicon, the Greeks have based their terminology on natural phenomena, observable and palpable, but ultimately beyond one's grasp. The shifting modalities of "smoke" and "wind" have been brought inside the Homeric being to charac- terize the strange phenomenon of one's existence, one's emo- tional power, and its vulnerability. Thus, in accounting for the phrase *áetai . . . thumós* in Aeschylus' *Choephoroi* (390-393), Schadewaldt remarks that "the 'stormy blasts' represent the 'irrational' force of emotion, which in Greek is so often felt as a force pressing on one 'from with- out'."[82] In similar fashion, the etymology of *átē* accords well with other developments in Greek by which a term that originally designated an external, natural phenomenon comes to refer to some aspect of emotional, psychological, and not merely physical being.[83]

APPENDIX: ODYSSEUS AND ELPENOR

Several influential scholars have questioned the effective- ness of the Elpenor-episode at the end of *Odyssey* 10. D. L. Page, for example, finds "that the description of Elpenor's death in the Tenth Book, though excellent in itself, is most uncomfortably placed in its present context,"[84] and G. S. Kirk has written that "the description at 10.551ff. certain- ly reveals a strained and unnatural composition."[85] On the contrary, I think that Elpenor's presence may serve a clear and important function and, at the risk of overreading the

episode in reaction to its current neglect, I shall briefly
support my contention that Elpenor represents Odysseus'
"double."

Though Odysseus does not reveal his actual name to the
Phaeacians until 9.19, I have suggested that already in
Book 8 he guardedly reveals his identity, through the transformation of one of his most distinctive epithets, in the
phrase πολλὰ γὰρ ἔτλην (8.182). Moreover, the next line reflects both his Iliadic and Odyssean experience (ἀνδρῶν τε
πτολέμους ἀλεγεινά τε κύματα πείρων). Throughout his reply
to Euryalus he is indeed the *anèr polútropos* of whom the
poet first asked the Muse to speak (1.1-2), a wanderer at
sea in search of homecoming, at Troy a sacker of cities. In
these terms, Elpenor may well represent a "foil to Odysseus,"
for Elpenor's portrait at *Odyssey* 10.552-553--almost the
sailor's epitaph--contrasts thoroughly with what we know of
Odysseus. Elpenor is neither *polúmētis* nor *polútropos*, and
he cannot be *polútlās*: he is simply *neōtatos* (10.552), and
from that fact derive his otherwise negative attributes
(οὔτε τι λίην / ἄλκιμος ἐν πολέμῳ οὔτε φρεσὶν ᾗσιν ἀρηρώς,
10.552-553). Unlike Polites, "marshal of men" (ὄρχαμος
ἀνδρῶν, 10.224), who, also "through lack of experience"
(ἀϊδρείῃσιν, 231), led the sailors into Circe's thrall,
Elpenor is not a "leader" in any ordinary sense and he is
not described as having any close association with Odysseus
(contrast Polites, 10.225): he is Elpenor *tis* . . .
neōtatos who in death becomes merely "wretched" (*dústēnos*,
11.76, 80).

Elpenor's name, I have suggested, itself contrasts with
the name of Odysseus: he is a man of "aspiration" (*elpís*),
not one of performance, a man of "trouble." As a corollary
of his extreme youth, he lacks Iliadic competence (οὔτε τι

λίην / ἄλκιμος ἐν πολέμῳ) and that distinctively Odyssean capacity to survive by his wits (οὔτε φρεσὶν ᾗσιν ἀρηρώς). In that he is neither *ptolipórthios* nor *polútropos*, Elpenor lacks those attributes which most particularly characterize Odysseus. His role is solely a passive one; drunkenness has blinded him (cf. 11.61) as it will blind Eurytion (21.295-302), and unlike Odysseus (cf. *peîrōn*, 8.183), he attempts nothing. Elpenor is inset within the larger frame which the presence of Circe describes around Odysseus' visit to the Underworld. Without past or story, *Elpḗnōr neōtatos* has no *nóstos*, no future; he will never reach maturity, for his "aspirations" are dashed, falling with him from Circe's roofbeam. He is newborn into the poem without any goal but to "lead" Odysseus into the Underworld as Polites led the sailors to Circe.

C. P. Segal has well remarked of Elpenor that "his weakness perhaps makes him a kind of ritual scapegoat for Odysseus' journey to the dead."[86] Though I would not exaggerate the "sacrificial" aspect of Elpenor's death or imply any precise analogy with Patroclus' Iliadic relationship to Achilles, certain aspects of Homer's account of Odysseus' preparation for and his return from his ordeal in the Underworld suggest that Elpenor may have a special role to play. It is significant enough that the *Nekyia* occupies the central position in the scheme of Odysseus' progressive survival against odds, especially the odds of death. Though Odysseus survives this present encounter with his mortality, in Hades he hears the nature of his own end foretold (11.119-137), and his capacity to go on outmaneuvering every obstacle is further qualified by the spectacle of his ancestor, Sisyphus (11.593-600). Once again Odysseus' safe passage is due to planning and preparation, not merely to chance

or to the mythological convention by which so many Greek heroes survive confrontations with death as the triumphant act
of their enterprise. Circe not only clothes Odysseus
(10.542), but also arms him with exact knowledge of apotro-
paic ritual (10.526ff.). Finally, when all these other prep-
arations are complete, Elpenor's *psyche* "went down to Hades"
(10.560),[87] and at that very moment Odysseus announces to
his companions that the Underworld is his own destination
(10.561-565).[88] Though Hades will not claim Odysseus this
time, he does keep Elpenor; and A. B. Lord compares the
death and burial of Menelaus' helmsman, Phrontes, at *Odyssey*
3.276-285, suggesting that "the death of a companion in this
configuration" should be seen as "sacrificial and a necessary element for the successful journey to the land of the
dead."[89] Then, once Odysseus has fled the Land of the Dead,
we are presented with one last instance of "doubling" between Odysseus and Elpenor: just as Elpenor's freefall co-
incides with Odysseus' departure for Hades, so his formal
burial takes place immediately upon Odysseus' return to
Aeaea (12.8-15). Elpenor's grave, at his own request (11.77-
78), is marked by an oar (12.15). According to Teiresias'
prophecy, Odysseus' own death will likewise be prefigured
and its ritual set in inexorable motion, if in a different
context, by the hero's action of implanting an oar in the
earth (11.129), which, as Segal observes, reflects his "par-
ticipation in common toil and risks, the sharing of the
years of wandering."[90]

NOTES

* I gratefully acknowledge assistance from Anna Morpurgo
   Davies and N. J. Richardson in preparing the final version
   of this essay.

1. Anne Amory, "The Gates of Horn and Ivory," *YClS* 20 (1966),
   23, note 27.

2. Paul Friedländer, *Plato: An Introduction*, tr. Hans Meyer-
   hoff (New York: Harper and Row, 1964), p. 32.

3. Manu Leumann, *Homerische Wörter* (Basel: Reinhardt, 1950),
   pp. 91ff.; Emile Benveniste, *Indo-European Language and
   Society*, tr. E. Palmer (Coral Gables: University of Miami
   Press, 1973), pp. 434ff.

4. See also Hesiod *fr.* 234 Merkelbach-West; Callimachus *fr.*
   496, with Pfeiffer's note.

5. Henry Hayman, *The Odyssey of Homer* 2 (London: Nutt, 1873),
   p. 179 (ad *Od.* 10.562).

6. Cedric H. Whitman, *Homer and the Heroic Tradition* (Cam-
   bridge, Mass.: Harvard University Press, 1958), p. 292;
   C. P. Segal, "The Phaeacians and the Symbolism of Odysseus'
   Return," *Arion* 1.4 (1962), 41.

7. Gregory Nagy, "The Name of Achilles: Etymology and Epic,"
   in Anna Morpurgo Davies and Wolfgang Meid, eds., *Studies
   in Greek, Italic, and Indo-European Linguistics Offered to
   Leonard R. Palmer = Innsbrucker Beiträge zur Sprachwissen-
   schaft* 16 (Innsbruck: 1976), p. 231, also p. 211 (with
   bibliography); J. H. Finley, Jr., *Homer's Odyssey* (Cambridge, Mass.: Harvard University Press, 1978), p. 71.
   On Odysseus and Elpenor, see the Appendix to this paper.

8. Robert Fitzgerald, tr., *Homer: The Odyssey* (Garden City,
   N.Y.: Anchor Press/Doubleday, 1961), p. 142.

9. Note also the Aeolic character of *polútlās* in terms of both its root vocalism and its accent (as opposed to Ionic *-tlḗs*; cf. Pierre Chantraine, *Grammaire homérique* 1, 2nd ed. [Paris: Klincksieck, 1958], pp. 21-22), an observation which might reflect upon Fick's now unfashionable thesis concerning an Aeolic origin for the myth of Odysseus. Ionic transformations of *polútlās* are attested in *polutlḗmōn* (*Il.* 7.152, Nestor of himself) and *polútlētos* (*Od.* 11.38, etc.); at *Od.* 18.319, the disguised Odysseus closes his address to the female servants of his house with the words, πολυτλήμων δὲ μάλ' εἰμί, perhaps again with an oblique reference to his true identity (beyond his present, disheveled appearance) comparable with the passage at 8.182.

10. The view of W. Whallon, "The Homeric Epithets," *YClS* 17 (1961), 97-142, as summarized by Adam Parry, "Language and Characterization in Homer," *HSPh* 76 (1972), 6.

11. Parry, 8.

12. For examples of the association of *átē* and *apátē*, see *Il.* 2.111-115 (= 9.18-22), 19.95-97 ("*apátēsen* . . . : schon fast Konkurrenzwort zu *aásato!*," H. Seiler, "Homerisch *aáomai* und *átē*," in *Sprachgeschichte und Wortbedeutung = Festschrift Debrunner* [Bern: Francke Verlag, 1954], p. 416). This interaction is discussed at length by Josef Stallmach, *Ate: Zur Frage des Selbst- und Weltverständnisses des frühgriechischen Menschens = Beiträge zur klassischen Philologie* 18 (Meisenheim am Glan: A. Hain, 1968), pp. 43ff. For the lexicological connections between *atasthalíē* and *átē*, see Hjalmar Frisk, "'Ἀτάσθαλος, ett omtvistat grekiskt adjektiv," *Eranos* 31 (1933), 21, 24 (cf. Pierre Chantraine, *Dictionnaire étymologique de la langue grecque* [Paris: Klincksieck, 1968-1980], 1:132, s.v.

atásthalos), and, for example, the collocation of *atastha-líē* and *aásthē* with *népios* (e.g., *Od.* 1.7-8 and *Il.* 16.685-686).

13. Cf. Hjalmar Frisk, *Griechisches etymologisches Wörterbuch* (Heidelberg: Winter, 1954-1972), 1:136, s.v. *aréskō*; (hereafter abbreviated *GEW*); Chantraine, *Dictionnaire étymologique* 1:107, s.v. *aréskō*.

14. Werner Jaeger, *Paideia* 1, 2nd ed., tr. Gilbert Highet (New York: Oxford University Press, 1945), p. 418, note 10.

15. According to the testimony of a Florentine scholiast *ad loc.* and Eustathius *ad Odysseam* 1422.19. The scholiast glosses *áros* as *epikouría* in his paraphrase: ἡ τῶν βρετέων ἐπικουρία βλάπτει με; and H. Friis Johansen prints *áros* in his recent edition of the text (*Aeschylus: The Suppliants* [Copenhagen: Gyldendal, 1970], p. 126).

16. Hansjakob Seiler, *Die primären griechischen Steigerungsformen* (Hamburg: Heitmann, 1950), pp. 116ff. On the remodeling of **áreios*, derived from *áros* as *téleios* from *télos*, to *areíōn*, see Frisk, *GEW* 1:135-136. The association of *areíōn* with *Arēs* is, pace H. Güntert (*Indogermanische Forschungen* 27 [1910], 67-68), a folk-etymological one.

17. For example, *níkē* (*Il.* 7.203; cf. Pind. *Isthm.* 6.60; Bacchyl. 2.5; Xenophanes 2.1; Hes. *Th.* 628); *timḗ* (*Il.* 1.159; 5.552; Hes. *fr.* 302.4 Merkelbach-West); *eûkhos* (*Il.* 7.203; 11.290; 21.297; Hes. *Th.* 628); *kléos* (*Il.* 5.273; 6.446; 17.16; 18.121; *Od.* 1.240; 13.422; 14.370; Pind. *Ol.* 9.101); *kûdos* (*Il.* 4.95; 9.303; 12.407; 14.365; 16.88; 17.287, 419; 20.502; 21.543; 22.207; *Od.* 22.253, etc.); *misthós* (*Il.* 12.435, see also Leumann, *Homerische Wörter*, p. 316 and note 105); *aéthlia* (*Il.* 9.124, 266,

269; 22.160), and *ápoina* (*Il.* 19.138).

18. For example, Hitt. *arnuzi-*, 'brings', Armen. *aŕnum* (aor. *aŕi*), 'takes', Avest. *ərənav-*, 'grants' (Frisk, *GEW* 1:146).

19. Bruno Snell, *The Discovery of the Mind*, tr. T. G. Rosenmeyer (New York: Harper and Row, 1960), p. 158; note also E.-M. Voigt in the *Lexikon des frühgriechischen Epos*, pp. 1229ff. (hereafter abbreviated *LfE*).

20. Snell, *Discovery*, pp. 158-159.

21. Moses I. Finley, *The World of Odysseus* (Harmondsworth: Pelican Books, 1962), pp. 138-139.

22. Cf. *LfE*, pp. 1289-1290, s.v. *áristos*, and such passages as Tyrtaeus 12.13-14 West.

23. A. W. H. Adkins, *Merit and Responsibility* (Oxford: Clarendon Press, 1960), pp. 66 and 81, note 13, in my judgement needlessly sees a moral overtone in Homer's use of *aretãn*.

24. M. L. West, ed., *Hesiod: Works and Days* (Oxford: Clarendon Press, 1978), p. 229. In this connection note the use of *ólbos* as a synonym for *areté* (cf. *LfE*, pp. 1231-1232, s.v. *areté* 4b).

25. Emile Benveniste, "Problèmes sémantiques de la reconstruction," *Word* 10 (1954), 251-264, reprinted in *Problèmes de linguistique générale* (Paris: Gallimard, 1966), pp. 289-307. To insist on such accuracy in glossing Greek words may in any case not necessarily be the hallmark of scholarly precision. Instead it can lead to the kind of anachronistic confusion I have already mentioned, since to distinguish in contemporary English between, for example, "prowess" and "achievement" may have little direct bearing upon the way in which the corresponding semantic field was articulated in Homer's Greek.

26. Philipp Buttmann, *Lexilogus*: *Beiträge zur griechischen Wörterklärung hauptsächlich für Homer und Hesiod* (Berlin: 1818), p. 1.

27. R. D. Dawe, "Some Reflections on Ate and Hamartia," *HSPh* 72 (1967), 96–97.

28. Frisk, *GEW* 1:2 (s. v. *aáō*, "unerklärt"); Chantraine, *Dictionnaire étymologique*, 1:3 ("étymologie inconnue").

29. See, for example, the suggestions reported by Emile Boisacq, *Dictionnaire étymologique de la langue grecque* (Heidelberg: Winter, 1907), p. 96. The most extensive attempt to connect *átē* with roots meaning 'strike a blow' etc. is that of Wilhelm Havers "Zur Semasiologie von griechischen ἄτη," *ZVS* 43 (1910), 225–244; but see Seiler's comments, "Homerisch *aáomai*" (above, note 12), 409–410.

30. "Reflections" (above, note 27), 96.

31. *LfE*, p. 10 (s.v. *átē*) and "Homerisch *aáomai*," 409–417.

32. E. R. Dodds, *The Greeks and the Irrational* (Berkeley and Los Angeles: University of California Press, 1951), pp. 2ff.

33. W. S. Barrett, ed., *Euripides: Hippolytus* (Oxford: Clarendon Press, 1964), p. 206 (ad v. 241).

34. *Ate* (above, note 12), p. 102.

35. In the following list I have cited the root shapes in their uncontracted form where the meter permits. (I do not include the ambiguous form *atéonta* [*Il.* 20.332], on which see Leumann, *Homerische Wörter*, p. 215, note 10; Chantraine, *Dictionnaire étymologique*, 1:133.) (i) ἄ(w)a- in the noun: *Il.* 1.412; 2.111; 8.237; 9.18, 504, 505; 10. 391; 16.274, 805; 19.91, 126, 129, 136, 270; 24.480; *Od.* 4.261; 12.372; 15.233; 21.302; 23.223); in the verb: *Il.* 8.237; 16.685; 19.91, 129 (*aátai* < *awá-etai*, cf. note 37), 113, 136; *Od.* 4.503, 509; 21.301. Compare the augmented

form, $\bar{a}(w)a$-:   *Il.* 9.116, 119; 19.137; *Od.* 21.296, 297.
(ii) $\breve{a}(w)\bar{a}$-:   *Il.* 9.537; 11.340; *Od.* 10.68.   (iii) $\bar{a}$-
(contracted after loss of digamma) in *thesis*:   *Od.* 11.61;
in *arsis*: *Il.* 6.356 = 24.28; 19.88.   Cf. Seiler, "Homerisch
aáomai," p. 410.

36. Note that the evidence of Doric and Aeolic requires us to
reconstruct a root shape **awa-* for Proto-Greek; cf. *auáta*
at Alcaeus *fr.* 70.12 and 10.7 Lobel-Page, Pind. *Pyth.* 2.
28, 3.24.   The denominative *awatatai* is attested in Crete
(*Gortyn Law Code* 4.30, etc.) and from the Laconian town-
ship of Gythium (*IG* V 1, 1155 = Schwyzer no. 51).   For
discussion of this and other epigraphic evidence, see
Stallmach, *Ate*, p. 64; and on the digamma, see Rolf
Hiersche, "Zu αὐειρομέναι und αὐάτα bei Alkman," *Glotta* 56
(1978), 43-48.

37. While *aãtai* could theoretically be analyzed as a themati-
cization of an old root present, it is best explained as a
secondary derivation from the sigmatic aorist by analogy
to thematicized models of the type *agáetai* (beside *ágatai*):
ēgassámēn; *eráomai* (beside *éramai*): *ērasámēn* (on which see
Chantraine, *Grammaire homérique* 1^2:   354-355, and Seiler,
"Homerisch *aáomai*," pp. 410-411).   As another secondary development found in the Ate of Zeus, note the irresolvably
disyllabic form of $\acute{\bar{a}}t\bar{e}n$ at *Il.* 19.88.

38. The voice of the Homeric verb paradigm can be summarized
as follows: (active) *Il.* 8.237; *Od.* 10.68; 11.61; 21.296-
297; (middle) *Il.* 9.116, 119, 537; 11.340; 19.137 (cf.
aãtai, 19.91 = 129); (passive) *Il.* 16.685; 19.113, 136; *Od.*
4.503, 509; 21.301; cf. Seiler, "Homerisch *aáomai*," p. 410.
Notice that the passive is restricted to verse final position (the Homeric *Hymn to Demeter* 246 provides an exception) while the middle never so occurs: the descriptive

difference for Homeric Greek may thus be one of formula,
rather than of lexical meaning (but see J. M. Bremer,
Hamartia [Amsterdam: Hakkert, 1969], p. 102, note 12). On
the relative chronology of the three formations, see also
below, note 68.

39. For a succinct statement of this principle, see W. Cow-
gill, *Language* 40 (1964), 351, note 38.

40. *Fr.* 296.10 Lobel-Page. Page (*Sappho and Alcaeus* [Ox-
ford: Clarendon Press, 1955], p. 298) despairs of any explanation for this form although he cites Hesychius' gloss,
kataésetai = *katapneúsei*, and compares Euripides' *Medea*
836ff., a passage in which Aphrodite is the subject of
katapneûsai (839). In my judgment, this evidence cogently
accounts for Alcaeus' *kataéssato*, which I therefore gloss
as 'breathed down' (rather than 'blew down, confounded'):
"the Cyprian-born goddess breathed down upon you . . .
Damoanactidas . . . beside the lovely olive trees." The
-*ss*- of *kataéssato* doubtless represents a redactional
variant, common enough in Lesbian poetry following a long
vowel, for an expected *kataésato*. The aorist participle
kataéssas, however, belongs with the paradigm of *aéskō*
and, pace Liddell and Scott (s.v. κατάημι), has nothing to
do with the root of *áēmi*.

41. Cf. E. D. Francis, *Greek Disyllabic Roots* (Diss. Yale University, 1970), pp. 196-198.

42. Dawe, "Reflections" (above, note 27), 98.

43. *Lexilogus*, (above, note 26), p. 5.

44. Anton Göbel, "Homerische Etymologien," *Philologus* 36
(1877), 32-63. On 34 Göbel analyzes *aw-áō* ("wind
machen") as a denominative from **áw-ē*. The morphology of
his suggestion is improbable, but Göbel was evidently also
seeking the explanation of the gloss *Verblendung* through a
connection with the root of *áēmi* (cf. 35ff.).

114   *E. D. Francis*

45. "Semasiologie" (above, note 29), 226.

46. Cf. Pind. *Ol.* 7.31 and the frequent association of *átē* with *para*-compounds, e.g., *paréoros* (*Il.* 23.603; cf. Leumann, *Homerische Wörter*, pp. 228-229; O. Becker, *Das Bild des Weges = Hermes Einzelschriften* 4 [Berlin: Weidmann, 1937], pp. 159-160), *parakopá* (Aesch. *Ag.* 223, "knocked sideways," Dawe, "Reflections," 110-111), *parágei* (Aesch. *Pers.* 96, cf. Theognis 402ff.). Note also the relation of *átē* to words like *hamartía* and *amplakía* (Dawe, 102-102).

47. On the collocation of *népios* and *aásthē*, see Dodds, pp. 5ff.; Stallmach, pp. 22-24; Bremer (above, note 38), pp. 101-104, and the Homeric *Hymn to Demeter*, 256-258.

48. On "strike," see Havers, "Semasiologie" (above, note 29), 232; and, for a recent discussion of metaphor, C. Moulton, "Homeric Metaphor," *CPh* 74 (1979), 279-293.

49. With *thumós*: *Il.* 9.537, 11.340, *Od.* 23.223; with *phrénes*: *Il.* 9.119; 16.805; 19.88, 137; *Od.* 15.233-234; 21.297 (cf. the compounds, *aesíphrōn*, *aesiphrosúnē*); with both: *Od.* 21.301-302. Cf. Stallmach, *Ate*, pp. 15ff., also pp. 48ff.; S. M. Darcus, "-*phrōn* Epithets of *thumós*," *Glotta* 55 (1977), 178-182; Bruno Snell, "φρένες--φρόνησις," *Glotta* 55 (1977), 34-64, esp. 47-48; Moulton, "Homeric Metaphor," 282.

50. Richmond Lattimore, tr., *The Iliad of Homer* (Chicago: University of Chicago Press, 1951), p. 428.

51. A. C. Moorhouse, "'ΑΑΑΤΟΣ and Some Other Negative Compounds," *CQ* n.s. 11 (1961), 16, note 3.

52. "'ΑΑΑΤΟΣ," 16-17. Quintus of Smyrna (1.217), may have thought, as the lexicographical tradition seems to have done, that *aéton* represented a metrical variant of *áāton*, 'inexhaustible' (: *áō*, 'satiate') and accordingly restored a hypercorrect -*ā*-. Alternatively, Quintus, perhaps

influenced by Apollonius' use of *aáatos* (2.77, 'unsusceptible to harm', hence 'invincible'; *contra*, Moorhouse,
ibid.), may have interpreted Homeric *áëton* as a contracted
variant of *a-ā(w)aton* and assimilated the vocalism to accommodate his mistaken hypothesis (note that the development of Proto-Greek *ā* as Ionic *ë* precedes the loss of intervocalic digamma). Cyril's gloss, *aáatos* = *aplérötos*,
seems to combine both these assumptions, but in my judgement forms an insubstantial basis for interpreting the
Epic usage of *áëtos*, etc.

53. Cf. Becker (above, note 46), p. 169. On the association
of *áëton* and *áëmi*, cf. *LfE*, pp. 193-194, s.v. *áëtos*; for
the formation, compare *plōtós* beside *plōō*. *Átë*, or rather
parakopá, and *thrásos* are associated by Aeschylus at *Ag*.
222-223 (on which see Mark W. Edwards, "Agamemnon's Decision: Freedom and Folly in Aeschylus," *CSCA* 10 [1978], 26).

54. Compare the exchange between Odysseus and Elpenor in the
Underworld: πῶς ἦλθες; Odysseus inquires (*Od*. 11.57), to
which Elpenor replies (61): ἄσέ με δαίμονος αἶσα κακὴ (cf.
Aeolus' query at 10.64) καὶ ἀθέσφατος οἶνος.

55. Cf. H. Fränkel, *Die homerischen Gleichnisse* (Göttingen:
Vandenhoeck and Ruprecht, 1921), pp. 17ff.; C. Moulton,
Similes in the Homeric Poems = *Hypomnemata* 49 (Göttingen:
Vandenhoeck and Ruprecht, 1977), pp. 33-45.

56. On the "third wind," see Hugh Lloyd-Jones, "Modern Interpretation of Pindar," *JHS* 93 (1973), 130. Aeschylus' narrative of Agamemnon's crisis at Aulis immediately following the Hymn to Zeus may illustrate how the imagery of the
wind reflects the direction of the king's will (cf. E.
Fraenkel, ed., *Aeschylus: Agamemnon* 2 [Oxford: Clarendon
Press, 1950], p. 115 [ad 187]), but Mark Edwards has recently argued that τροπαίαν at verse 219 refers not to any

"vacillation in the mind of Agamemnon," but to the actual "change of wind" that permits the fleet to sail from Aulis ("Agamemnon's Decision," 26 and note 41).

57. On this passage, see G. Müller, "Der homerische Ate-Begriff und Solons Musenelegie," in *Navicula Chiloniensis = Festschrift Felix Jacoby* (Leiden: Brill, 1956), pp. 11ff.

58. Cf. West, *Works and Days*, p. 214.   It is perhaps best to regard this usage as an instance of *átē* (iii) (see below, pp. 100-101).   Note the similar semantic relationship between "disaster" and "blight" in the etymology of Lat. *calamitas* which, however, generalizes rather than restricts the original usage.

59. While *aasíphrōn* seems to be the original form (: aor. *áasa*, cf. *talasíphrōn : etálasa, olesi- : ólesa*, etc.), the attestation of variants in *aesi-* may well suggest folk-etymological association with the root of *áēmi* and its derivatives (cf. *aellós = mainómenos*, Hsch.).

60. W. Schulze, *Quaestiones Epicae* (Gütersloh: Bertelsmann, 1892), p. 512.

61. "'ΑΑΑΤΟΣ" (above, note 51), 10-11.   Note, however, that the form *aáspetos*, coined by Quintus of Smyrna (3.673, 7.193) can certainly be explained as analogical to *aáskhetos*.

62. "'ΑΑΑΤΟΣ," 13ff.   Apart from the existence of strong morphological arguments against Moorhouse's connection of *aáatos* with the root of *áō*, 'satiate,' he takes insufficient account of the testimony of Hesychius' corrupt (?) gloss, *aábaktoi = ablabeĩs*, which seems to imply the existence of a form *aáatos* derived from *átē*.

63. It may be possible that *aáaton* continues a form **a(n)áēton* 'where no wind blows,' (of an Underworld river), with metrical lengthening to *a(n)áēton*, subsequently rebuilt

by folk-etymological association with $a(w)át\bar{e}$, but I doubt that this is the case.

64. "Reflections" (above, note 27), 99, but see Bremer's remarks (*Hamartia* [above, note 38], p. 111). Note also Telemachus' description of the suitors' *húbris* and *atasthalíē* (e.g., at *Od.* 16.86, cf. 23.64), with Odysseus' reply (16.91-111, esp. 93).

65. W. B. Stanford, interpreting *aáatos* as "most destructive," suggests that Antinous construes *mnēstéressin* with *kat'*. . . *lipónte* in the previous line (*The Odyssey of Homer* 2 [London: Macmillan, 1948], p. 360). On the other hand, if, as I prefer, we understand the initial *alpha* as privative, not intensive, then *mnēstéressin* can be taken *apò koinoû* with both *kat'*. . . *lipónte* and *aáaton*.

66. Cf. Stanford, p. 366 (ad 296); note Odysseus' earlier characterization of the drunk and disorderly suitors in *Od.* 16.105-111.

67. Ajax would have been safe on the promontory of Gyrae εἰ μὴ ὑπερφίαλον ἔπος ἔκβαλε καὶ μέγ' ἀάσθη (*Od.* 4.503). At *Od.* 21.285ff., as the suitors express their frustration about the bow, Antinous turns on Odysseus in angry scorn: οὐκ ἀγαπᾷς ὃ ἔκηλος ὑπερφιάλοισι μεθ' ἡμῖν / δαίνυσαι (289-290). He then proceeds with the cautionary tale of the Lapith Wedding and Eurytion's *át\bar{e}*. Just as he is insensitive to the way in which this scene prefigures the destruction not of Odysseus, but of the suitors, so the peculiar pride he takes in their being *huperphíaloi* leaves him heedless of the potential consequences of that state: καὶ μέγ' ἀάσθη (with Zeus' approval, 21.413-415).

68. I have suggested that the sigmatic aorist most probably developed from a passive (or at least stative) formation. Seiler ("Homerisch *aáomai*" [above, note 12], 412ff.) argues

that the verb was characteristically used first as a middle
and that the attested active and passive uses were relatively younger. It is certainly the case that the metaphorical use of *áēmi* in the Iliadic phrase *thumòs áēto* is
medio-passive and I therefore suspect that Seiler is basically correct: once it is possible to say, for example,
oínōi aásato phrénas, one can then say *oînos áase phrénas*.

69. Though Dodds (above, note 32), pp. 5-6, argues vigorously
    that, in Homer, *átē* cannot be seen as "the punishment of
    guilty rashness," I am impressed by the fact that *áasa* etc.
    often occur in conjunction with *hupér* and its compounds:
    if "guilty rashness" is not at issue then surely "excessive
    behavior" is. For example, in the *Iliad* (8.236-237) Ajax,
    son of Telamon, asks Zeus: τιν'. . . ὑπερμενέων βασιλῆων
    / τῇδ' ἄτῃ ἄασας . . .; (for the *Odyssey*, cf. note 67). In
    the classical period, the Ghost of Darius has no doubt that
    the harvest of Hybris is Ate (Aesch. *Pers.* 821ff.; cf.
    Solon 4.30-35 West; Pind. *Pyth.* 2.28ff., *Ol.* 1.57), a no-
    tion at least already latent in the Homeric passages I have
    cited. For the development of this theme, see Stallmach
    (above, note 12), pp. 59-63.

70. For discussion of the connections between *átē* and *blabé*,
    etc. see Dawe (above, note 12), 104-105; Seiler, "Homerisch
    áaomai" (above, note 12), 415-416; Becker (above, note 46),
    p. 159 (ad *Il.* 15.724). The fact that the Homeric passages
    (*Il.* 9.505-507, cf. 512; 19.91-94; *Od.* 21.293-298; cf. 23.
    11-14) plainly associate the words does not oblige us to
    regard them as necessarily synonymous, or to derive *átē*
    from a root meaning 'strike.' Nevertheless, the Iliadic
    passages make it clear that a function of Ate is to "harm
    humanity" (cf. Hesiod's *Works and Days* 216, with West's
    note), and the classical sense of "ruin" developed in part
    under the influence of such contexts.

71. Note that the root shape $a(w)\bar{e}$- was indeed generalized to medio-passive forms (e.g. *aémenos*, *Od.* 6.131; *áēto*, *Il.* 21. 386), perhaps replacing a zero-grade formation (cf. *áeto* = *diépnei*, Hsch.?; *áethlon*, etc.). Forms like *ā́(w)āsan* (*Od.* 10.68) and *ā́(w)ásato* (*Il.* 11.340) might continue the expected quantity of an inherited *awĕsai* with the vowel quality redactionally altered, but they remain more plausibly explained as the result of metrical lengthening. It is also conceivable, but in my judgment unlikely (cf. note 37), that *aắtai* continues the redactional transformation of an athematic *áētai*.

72. E. L. Harrison, "Notes on Homeric Psychology," *Phoenix* 14 (1960), 64.

73. Norman Austin, *Archery at the Dark of the Moon* (Berkeley and Los Angeles: University of California Press, 1975), pp. 98-100.

74. Ibid., p. 116.

75. Ibid., p. 271, note 32. For a recent bibliography on the subject, see Moulton, *Similes* (above, note 55), pp. 156-158.

76. Austin, p. 117.

77. Cf. Austin, p. 104.

78. *Dictionnaire étymologique* 2:446.

79. Cf. Frisk, *GEW* 1:694 s.v. *thumós*.

80. *Indo-European Language and Society*, p. 486; cf. Richard B. Onians, *The Origins of European Thought* (Cambridge: Cambridge University Press, 1954), pp. 44ff.

81. *Thumiáō* is probably attested first at Sappho *fr.* 2.3-4 Lobel-Page (cf. Hipponax *fr.* 175 West; cf. *thumíama*, 'incense,' *thumiatḗrion*, 'censor,' Hdt.+). Frisk (*GEW* 1: 693-694) suggests that the unexpected formation of *thumiáō* is analogical to *koniáō*, straightforward beside *konía*, *konís*; but the semantic distance between *thumiáō*, 'smoke'

and *koniáō*, 'plaster,' combined with the fact that the attestation of *koniáō* and its derivatives substantially post-
dates that of *thumiáō*, etc. causes difficulty for this explanation.

82. W. Schadewaldt, "Der Kommos in Aischylos' *Choephoren*,"
Hermes 67 (1932), 333; cf. Becker (above, note 46), pp.
169ff., and my account of *thūmòs áēto* above. The etymology
of *psukhḗ*, uncertain though it still is, may involve a similar semantic development (cf. Frisk, *GEW* 2:1142). Ar-
chilochus' use of *kukōmene* in his apostrophe to his *thumós*
(*fr.* 128.1 West) provides a striking instance of the development I am invoking: a word which previously characterized, for example, the whirlpool of Charybdis (*Od.* 12.238,
241) now expresses the turbulence of the poet's *thumós* (cf.
Hesychius' gloss, *aellós = mainómenos*).

83. In thus attempting to account for the semantic prehistory
of a set of terms which the Greeks found particularly compelling, I have not intended, for example, to define in detail the productive usage of *átē* in Homer, let alone reconstruct "the historical development of Greek beliefs
about atē" which John Herington has called "the most significant side of the subject" (*CW* 63 [1970], 274). Beside
more widely recognized developments, however, some of the
specialized contexts in which *átē* became productive are
worthy of brief mention. For example, *átē* is already invoked in Homer as a precondition of adultery (*Il.* 3.100
Zenodotus, 6.356; *Od.* 4.261, 23.223, cf. Bremer [above, note
38], p. 104), and this usage is also attested in Pindar (of
Coronis, *Pyth.* 3.24), Aeschylus (*Ag.* 1192), and Euripides
(of Phaedra, *Hipp.* 241); on *xennapátas* (of Paris, Alcaeus
fr. 283.5 Lobel-Page, see above, page 81), and note the

collocation of *átē* with *dólos* and its derivatives already
in *Iliad* 19.95-97, 112-113 (cf. Aesch. *Pers.*94-98, *Ag.*
1523; Soph. *Trach.* 850-851; Eur. *Tro.* 530; cf. Stallmach
[above, note 12], pp. 90-91). Onians (above, note 80), p.
327, considers the use of *átē* and related forms in predica-
tions which include a word of "binding" (e.g. *Il.* 2.111 =
9.18; cf. 19.93ff.; Hes. *Th.* 502ff.; Aesch. *PV* 1078-1079)
basic to an understanding of "the *daímōn Átē.*" At any
rate, such usage sponsors the connotations of liability
which Dodds has discussed (pp. 3ff.) and, combined with the
sense of calamity and loss I have already mentioned, accounts for the technical use of *ata* and its denominative
atáomai in the Gortyn Law Code to refer not only to "damage" (6.23,43; 9.14), but to "obligation, indemnity, loss
in a law-suit" (e.g. 10.23-24; 11.34-35, 41), on which see
Hiersche, *Glotta* 56 (1978), 46, and E. Bourguet, *Le
Dialecte laconien*, (Paris: Honoré Champion, 1927), pp.
56ff.

84. D. L. Page, *The Homeric Odyssey* (Oxford: Clarendon Press,
    1955), p. 44.

85. G. S. Kirk, *The Songs of Homer* (Cambridge: Cambridge
    University Press, 1962), p. 239; see also Herbert Eisen-
    berger, *Studien zur Odyssee = Palingenesia* 7 (Wiesbaden:
    F. Steiner, 1973), pp. 165-167.

86. C. P. Segal (above, note 6), 41.

87. For a comparison with Patroclus' death at *Il.* 16.851ff.,
    see E. Rohde, *Psyche*, tr. W. B. Hillis (London: Kegan
    Paul, 1925), pp. 19, 36.

88. See Page, p. 44, on the phrase ἐρχομένοισι δὲ τοῖσιν.

89. A. B. Lord, *The Singer of Tales* (Cambridge, Mass.: Har-
    vard University Press, 1960), p. 168.

90. Segal, 41; cf. Finley, *Homer's Odyssey* (above, note 7),
    pp. 115-116.

Mycenaean Greece and Homeric Reflections

R. Hope Simpson

(This paper, as delivered, was in three sections, of which
the second was an informal presentation of selected slides.
These were chosen to illustrate Mycenaean structural engineering, sites discussed in connection with the Homeric Catalogue of the Ships, and the topography of Ithaca. The author
here summarizes the main arguments made in this central section, but he cannot, of course, reproduce the visual presentation. Both in this section and in the others, he has, like
Thucydides, tried to adhere as closely as possible to the
gist of what was actually said.)

I have always been most grateful to the late Professor
Wace for encouraging me to undertake fieldwork in Laconia.
The survey of Laconia was begun by scholars of the British
School of Archaeology before World War I and continued by
Helen Thomas (now Lady Helen Waterhouse) in 1936-38.[1] My own
work, in 1956-58,[2] became a prelude to a broader survey of the
topography of Mycenaean Greece and to the study of a subject
which may be loosely termed "Homeric Geography."

Most of my travels in connection with this broader survey
were in the company of John Lazenby, and we eventually produced a book[3] in which we discussed the relationship between
the patterns of Mycenaean and later settlement in Greece, and
the names of people and places in the Catalogue of the Ships
in the *Iliad*. Of our reviewers,[4] some compromised by on the
one hand praising the archaeological fieldwork and on the
other hand rejecting the conclusions on the "Homeric" side.
Scepticism was, of course, to be expected; and, as often

happens in reviews, some misunderstandings and even misrepre-
sentations occurred, in cases where conclusions were taken out
of context or our careful qualifications were not taken into
account.[5] Our main conclusion was, and still remains, that
the Achaean section of the Catalogue of the Ships in the
Iliad is a remarkably good reflection of Mycenaean Greece as
so far revealed by archaeology. It is, of course, a poetic
reflection, and there are obvious limits as to the inferences
we may draw from it. Nevertheless, it should not be rejected
out of hand as a potential source of information about
Mycenaean geography.

I will first discuss "Homeric Geography" in general, before
giving the particular reasons for the *special* value that we
place on the Catalogue of the Ships. The term "Homeric Geography" could be misleading. Geography nowadays implies precision and a scientific outlook, whereas Homer was a poet,
living at a time when map-making was in its infancy. Further
confusion has been caused by romantics such as Mr. Ernle
Bradford, whose account of his Mediterranean voyages was
given "in color on C.B.S." on January 11, 1966. The *New York
Times* was enthusiastic, and I quote from their account:

> Mr. Bradford was engaged by the Columbia Broadcasting
> System to narrate his own story demonstrating the fac-
> tual accuracy of "The Odyssey," with James Mason, the
> actor, reading illustrative lines from Homer. The
> British historian and sailor then offered his own evi-
> dence for believing that the Odyssey was good report-
> ing and not myth.

I will forego here a detailed discussion of the locations
proposed by Mr. Bradford for the various "stopovers" made by
Odysseus on his travels. For it is abundantly clear that
Odysseus, on his return home to Ithaca from Troy, spends most

of his time in an Ancient Greek Fairyland. He enters Fairyland after he passes by the island of Kythera (*Od.* 9.81), and
he does not leave it again until his final landing on Ithaca
(*Od.* 13.95ff.). His travels among Lotus-Eaters, Sirens, and
Clashing Rocks are reminiscent of the travels of Sinbad the
Sailor, as are the witches and bitches, the one-eyed giants
and the whirlpools. Mr. Bradford, like that other hopeless
romantic who tried to demonstrate that Stonehenge was a primeval observatory,[6] is looking for precision where no precision can be expected.

Homer, the poet, has a poetic vision of the real world also. He thinks of the Earth itself as a flat circular disc,
surrounded by the stream of Ocean, from which all rivers, all
seas, all fountains, and all wells originate:[7]

> ἐξ οὗ περ πάντες ποταμοὶ καὶ πᾶσα θάλασσα
> καὶ πᾶσαι κρῆναι καὶ φρείατα μακρὰ νάουσιν.

(Il. 21.196-197)

The sun rises out of this ocean and sinks again into it.
There are no points of the compass, but the four main winds
are named, and are given stock descriptions. East is "towards the dawn and the sun," πρὸς ἠῶ τ' ἠέλιόν τε, and west
is "towards the misty gloom," ποτὶ ζόφον ἠερόεντα.

These are, of course, rough directions, not exact points.
Distances, and the time taken to cover them, are also not exact. When Telemachus sets out from Pylos to Sparta, there is
no mention of the formidable Mount Taygetos which lies in his
path, and for which an extra day's journey would have been
needed (*Od.* 3.487-490 = 15.185-188). Another example concerns the plunder taken from the Eleians by Nestor (*Il.* 11.
670-681). Pigs are slow-footed animals (as those who have
seen them being loaded into a Greek boat will remember). Yet
if we accept that Nestor's palace has been discovered in

Messenia, we would have to suppose that no less than fifty
herds of swine were made to move from somewhere north of the
Alpheios all the way to Pylos, some fifty miles away,
overnight!

These examples are taken from the Greek Mainland. We
should expect even less precision with regard to the Black
Sea and the Western Mediterranean, both of which appear to
have been unknown to Homer. Homer does mention most of the
big rivers and mountains in Mainland Greece south of Mace-
donia, and he had apparently seen parts of the Aegean with
his own eyes before (supposedly) going blind, as seems indicated by his graphic description of the distant hills of
Samothrace viewed from the plain of Troy. He is, however,
usually careful not to add any knowledge concerning the geography of Asia Minor of his own day (presumably the latter
part of the 8th century B.C.). But it is clear that in much
of his description of Mainland Greece, and probably also of
Ithaca, he is merely giving the traditional details of people
and places, as handed down by oral poets before him. He is
obviously ignorant of the locations of many places mentioned
in the Achaean section of the Catalogue of the Ships, the
list of the Greek forces which assembled at Aulis in Boeotia
for the expedition against Troy. This ignorance is especially revealed in the Peloponnesian "Kingdoms" (apart from those
of Agamemnon and Diomedes), and in many of the Thessalian
"Kingdoms." It is clear that by the time of Homer, this Catalogue was very old and venerable. It gave the names and
pedigrees of the commanders, the number of ships and the
places that provided them, and occasionally the numbers of
men in each ship. It was also necessary to the plot of the
Iliad, as a sort of list of characters, most of whom were
destined to become, as it were, "cannon fodder" in the fighting before Troy.[8]

The list divides the Greeks into specific territorial
units, and thus invites comparison with the archaeological and
literary evidence concerning these districts and places. However, since the list was handed down by oral tradition, we
must expect that some changes may have occurred in the process, particularly some omissions.

Archaeological excavations have already demonstrated that
the names of most of the main centers are based on fact:
these include Troy, Mycenae, Tiryns, Pylos, Thebes, Iolkos,
Knossos, and Phaistos. But if our object is to test the truth
of the tradition in detail, we must test the historicity of
the less important names in the traditional list. Only a few
of the relevant ancient sites have been excavated. Of the
places which are both securely identified and at the same
time of lesser importance in the list, only Eutresis and
Haliartos in Boeotia and Krisa near Delphi in Phocis have been
investigated "by the spade." It may be significant that all
of these have the thick Cyclopean defense walls that are a
feature of many major Mycenaean settlements, and that two of
them at least (Eutresis and Krisa) were deserted for a time
after the Mycenaean Age. Indeed, Eutresis was never again of
importance. There is a larger category of excavated Mycenaean sites which are probably, but not certainly, to be
equated with places named in the Catalogue. Such are Malthi-
Dorion in Messenia (Homeric Dorion?), Teichos Dymaion in Elis
(Homeric Myrsinos?), the Menelaion in Laconia (Sparta?), and
Pheneos in Arcadia. For other such places, we usually have
only the evidence of broken potsherds on the surface of the
sites where the names are traditionally located. The most
valuable test cases are those where the identification is
backed by a reliable ancient source, as for instance when
Thucydides tells us that Mykalessos in Boeotia was ravaged by

Thracian mercenaries in the Peloponnesian War.[9] Somewhat less valuable are cases like Messe in Laconia and Araithyrea in Agamemnon's kingdom, where the identification rests on accounts of antiquarians of the Roman period, such as Pausanias the traveller and Strabo the geographer.

There are, of course, similar problems with the districts in the Catalogue. It has often been argued that the split in the Argolid between the Kingdoms of Agamemnon and Diomedes does not accord well with the sizes and locations of the major fortresses of Mycenae and Tiryns or with the evidence for Mycenaean highways in the area. The division indeed appears more consistent with the period *after* c. 1200 B.C. than with the preceding period, when Mycenaean power was at its height, and when authority was apparently more centralized, at least in this northeast part of the Peloponnese.[10] In the LH IIIB period, Mycenaean highways apparently linked Mycenae with the Corinthia;[11] the road which has been traced between Mycenae and the Heraion almost certainly continued to Tiryns; and the Cyclopean bridge at Kasarma,[12] half-way between Tiryns and the port of Epidauros, is almost certain proof that Tiryns and this port were similarly linked. The highways themselves, and their bridges and culverts, are constructed in a manner almost identical with that of the walls of the fortresses, with the same massive Cyclopean retaining walls and arches. The massive ancient dam near Tiryns has retaining walls of similar construction,[13] and both the dam and the channel dug to accommodate the diverted stream[14] must have involved great expenditure of time and energy, involving a considerable labor force. The dam apparently saved the rich farming area around Tiryns from disastrous flooding. Great resources would also have been needed for the construction of the Mycenaean wall at the Isthmus of Corinth,[15] a wall surely intended to provide a deterrent, if not a barrier, to invasion from the north.

A similar problem is presented by the Catalogue's division
of Boeotia between the Boeotians and the Minyans. In particular, it seems odd that most of Lake Copais is apparently in
the hands of the former, when the system of fortresses and canals would appear to have served mainly the latter.[16] A successful or even a partially successful drainage system in
Copais would have benefited mainly Orchomenos, since the
plain or marshland around Orchomenos is the highest in Copais
and would have been the first to be drained. Although the canals and dykes have not yet been proven to be of Mycenaean origin, there are compelling arguments in favor of this hypothesis. Mycenaean highways have been discovered leading both
from the north and the south gates of the great Mycenaean
fortress of Gla, which is known to have been destroyed c.
1200 B.C.[17] Without at least a partial drainage of the lake,
these roads could not have been built. The retaining walls
of the dikes are built in very much the same manner as the
walls of Gla.[18] The building of the dykes and the digging of
the canals (of which the largest was estimated by André Kenny
to have been about 180 ft. in width) would have demanded an
enormous amount of time and labor. Exploration has revealed
that the shores of the lake were very thickly inhabited in
the Mycenaean period; and all the fortresses around the lake,
and especially those in the vicinity of the most important canals in the northeast, have been certified as either definite-
ly or probably Mycenaean in origin (with the exception of the
Hellenistic circuit walls of Orchomenos itself). Obviously
the fortresses were necessary for the protection of the canal
system and the rich agricultural land secured by the system.

Again, as in the case of the bisection of the Argolid in
the Catalogue, the division of Boeotia and particularly of
Lake Copais would better suit the more disturbed period *after*

c. 1200 B.C., when the canal system may have failed.[19]   And
Thucydides tells us that the Boeotians did not enter Boeotia
until sixty years after the Trojan war.[20]   In general, many
of the divisions in the Catalogue appear to fit better with a
period when the main central power and authority had been
weakened by the series of attacks c. 1200 B.C.

Yet the place names themselves, as opposed to the districts
in the Catalogue, often accord best with the pattern of the
main Mycenaean centers *before* c. 1200 B.C. Many of the sites
associated either securely or tentatively with the names in
the Catalogue have Cyclopean fortifications, and most are
known to have been occupied by Mycenaeans in the period immediately preceding c. 1200 B.C. Leaving aside certain particular difficulties regarding the identification of some of
the place names, the pattern of their locations agrees remarkably well with the overall distribution of known Mycenaean
settlements.

I turn now to another and somewhat different example of
"Homeric Geography," namely Odysseus' description of Ithaca
(*Od*. 9.21-27). This description, or rather a misunderstanding
of it, has even caused some scholars to doubt that Homer's
Ithaca is modern Ithaca.[21]   I hope that the following translation of the passage in question is sufficiently accurate to
serve the arguments which follow:

> I live in Ithaca, the island seen in the distance. In
> it is a mountain called Neriton, thickly wooded and
> prominent; round about lie many islands, very close to
> one another, Doulichion and Same and wooded Zakynthos.
> Ithaca itself is the lowest and lies farthest in the
> sea towards the darkness. The rest lie apart from it,
> towards the dawn and the sun.

This description, whatever its time of origin, is clearly
that of a sailor or passenger approaching by sea; and it is
important to determine the direction from which Ithaca is being observed. If the viewpoint is towards the west, Ithaca
is certainly not the lowest or furthest. But the *normal* approach to Ithaca is from the southeast, and from this direction Ithaca does appear both low and far. And there is greater and brighter light to the *south* of Ithaca.

In the more detailed topography of Ithaca in the *Odyssey*,
we are given a mixture of fact and fancy. But the Harbor of
Phorcys, where Odysseus lands, and which is described as a
narrow inlet between steep promontories (*Od*. 13.96-101), suggests the Vathy Sound,[22] which resembles a fjord. After landing, Odysseus hides in a cave the treasures which the Phaeacians have given him. Among these are a tripod from Antinous
and a tripod from each of his twelve fellow nobles. The cave
is described as having stone bowls and jars in it, and long
stone looms where the Nymphs weave garments of sea purple.
It has two doors, one on the north and the other on the south,
the latter described as so small that only immortals can enter (*Od*. 13.102-112). Odysseus, after hiding the gifts in the
cave, journeys to find the swineherd Eumaeus. He takes a
rocky path over hills and through woods until he comes to the
Raven's Rock and the Fountain Arethusa (*Od*. 13.408). The
Raven's Rock, the Fountain Arethusa, and even the pigsties of
Eumaeus have all been convincingly identified by the natives
of Ithaca, and all lie in the south part of the island, to
the south of the Gulf of Molo. For the Cave of the Nymphs
there are, unfortunately, two rival candidates. The Marmaro-
spelia cave is closest to the Gulf, and it has the required
stalactites and a hole in the roof of the required diminutive
dimensions. But the excavations at the Polis cave produced

the required fragments of thirteen tripods of the Geometric period, and inscribed sherds prove that the cave was, at least in later times, sacred to the Nymphs.[23] For the moment, therefore, we have a sort of "composite" cave, probably reflecting the remembered features of two actual caves.

The element of uncertainty still involved in "the Ithaca question" will, I hope, illustrate the folly of placing too literal an interpretation on some aspects of "Homeric Geography." But, as in the case of the Ithaca of the *Odyssey*, the Greece of the Catalogue of the Ships is, we would argue, a reflection, however partial and distorted, of Mycenaean Greece. It would, however, be as useless to ask, for instance, why it omits the Cycladic Islands as to ask why Mycenaean Miletos is, so to speak, "on the wrong side" (i.e., listed as among the *Trojan* allies). Another "omission" often cited by sceptics is that of most of Attica, since Athens alone is mentioned in the contingent of the Athenian commander υἱὸς Πετεῶο Μενεσθεύς.[24] For the benefit of those who believe that the Catalogue is mainly an eighth or seventh century B.C. creation,[25] I here demonstrate (by plagiarizing from the Homeric Hymns, etc.) how such a supposed eighth or seventh century B.C. rhapsody might go about stitching together an Attica section. This rhapsody might read somewhat as follows:

οἳ Θορικόν[26] τε νέμοντο καὶ ἠνεμόεσσαν ᾽Αφίδναν[27]
οἳ δ᾽ εἶχον προλίεθρον ᾽Ελευσῖνος[28] θυοέσσης
Δήμητρος τέμενος, Μαραθῶνα[29] τε . . .

An interesting consideration is raised by one of our reviewers, who remarked as follows:

An argument which the authors use to good effect is
that oddities in the Catalogue are actually reasons
for believing that "it does correspond with reality,"
since a late innovator would be likely to make things

look more sensible. He would, for instance, have given
Agamemnon a more "appropriate" realm.[30]

While we welcome the implied support, it must be admitted
that an accusation of sophistry, of the use of the *adikos
logos*, could here be leveled against us, if this was indeed
the lynchpin of our argument. Actually, however, our strongest points were more positive. Our main argument, although
it is admittedly somewhat "circular," remains the general co-
incidence of the names and regions in the Catalogue with the
observed pattern of Mycenaean settlement. A second argument,
which I have presented elsewhere,[31] is that the Greeks of the
eighth to seventh century B.C., just like those before and
those after, were themselves very much concerned with keeping
their oral traditions pure and accurate, and with excluding
anachronisms. It is not without reason that the poet calls
upon the Muse of Memory before reciting the Catalogue. As I
wrote, "for so difficult a feat of memory to be performed, a
special motivation is required." It is clear to me that Homer adapted for his purpose a pre-existing Catalogue (or Cata-
logues), and that he had neither the desire nor the need to
invent a new one. But how old was this Catalogue? It is often pointed out that the language used is comparatively
late.[32] And both the ship numbers and the epithets have been
singled out as "at the mercy of the meter."[33] The constant
repetitions of *tessarakonta* and *euktimenon ptoliethron* are
particularly noticeable in these two categories respectively.
But we would argue that it is the names which constitute the
kernel of the oral tradition, so that it is in this category
that the best memory work would be expected. It has often
been suggested that Achilles is a hero added to the Trojan
War saga somewhat late in its development.[34] But there is no
need, for this reason alone, to regard the Thessalian or

Aeolian division of the Catalogue as necessarily later in
composition than the main body of the Achaean section. We
must still apply the same *archaeological* critèria in the case
of the Thessalian contingents. There are, of course, some
rather more complicated topographical problems involved
here;[35] but despite the fact that this was a remote area of
Mycenaean Greece, and perhaps less well known by poets, the
names of the places and the kingdoms are even here reasonably
compatible with the known pattern of Mycenaean settlement in
Thessaly.

   In our arguments we stressed the importance of the less important names in the Catalogue, whose locations have been more
or less securely identified. There is some "news" concerning
such places from recent archaeological work. In central
Greece, Mycenaean surface sherds have been found at Ancient
Koroneia in Boeotia;[36] and Mycenaean sherds and a figurine
fragment on the acropolis of Ancient Eretria.[37] In the Peloponnese, stratified deposits of LH IIC pottery and house foun-
dations have been found on the acropolis of ancient Aigeira,[38]
whose former name was, according to Pausanias, Hyperesia; the
rich contents of the LH III chamber tomb cemetery at Aigion
have recently been published;[39] dedications both to Menelaus
and Helen have been found at the Menelaion, adjacent to successive Mycenaean "Mansions,"[40] strengthening the argument
that this was the Sparta of the Catalogue; in Arcadia a can-
didate has been proposed for the elusive "Windy Enispe,"
namely a site overlooking the village of Dimitra, where numerous Mycenaean surface sherds have been found[41] (the claim
for the identification of this name with this particular site
is, however, difficult to evaluate). In northwest Greece,
Mycenaean sherds have now been certified at the site of "Old
Pleuron";[42] and a few Mycenaean sherds, and some imitating

Mycenaean, have been found at Dodona.[43] And in Thessaly Mycenaean vases have been found at Elasson,[44] presumed to be
the site of the Oloosson of the Catalogue.

No great stress should be laid on these recent finds in
particular, since they constitute only a small proportion of
the recent archaeological discoveries relevant to the question. Indeed it could be suggested that the growing number
of Mycenaean settlements discovered may prove an embarrass-
ment to those seeking to identify certain Homeric place names,
since the choice would in some cases be too wide.

Another attack on our point of view seems at first sight
even more damaging. John Chadwick has recently pointed out
that, despite previous hopes, little or no correspondence can
be demonstrated between the Pylian section of the Catalogue
and the names recorded in the Linear B tablets excavated at
Mycenaean *Pu-ro* (modern Ano Englianos).[45] But, as I argued
several years ago, there is in fact no compelling reason to
expect such a correspondence between a set of bureaucratic
records and a fragment of oral tradition preserved in poetry.[46] Further, in most cases we do not know whether the Linear B names in question refer to individual settlements, i.e.,
"towns" or "villages," or to districts, or even to natural
landmarks. It is therefore quite impossible to prove that
there is any actual discrepancy between the two sets of names,
still less that this section in the Catalogue is either anachronistic or a creation of fantasy. There are in any case
no examples of direct conflict between known locations of
names in either category. I have argued this case more fully
elsewhere, in a recent book, in which I have also joined in
the attempt at locating the main names listed in the two "pro-
vinces" of Mycenaean *Pu-ro*.[47] Naturally I agree fully with
Chadwick that Homer "was a poet not an Historian."[48] I also

agree that Homer did not have any detailed knowledge of the geography of this part of Greece. Indeed I would be extremely suspicious of Homer's account if I thought he had added most of the (supposedly Mycenaean) topography in the Catalogue from eyewitnesses of his own day. Homer was neither a "pseudo-historian"[49] nor a pseudo-geographer, for the simple reason that he relied on tradition, and his own memory, for the main names in the Catalogue(s). He has, characteristically, added "story-additions" and other embellishments, mainly to bring the list of a First Year muster of forces into line with the needs of a Tenth Year *Achilleid.*[50] But he and his audience obviously shared a desire for faithful accuracy, since the oral tradition was their only vehicle for the transmission of their history. For this reason, in the Catalogue the great creative singer subordinates creativity to Memory.[51]

NOTES

1. *ABSA* 51 (1956), 168-171.
2. H. Waterhouse and R. Hope Simpson, *ABSA* 55 (1960), 67-107, 56 (1961), 114-175.
3. R. Hope Simpson and J. F. Lazenby, *The Catalogue of the Ships in Homer's Iliad* (Oxford: Clarendon Press, 1970); hereafter *CSHI.*
4. The following is a selected list of significant reviews:
   W. McLeod, *Phoenix* 24 (1970), 256-260
   Y. Bequignon, *RA* (1971), 130-131
   C. R. Beye, *ACR* 1 (1971), 84-85
   J. M. Cook, *CR* n.s. 21 (1971), 173-174
   G. Fischetti, *Maia* 23 (1971), 151-160

A. Heubeck, *BO* 28 (1971), 91-92

C. Matsudaira, *JCS* 19 (1971), 99-101

W. B. Stanford, *Hermathena* 111 (1971), 74-75

C. G. Thomas, *CW* 64 (1971), 236

P. Wathelet, *AC* 40 (1971), 231-232

M. L. West, *The Oxford Magazine* (1971), 322-323

F. M. Combellack, *CP* 67 (1972), 72-73

M. L. Lang, *AJP* 93 (1972), 602-605

J. K. Anderson, *CJ* 69 (1973), 180-182

J. Kerschensteiner, *Gymnasium* 80 (1973), 319-321

There was also a brief and blandly descriptive review, unsigned, in the *Times Literary Supplement*. Cook, West, and McLeod in particular seem to share the view that the Catalogue probably owes more to eighth and seventh century B.C. invention than to genuine tradition.

5. McLeod and West appear to be under the mistaken impression that we were unaware of the relatively late linguistic form in which the Catalogue is preserved. They therefore administer elementary lessons (concerning *-oio* genitives and the Ionic form *nees*), while adroitly using their reviews as vehicles for propaganda of their own.

6. The romantic in question was well disposed of by R. J. C. Atkinson in *Antiquity* 40 (1966), 212ff., in a review entitled "Moonshine on Stonehenge."

7. I here borrow respectfully from the excellent account of "Homeric Geography" given by H. Thomas and F. H. Stubbings under the heading "Lands and Peoples in Homer," in A. J. B. Wace and F. H. Stubbings, eds., *A Companion to Homer* (London: Macmillan, 1962), pp. 283-310 (hereafter *CH*).

8. C. R. Beye, *HSPh* 68 (1964), 345-373; R. Hope Simpson, *SMEA* 6 (1968), 39-44, especially note 8.

9. Thucydides 7.29.2-4.

10. C. G. Thomas, *JHS* 90 (1970), 184ff.; cf. *CSHI*, pp. 70-72.

11. H. Steffen, *Karten von Mykenai* (Berlin: 1884); G. E. Mylonas, *Mycenae and the Mycenaean Age* (Princeton: Princeton University Press, 1966), pp. 86-88; J. M. Balcer, *AJA* 78 (1974), 148-149.

12. *CSHI*, Plate 5. The dromos of the tholos tomb nearby to the east faces south, toward the modern road, which is probably on more or less the same line as the ancient road (*AD* 22 [1967], Chronika 179; *AD* 24 [1969], Chronika 104). We may compare the situation of the tholos tomb near the Argive Heraion (A. J. B. Wace, *Mycenae* [Princeton: Princeton University Press, 1949], p. 27; *ABSA* 25 [1921-1923], 330).

13. *AA* 1930, 112; *MDAI(A)* 78 (1963), 5 note 4, Beilage I, Tafel II; J. M. Balcer (above, note 11), 141-149.

14. J. L. Bintliff, *Natural Environment and Human Settlement in Prehistoric Greece* = *British Archaeological Reports* Suppl. 28 (Oxford: 1977), pp. 280-282.

15. O. Broneer, *Hesperia* 24 (1955), 124; 35 (1966), 346-362; 37 (1968), 25-35.

16. For a discussion and bibliography on the Copais drainage, see R. Hope Simpson, *Mycenaean Greece* (London: Noyes Press, 1981).

17. *PAAH* 1960, 23ff.; 1961, 28ff.; G. E. Mylonas (above, note 11), pp. 84-85.

18. *CSHI*, Plate 2.

19. Cf. Pausanias 9.38.7 for the tradition that Heracles blocked the swallow-holes.

20. Thucydides 1.12.3.

21. Further discussion of the "Ithaca question" and excellent illustrations are given by F. H. Stubbings in *CH*, pp. 398-421, and most recently by J. V. Luce, *Homer and the Heroic Age* (New York: Harper and Row, 1975), pp. 141-155; cf. *CSHI*, pp. 101-106.

22. *CH*, pp. 414–416. But J. V. Luce (above, note 21), pp. 144–146, prefers the Dexia Bay, and this may well be more appropriate.

23. *CH*, pp. 418–419.

24. *CH*, p. 289; *CSHI*, pp. 56–58.

25. G. Jachmann, *Der homerische Schiffskatalog und die Ilias* (Köln: Westdeutscher, 1958); A. Giovannini, *Etude historique sur les origines du Catalogue des Vaisseaux* (Bern: 1969).

26. *Hymn to Demeter* 126.

27. *Cypria* fragment 10 Allen; cf. Herodotus 9.73.

28. *Hymn to Demeter* 97, 318, 356, 490.

29. *Od.* 7.80; cf. *Vita Herodotea* 1.397.

30. F. M. Combellack (above, note 4), 73.

31. Above, note 8.

32. Above, notes 4 and 5.

33. Cf. D. L. Page, *History and the Homeric Iliad* (Berkeley and Los Angeles: University of California Press, 1959), p. 152.

34. E.g., by West (above, notes 4 and 5).

35. *CSHI*, pp. 126–151.

36. J. M. Fossey, *Euphrosyne* 6 (1973–1974), 9.

37. *AAA* 2 (1969), 26; *AE* 1969, 143.

38. *AAA* 6 (1973), 197; 7 (1974), 157ff.; 9 (1976), 162ff; *BCH* 101 (1977), 568.

39. A. J. Papadopoulos, *Excavations at Aigion--1970* = *Studies in Mediterranean Archaeology* 46 (Göteberg: Paul Åström, 1976). The chamber tombs contained mainly LH IIIB and LH IIIC pottery.

40. *AR* 23 (1976–1977), 24–42.

41. *ABSA* 68 (1973), 193–205.

42. *AD* 26 (1971), Chronika 326–327; *AR* 22 (1975–1976), 17.

43. *PAAH* 1967, 39; 1968, 56; 1969, 26; 1972, 97.

44. *AD* 23 (1968), Chronika 269.

45. J. Chadwick, *The Mycenaean World* (Cambridge: Cambridge University Press, 1976), pp. 35–59, 180–186 (hereafter *MW*); cf. J. Chadwick, *Documents in Mycenaean Greek*, 2nd ed. (Cambridge: Cambridge University Press, 1973), pp. 415–417; and in *Minos* 14 (1973), 55–59.

46. *ABSA* 61 (1966), 130.

47. *Mycenaean Greece* (above, note 16).

48. *MW*, p. 186; cf. *CSHI*, p. 169.

49. *MW*, chapter 10.

50. *SMEA* 6 (1968), 40–41 and note 9.

51. C. R. Beye, *The Iliad, the Odyssey, and the Epic Tradition* (New York: Anchor, 1966), p. 90, rightly terms this feat of memory a "tour de force."

Reverberation and Mythology in the *Iliad*

Mabel L. Lang

The relationship between non-Trojan-War *exempla* and the *Iliad* episodes or situations which they illuminate has been defined in two opposite and apparently mutually exclusive ways. One view sees the *exemplum* as a model from which the *Iliad* episode was adapted; the other holds that the *Iliad* situation has priority, and that the *exemplum* was invented to fit it. In both these cases the relationship is viewed as it would be in a literary work which was composed once and for all by an individual poet. The *Iliad*, however, is presumed to be the end product of many re-creations, and in this case it is almost inevitable that both types of relationship operated. What we have to allow for then is a process of reverberation between inherited material influencing the *Iliad* narrative and also the *Iliad* narrative influencing inherited material. Imitation and innovation go hand in hand on a two-way street.

How reverberation would have operated may be illustrated with the first *paradeigma* in the *Iliad* (1.259ff.), by which Nestor urges the heroes to heed his words even as his old fighting comrades the Lapiths had done. First an assumption must be made about Nestor's presence at Troy: is it possible that at some early stage of the Trojan War story, or even of the *Iliad* itself, Nestor was added to the Greek warriors to provide a different, older-generation type (as Odysseus, Ajax, Agamemnon, and Diomedes were respectively types of resourcefulness, brute strength, authority-figure, and all-roundness)? Or was Nestor always part of the group and only gradually specialized into a type? It is easier to accept the former alternative and to think of him as imported into the Trojan War

from another time and context. Only so does the unprecedent-
ed and elaborate introduction provided for him make sense (1.
248ff.): it serves as an apology for including him in a generation which everyone knew was "after his time." Only Cal-
chas is similarly introduced, and that case has been properly
explained as a necessary guarantee of his prophetic authority.
In addition, it is clear that the *arete* of Nestor as the older-
generation type was not his military prowess but his speech,
or advice. Thus his reminiscences of pre-Trojan-War experi-
ences could be used to defuse (or diffuse) quarrels among the
heroes. Thus in some early version of the quarrel between
Achilles and Agamemnon he was used to urge reconciliation; he
gave authority to his words simply by reminding them that he
had associated with far better men than they, to wit, the Lapiths, who had respected him, and together they had faced the
most frightful enemy such as no present warrior could take on.
That is pretty much the *exemplum* which appears in our text,
except for the lines: "These listened to the counsels I gave
and heeded my bidding. / Do you also obey, since to be persuaded is better." (273-274, tr. Lattimore). Instead of these
words the original version might have had the single line
which is known from the Homeric *Hymn to Apollo* (line 486),
with very close relatives in the *Iliad* (2.139; 9.26, 704; 12.
75; etc.): ἀλλ᾽ ἄγεθ᾽, ὡς ἂν ἐγὼ εἴπω, πείθεσθε τάχιστα (But
come and quickly obey whatever I say).

In later re-creations of this scene the obedience which
Nestor asks for in the *Iliad* narrative must gradually have
found a place in the *exemplum* as well. That it did not originally belong there is suggested by the inherent improbabili-
ty of battle-hardened Lapiths seeking advice from a young
foreigner. Nevertheless, because the situations were similar
enough, they must have exerted a mutual attraction on each

other which increased the similarity, by adding to the *exemplum* a detail which really makes better sense in its *Iliad*
context. The parallel was made more pointed thereby, and also the ring composition was extended. That is, the original,
now the outer, ring started: "Yet be persuaded. Both of you
are younger than I am," and would have ended: "But come and
quickly obey whatever I say." The mid-part merely moved from
Nestor's association with the Lapiths to their joint ventures
against the Centaurs. But the present version makes an inner
ring around the battle verses: thus, at the beginning, "Yes,
and in my time I have dealt with better men than / you are,
and never once did they disregard me," and then the echo,
"These listened to the counsels I gave and heeded my bidding."

If a *paradeigma* is viewed in this fashion, not as the product of a single act of innovation but as part of the development that comes with successive re-creations, it is clear
that the whole "chicken and egg" question of priority which
has been so hotly argued (particularly with regard to the
wrath-stories of Meleager and Achilles in Book 9) is unanswer-
able. The reverberation or echo-effect between the original
tale, whichever it was, and its parallel would cause changes
in both, bringing them closer together and hopelessly blurring
priority.

Although this first *paradeigma* in the *Iliad* could well have
been inherited material that established Nestor as a warrior
among warriors, the end result of its association with the
wrath-story is very much the same as that pointed out by
Kakridis for the last *paradeigma* in the poem: "Niobe in book
24 eats for the simple reason that Priam must eat."[1] So here
in Book 1 the Lapiths listen to Nestor because Achilles and
Agamemnon ought to listen. And it is because Achilles and
Agamemnon do *not* listen that the whole *Iliad* follows. Thus

the epic comes full circle in this as in other ways: a *para-deigma* that fails to persuade opens up the wrath-story, which is finally brought to a close with a *paradeigma* that succeeds in persuading.

Can we discern the mechanics of reverberation at work in the Niobe *paradeigma*? And must we do so, or can the difficulties this episode presents all be met by assuming simple, one-way innovation? Here is the whole passage in Richmond Lattimore's translation:

> Now you and I must remember our supper.
> For even Niobe, she of the lovely tresses, remembered
> to eat, whose twelve children were destroyed in her
>   palace,
> six daughters, and six sons in the pride of their
>   youth, whom Apollo
> killed with arrows from his silver bow, being angered
> with Niobe, and shaft-showering Artemis killed the
>   daughters;
> because Niobe likened herself to Leto of the fair
>   colouring
> and said Leto had borne only two, she herself had
>   borne many;
> but the two, though they were only two, destroyed all
>   those others.
> Nine days long they lay in their blood, nor was there
>   anyone
> to bury them, for the son of Kronos made stones out of
> the people; but on the tenth day the Uranian gods
>   buried them.
> But she remembered to eat when she was worn out with
>   weeping.
> And now somewhere among the rocks, and the lonely
>   mountains,

> in Sipylos, where they say is the resting place of the
>   goddesses
> who are nymphs, and dance beside the waters of
>   Acheloios,
> there, stone still, she broods on the sorrows that the
>   gods gave her.
> Come then, we also, aged magnificent sir, must remember
> to eat, and afterwards you may take your beloved son
>   back
> to Ilion, and mourn for him; and he will be much
>   lamented.

(24.601-620)

Some of the unlikely details in the Niobe story can be explained as simple innovations inspired by the main narrative
and introduced in order to improve the parallel between Niobe
and Priam: thus she eats because Priam must eat; her children
must lie unburied because Hector so lies (the petrifaction of
the populace may then have been introduced, by analogy with
Niobe's petrifaction, to explain the lack of burial); and,
finally, the otherwise unsuitable burial by the gods could
have been invented to parallel the gods' concern in Book 24
for Hector's burial. But one difficulty cannot be explained
as simple, one-way innovation; that is the inconcinnity between Niobe's remembering to eat when she tired of weeping
and her subsequent petrifaction from grief. So awkwardly do
the lines about her becoming stone fit that they were thought
by Aristophanes and Aristarchus to be interpolated, and by
some modern commentators as well. We can meet this final objection only by imagining that the Niobe story evolved, gradually becoming more parallel to Priam's situation, with both
being changed in the process of mutual attraction and reverberation. How might this process have worked? Let us assume
that in some original version the poet wished to make a

transition from the difficult, because unique, ransoming
scene to the familiar ground of a standard hospitality theme,
and so had Achilles say: "Now you and I must remember our
supper / For even Niobe, she of the lovely tresses, ceased to
wail" (that is, "ceased to wail" instead of "remembered to
eat" or *lēge klauthmoio* instead of *emnēsato sitou*). Achilles
would then have continued as in the present text through the
twin gods' slaughter of the Niobids and its cause in Niobe's
attempt to rival Leto. Then, making no mention of the Niobids' unburied state, Achilles would have returned to his
original statement not with the present line, that is, "but she
remembered to eat when she was worn out with weeping" (ἡ δ᾽
ἄρα σίτου μνήσατ᾽, ἐπεὶ κάμε δάκρυ χέουσα), but with this one:
"But she ceased to wail when she was worn out with weeping"
(ἡ δ᾽ ἄρα λῆγε γόοιο, ἐπεὶ κάμε δάκρυ χέουσα). The lines
about her petrifaction then follow with perfect propriety, and
Achilles' speech would conclude not with encouragement to eat,
but with a plea to cease from grief: not ἀλλ᾽ ἄγε δὴ καὶ νῶϊ
μεδώμεθα, δῖε γεραιέ, / σίτου but ἀλλ᾽ ἄγε δη καὶ νῶ λήγωμεν,
δῖε γεραιέ, / κλαυθμοῦ (But come, aged sir, let *us* also cease
our weeping).

    Thus the original *paradeigma* would have given the usual
Niobe story, and only in subsequent re-creations would the mutual attraction between the similar plights of Niobe and Priam
have caused interaction and changes in both tales. The first
effect may have been the inclusion in Achilles' earlier speech
of the lines (530ff.) which remind us that Peleus had only one
son who was bringing grief to Priam and his children. Simultaneously, Priam's earlier speech would have been expanded
with the lines (495ff.) counting his fifty sons and mourning
the many killed. At least the contrast between the two children of Leto and the twelve of Niobe has more point for that
story than does the contrast between Peleus' one and Priam's

fifty sons for the *Iliad* story; any influence therefore is
more likely to have gone from the inherited material to the
Iliad than in the other direction. The next change may have
been the addition of Niobe's eating to the *paradeigma*. That
is, the way in which the main narrative turned immediately to
formulas of feasting combined with the pressure of ring-
composition to make it seem natural for Niobe also to take up
eating instead of merely ceasing to weep. The mere association of Niobe and Priam in re-creation after re-creation must
have set up the kind of bond that prevented the addition of
the eating detail from seeming to be a gratuitous invention.
And because the original detail of her petrifaction was so
generally accepted a part of her story, and had had its right-
ful place in the original *exemplum*, there would have been no
impulse to remove it from the later version. Thus Niobe eats
because Priam must eat, but she becomes stone because she had
always done so. Still later, perhaps, continued reverberation between *paradeigma* and narrative resulted in the Niobids
taking on Hector's unburied state and, like his body, attract-
ing divine concern. The reason is clear in the *Iliad* why Hector lies unburied, but once this detail was added to the *exemplum* it required some explanation there. The poet's solution
was one more addition to the Niobe story: potential buriers
were all turned to stone, a detail obviously patterned on Niobe's own fate.

Thus there is no question that innovation has taken place,
even as Kakridis and Willcock have indicated, but two things
about it have not been sufficiently appreciated: 1) that it
is not a one-time, or necessarily even a one-poet, operation
but rather a function of re-creation; and 2) that it is a two-
way street, with *paradeigmata* creating parallels in the narrative as well as the narrative demanding parallels in the
paradeigmata. These two principles combine to answer the

objection most often made to demonstrations of mythological
innovation by Homer: that if the myth which is presented as
a *paradeigma* has suffered very much in the way of innovation
it will have lost its persuasive power as a precedent to be
respected. But this is not a danger if, as suggested, the innovations occur in both main narrative and *paradeigma*, and if
they evolve naturally and gradually out of the pressures of
propinquity and from a desire to strengthen the parallel. In
this case the tales will remain familiar through constant retelling, and there will be no suspension of belief.

In order to test whether the two principles stated above
have any validity beyond these two *exempla*, it seems right and
proper to examine other *paradeigmata* and their contexts, to
see if we can find traces of reverberative innovation through
successive re-creations. In order to make the examination
more challenging and more revealing about the extent to which
paradeigmata include inherited material, we shall limit ourselves here to the *exempla* which primarily concern divinities.
These are more challenging because, given the largely human
subject matter of the *Iliad*, there is less room for reverberation between such *exempla* and the main narrative; they may also be more revealing because most of them fit together in such
a way as to suggest that each is not a self-contained episode,
but part of a larger whole which might be reconstructed.

Perhaps the easiest illustration of the way several *paradeigmata* may be fitted together is the theme of conflict on
Olympus.

1) Thetis freed Zeus when Hera, Poseidon, and Athena
    conspired to bind him (1.396ff.).
2) Poseidon and Apollo were punished by Zeus, who sent
    them to serve Laomedon, building the walls of Troy
    and herding his cattle (21.441ff.).

3) Zeus punished Hera by hanging her up and then
hurled to earth any divinity who tried to free
her (15.16ff.).

4) Hephaestus was hurled to earth by Zeus when he
tried to help his mother Hera (1.586ff.).

In the binding of Zeus (no. 1) no punishment of Hera, Poseidon, and Athena is mentioned, and in the punishment of Poseidon and Apollo (no. 2) no crime is given, since in neither
case is the omitted detail relevant; but the two tales complete each other, with Poseidon as the link. How Hera and
Athena may have been punished we cannot know, since serving
a mortal king by wall-building and cattle-herding is not appropriate for goddesses. Apollo, though punished in no. 2,
is absent from the list of rebels in no. 1; this might suggest that the two passages are not part of the same tale.
Further, the three rebels in no. 1 are also the three chief
divine supporters of the Greeks; this equation has been taken
as evidence that the revolt is an innovation to parallel the
plot of the *Iliad*.[2] But since both Zenodotus and others read
Phoebus Apollo instead of Pallas Athena at the end of the reb-
el list, the reverse could as well be the case: Apollo as the
original reading may have given way in later versions to Athena, because the mention of Hera and Poseidon recalled the traditional pro-Greek triad in the *Iliad*. In that case we would
have a trace of the original story in no. 2, with the punishment of the two rebels who really mattered to Zeus. (We have
his own word for the hopelessness of trying to discipline Hera: "Yet with Hera I am not so angry, neither indignant, /
since it is ever her way to cross the commands that I give
her," 8.407f.)

The three rebels listed in no. 1 might also be only repre-
sentatives or ringleaders of a far larger group, since if
these three alone were involved the other divinities on

Olympus could have freed Zeus, and there would have been no
need for the intervention of a sea-goddess like Thetis. However that may be, the connection between these two *paradeigmata* is further strengthened by the way in which it is echoed
in the second pair: again, no. 3 and no. 4 so complement each
other that both are needed to tell the full story.   In no. 3
we are not told what gods were hurled to earth for attempting
to release Hera, and in no. 4 we do not hear why Hera needed
the help which Hephaestus offered, and for which he was hurled
to earth. This pair introduces still another pair which
bring Heracles and Hypnos into the Olympian quarrel.

   5)   Hera's punishment was for the storm by which she
        drove Heracles off-course (15.26ff.).
   6)   So that Hera could thus vent her wrath on Heracles
        as he sailed from Troy Hypnos lulled Zeus to sleep
        and as a result would have suffered a fate like
        that of Hephaestus if he had not been protected by
        Night (14.247ff.).

Here again it takes two *paradeigmata* to tell one story since
no. 6 omits all reference both to Zeus' rescue of Heracles after his awakening and to his punishment of Hera while no. 5
explains neither how Hera could have sent the storm without
Zeus' knowledge nor what Heracles was doing at sea. That he
was sailing from Troy brings in still another pair of *paradeigmata* (see below) that will take us back to the original
revolt on Olympus and so make a complete story of Olympian
strife. This story is presented in seven different passages;
they make up four complementary pairs, appearing in six widely spaced books (1, 5, 14, 15, 20, and 21). Therefore it is
highly unlikely that all these references were invented separately to illuminate particular situations in the *Iliad*. Even
a writing poet might have difficulty in constructing such

a consistent and organic whole out of parts which he was inventing on an *ad hoc* basis.

The fourth pair of *paradeigmata* concern Heracles at Troy.

7) His sack of the city when he was disappointed of the
horses of Laomedon for which he had come (5.635ff.).

8) The wall which was built for him on the Trojan plain
as security against the sea-monster (20.145ff.).

The story in Book 5 (no. 7) tells us that Heracles sacked
Troy because as Laomedon's benefactor he was cheated of his
reward--but there is no mention of the way in which he benefited Laomedon. In Book 20 (no. 8) we learn what was presumably the benefit he conferred on Laomedon, for there he met
the attack of a sea-monster, apparently on behalf of the Trojans (who joined with Athena in building the wall for him)--
a feat for which he might well have been promised the divine
horses. Again the two episodes combine to tell the full story: the tale of the sack (no. 7) provides a sequel to the
tale of benefaction (no. 8), while the sea-monster in no. 8
gives point to Heracles' disappointment and consequent sack
in no. 7. The only loose end is then the origin or *raison
d'être* of the sea-monster, and this is where a Homeric link
is missing. But given Poseidon's anger at being cheated by
Laomedon (21.441ff.) as a parallel to Heracles' vengeance for
a similar disappointment at Laomedon's hands, it almost goes
without Homer's saying so that the sea-monster of Book 20 is
Poseidon's response to Laomedon's treatment of him and Apollo.

We have thus come full circle: the conflict on Olympus led
to the enforced servitude of Poseidon and Apollo, Poseidon's
dispatch of a sea-monster to punish Laomedon's failure to pay
for their service, Laomedon's hiring of Heracles to dispose
of the sea-monster, Heracles' sack of Troy to punish Laomedon's failure to pay up, Hera's bribing of Hypnos to distract
Zeus so she could drive Heracles off course, Zeus' punishment

of Hera and threat to hurl to earth anyone who tried to help
her, and Hephaestus being thus hurled for trying. Are there
other conflicts among the gods which are used in the *Iliad*
for illustrative purposes? If so, are they tied in to those
we have looked at; and how much interaction is there between
such presumably inherited material and the *Iliad* narrative?
Was there pre-Iliadic precedent for Hera's resentment of Zeus'
power and of those whom he favors, which is so basic to the
Iliad story (1.518ff., 540ff.; 4.25ff., 50ff.; 8.408; 16.440
ff.)? Does their preexisting enmity explain their support
of opposing forces in the Trojan War so that conflict on earth
reverberates with conflict on Olympus?

The tales of earlier (that is, pre-Trojan-War) strife among
the gods are so complex and so consistent that, as we have
seen, the various episodes or parts of episodes are not likely
to have been invented independently, to parallel details of
the *Iliad* plot. The probability is rather that the divine
strife of the *Iliad* story had its origin in such precedents
as appear in the *paradeigmata*. This probability is strengthened by the fact that several of these *paradeigmata* do not at
all parallel the episodes in which they appear, and so there
is no reason to suppose that they were created for their particular contexts. Neither Thetis' rescue of Zeus from revolting gods (1.396ff.) nor Poseidon's reminder to Apollo of their
suffering at the hands of Laomedon (21.441ff.) is in any way
parallel to its context. Zeus' anger at Hera over her deceit
and her treatment of Heracles does parallel his wrath over
Hector's suffering by her wiles; yet even here the *paradeigma*
clearly has priority. Hera's persecution of Heracles is many-
faceted and essential to that tale, quite unlike the contingent and one-shot character of her hostility to Hector. Indeed, that the conflict over Heracles is basic is confirmed
by another *paradeigma* which has only limited relevance to its

Iliad context. Agamemnon apologizes (19.91ff.) for his treatment of Achilles, blaming *Ate*, the blindness that deceived
even Zeus, who boasted that the one born of his line that day
would be lord of all his neighbors, but then was lured by Hera into confirming his boast with an oath, while she arranged
to delay Heracles' birth and hasten that of Eurystheus. Only
in the action of *Ate* is the *exemplum* parallel to Agamemnon's
situation, since no one had lured him into fulfilling his
threat to take Briseis; Achilles may have provoked him to
take action, but there is nothing to compare with Hera's elaborate machinations to thwart Zeus' will. Here again the *Iliad*
uses as a parallel a conflict between Zeus and Hera over Heracles. This recurrence of the Heracles theme helps to confirm
that there was a detailed tradition of Heracles as the object
of divine favor and hostility, and, more important, that Zeus'
and Hera's conflict over Hector was most likely modeled on
that tradition. That the Zeus-Hera strife in the *Iliad* may
indeed have been borrowed from the Heracles story is indicated
by the fact that it is not so much an integral part of the
Trojan War as it is a mechanism to make the wrath-story work:
that is, it belongs not to the original Trojan War chronicle,
but to the Wrath as encapsulating the War. For Zeus' support
of Hector and the Trojans, which brings him into conflict with
Hera, is the direct result of his favoring the Greek Achilles,
whom Hera supports. Thus for the greater part of the *Iliad*
Hector seems to inherit Hercles' uncomfortable situation as
object of the divine quarrel, while it is Achilles who is supported by both Zeus and Hera. This is shown particularly by
Athena, who serves as Hera's agent just as in the Heracles
"model" she was Zeus' agent in helping Heracles. The *Iliad*
makes bold use of this apparent switch when it makes Athena
speak reproachfully (8.360ff.) of the way in which Zeus

thwarts her and does not remember how he was always sending
her to help Heracles. Thus in the very act of associating
Athena (Heracles' helper) with Hera (Heracles' tormentor) in
a pro-Greek alliance against a temporarily pro-Trojan Zeus,
the poet is irresistibly reminded of the "pattern" alliance
between Athena and Zeus in the Heracles story. It is presumably only his "early Greek capacity for viewing things separately"[3] that allows him conveniently to ignore at the same
time the irony of Athena's present alliance with Hera: it
was Hera, after all, who caused the sufferings of Heracles
which Athena was so often sent to relieve.

Only two of the *exempla* in the *Iliad* which deal with inter-
relations among divinities do not fit into the cycle of divine
strife centered either on Olympus or on Heracles. Together
they involve Hera in apparent contradiction. While in 1.
586ff. it was for his attempt to help Hera that Hephaestus
was hurled from Olympus by Zeus, in 18.395ff. it is Hera who
caused his fall into the deep, where he was rescued by Thetis
and Eurynome. It is often assumed that the latter version is
a Homeric innovation to provide Hephaestus with a motive to
do whatever Thetis wants, but in that case it is odd that
Eurynome is given such prominence as a whole line to herself.
It is perhaps easier to assume a doublet in the tradition,
partly because Hephaestus' lameness marks him as accident-
prone, and partly because both hurling out of heaven and res-
cues by Thetis seem to have been popular motifs which were
useful in a variety of circumstances. The lameness of Hephaestus, essential in a smith-god, could be the *cause* of his
hurling out of heaven, given Hera's likely reaction to a de-
formed offspring (cf. Book 18); but it could also be the *effect* of such hurling, given the strife between Zeus and Hera
(cf. Book 1). And while story-tellers were exploring the

possibilities inherent in the hurling motif, they might also
have toyed with the alternatives of earth or sea landing, and
have considered as appropriate refuges for a fallen smith-god
both a volcanic island and a sea-goddess who made a specialty
of rescue (witness her deliverance of Zeus in 1.396ff., and
her rescue of Dionysus in 6.130ff.).

   Indeed, the otherwise unmotivated hostility which Hera
seems to display toward Thetis in Book 1, along with her regu-
lar resentment of any action taken by Zeus, almost requires
that the tradition provided some instance in which Thetis had
thwarted Hera's will. Completely different but perhaps relevant is the connection between Hera and Thetis as presented
by Hera in 24.59ff.; there she reminds Apollo that he played
at the wedding of Thetis, whom she herself had nurtured and
given in marriage to Peleus. The usual explanation of this
about-face on Hera's part is Homer's willingness to deal with
one situation at a time and to ignore contradictions that
might result. So now that Achilles is back fighting for the
Greeks all the pro-Greek divinities are happy to welcome Thetis (24.100f.); and the present Iliadic situation colors the
past so that these kindly feelings are allowed to flood back
to earlier days in the *paradeigma*. A very similar backcast-
ing is to be noted in 1.520f., where Zeus says to Thetis that
Hera is always reproaching him for helping the Trojans, even
though it is apparent that his support for the Trojans will
stem from his agreement with Thetis' request to make the
Greeks suffer, and will be a change from his usual pro-Greek
policy. But is it possible that the original tradition about
the revolt in heaven, noted in 1.396ff., incorporated details
that might motivate an actual change in the relationship of
Hera and Thetis? If indeed Thetis was brought up by Hera, as
"a daughter of the house" she would have been in the most

favorable position both to want and to be able to help Zeus
when the other gods ganged up on him; she would also, as in
the version from later poets, be in a position most likely to
attract Zeus' attention and wandering eye. Both of these situations could reasonably be expected to turn Hera against her
nursling out of frustration and jealousy. In that case she
would have been happy to marry Thetis off to Peleus, even
without any prophecy that Thetis would bear a son greater
than his father. This is pure speculation and perhaps an over-
ly ambitious attempt to historicize bits of myth, but surely
we have a right to assume that cause and effect operated even
in pre-Homeric tradition.

The other three *exempla* concerning divinities in the *Iliad*
all have more to do with divine-human relations than with intramural activities on Olympus. Two of them represent a reversal of the Heracles episodes we have already considered in
that they deal with mortals acting on divinities, instead of
divinities on mortals. An exact reversal would involve one
mortal harming and another helping one divinity, just as Hera
harmed and Zeus helped Heracles. Instead, presumably because
there is greater impiety in rescuing a god than in damaging
him, the helper in these cases is another divinity. And yet
the inclusion of a third party links these situations with
those in which divinities act on mortals and suggests that
they are variations on a single theme. For example, in 6.
129ff. Diomedes backs up his reluctance to fight with a divinity by citing the example of Lycurgus, who did not survive
long after he pursued Dionysus' nurses and frightened the god
into the sea (where Thetis rescued him). The other case is
5.385ff., where Dione cites three examples in order to reconcile Aphrodite to the rough treatment she has received at
Diomedes' hands: 1) Ares was imprisoned by Otus and Ephialtes

and only released by Hermes; 2) Hera was wounded by Heracles;
3) Hades was shot by Heracles and only cured by Paieon. Surely it is significant that only Hera has no god to help her,
as if to intimate that the untended wound rankled and justified her constant harassment of Heracles.

These further details of Heracles' adventures raise again
the question whether the *Iliad* poet is inventing examples of
gods suffering from mortals, or making use of already elaborated episodes. In the case of invention, we would expect
the poet to create a better parallel to Aphrodite's situation
in at least one of the examples Dione uses to console her.
Yet no one of the three damaged divinities was wounded by a
spear, nor was the afflicted part a hand; and for even loose
parallelism the imprisonment of Ares is far-fetched. Given
the relative inappropriateness of that tale and the way in
which the two adventures of Heracles can be tied in with
other episodes in the *Iliad* (like Nestor's account of
Heracles' raid on Pylos in Book 11), it is easier to assume
that the poet was drawing on pre-existing tales. It may be
that the two lines in which Paieon applies drugs both to
Hades' wound (5.401-402) and to Ares when he too is wounded
by Diomedes (5.900-901) originally belonged to only one episode and were added to the other, but it is impossible to ascertain which was the prior use. Thus the effects of reverberation can be discerned even where the process cannot be
followed.

The last of the divine *paradeigmata* is Zeus' urging of
Hera (14.313ff.) to make love because he has never before in
the course of his philanderings been so smitten. The list of
females he has loved is most closely related to Dione's list
in 5.385ff.: in both the one-line recommendation ("endure"
in the one and "let's go to bed" in the other) is followed by

two lines of generalized reason introduced by *gar*, and then
by the items of the list. Dione's examples are only three,
and take up respectively seven, three, and eight lines; whereas Zeus' list includes eight examples, no one of which ex-
ceeds two lines. Dione's speech concludes with a long section
on Diomedes' rashness and a veiled threat concerning his fate.
There is no return to the general reason for the recommendation to endure; perhaps this implies that the thought of vengeance to come will soothe Aphrodite more than a further reminder that she is not alone in her suffering. Zeus' list
does come full circle not only back to his generalized reason
but also, tactfully, to Hera herself, without however repeating his recommendation. Though little more than a bare list,
it still acts as a hortatory *paradeigma*, and as has often
been noted it probably presumes a catalogue of divine offspring. Whether or not its inclusion here is meant to mock
the god and his philanderings, it is likely that his reputation along those lines suggested Hera's ploy for distracting
his attention from the battlefield. That is, whenever and
wherever Hera first tricked Zeus, whether it was in some
Ur-Iliad or in some scandalous popular tale, the inspiration
likely came from his reputation as a great lover (with which
he must have been saddled largely to provide divine paternity
for heroes and godlings of all sorts).

What then of re-creation and reverberation can be identified in the various divine *paradeigmata* and the surrounding
narrative? Proceeding as before from those which are primarily intramural on Olympus, let us take up first the binding
and loosing of Zeus in 1.396ff., and the question whether the
frequency of the motif is a matter of borrowing from several
inherited anecdotes or of reverberation between such anecdotes and the action of the *Iliad*. The instances involving

158 *Mabel L. Lang*

both divinities and men may be summarized as follows.

BINDING	LOOSING
Inherited	
Other gods bind Zeus (Book 1)	Thetis looses Zeus (1)
Otus and Ephialtes bind Ares (5)	Hermes looses Ares (5)
Laomedon threatens to bind Apollo and Poseidon (21)	Other gods loose Hera (15)
Iliad action	
Zeus binds Agamemnon with *ate* (2, 9)	
Dolon asks to be bound (10) (regular way of taking captive [2])	
Achilles binds Trojan youths (21) and Hector to be dragged (22, 24)	

Except for the figurative binding with *ate* no *Iliad* action involves divine binding, unless we wish to see in the joint operation of Hera and Hypnos in Book 14 a figurative binding of Zeus that was inspired by his physical binding of Hera. Otherwise the theme of binding is so variously used in the inherited tales that it is difficult to find any common ground, except that for deathless beings it substitutes for death, whether the aim is usurpation (Book 1), punishment (15), or riddance (5, 21). It might be, then, that the use of binding in war as a fate next to death was the original source, and that divine binding in these anecdotes was an echo or reverberation from heroic epic. As far as loosing goes, there is a possible figurative reverberation if Zeus is thought of as "bound" by his oath to Thetis (1), and Hera and the other gods keep trying to free him from that oath. Certainly in a more general sense the inherited conflict of Zeus and Hera is invoked for the action of the *Iliad* at the same

time that inherited instances illustrating it are used as
exempla.

It was suggested that the revolt against Zeus was the act
which he punished by sending Apollo and Poseidon to serve
Laomedon (21.441ff.). This would link the *exemplum* used to
motivate Zeus' decision to favor the Trojans with that used
by Poseidon for an equal but opposite purpose, to undermine
Apollo's allegiance to the Trojans. There is an obvious relationship between Laomedon's refusal to give the promised
payment for the wall which the god built him (21) and
Laomedon's refusal to give Heracles his promised payment
(5.635ff.). The connection works in at least two ways. Not
only do both episodes use the same motif, perhaps, as so
often in doublets, in order to explore different outcomes
(Heracles' sack of Troy and Poseidon's dispatch of a sea-
monster), but they are also connected causally, with Laomedon
hiring Heracles in one episode to dispose of the very sea-
monster sent in the other. Furthermore, both these Laomedon
exempla seem to be reflected in Paris' refusal (7.357ff.) to
keep his promise that Helen go with the victor of the duel
(3.69ff.). That is, the refusal to give up Helen which presumably brought on war in the first place exemplifies a motif
that has many parallels as an explanation of conflict, but
that cause has here not only been renewed but also converted
into a failure to deliver on a promise which may well have
been patterned on Laomedon's refusal to live up to his agree-
ments about both horses and wages. Thus the duel between
Paris and Menelaus which properly belongs to the first year
of the war has been brought into the tenth year, and into the
Iliad, both to give the illusion of the conflict's beginning
and to make the Trojans' refusal to give up Helen into the
same sort of breach of promise that had justified Heracles'

sack of Troy and Poseidon's dispatch of the sea-monster.
Thus justification for the new fall of Troy is provided both
through the breaking of the truce in Book 4 and by Paris' refusal to keep his promise, a motif inherited from his grand-
father and reverberating for the bard from the earlier traditions about Troy.

The next pair of *paradeigmata* involving divine crime and
punishment concerns Hera's driving Heracles off course, Zeus'
vengeance on her for this action, his punishment of those
gods who tried to loose her, and Hephaestus as one who was so
punished (15.16ff.; 1.586ff.). In both these passages the
punishment is hurling from heaven, a feat in which Zeus in-
dulges, in fact or intent, on three other occasions, and
which Hera imitates for her own purposes in another
paradeigma. Hurling from heaven, even more than binding, is
a way of disposing of immortals, since at least in one case
(8.13ff.) it involves descent to Tartarus and the underworld.
And surely Zeus' habit of expressing his displeasure thus in
the old stories that are quoted in the *Iliad* has rubbed off
or reverberated on the *Iliad* narrative itself:

Inherited	*Iliad narrative*
Zeus hurls Hephaestus (Book 1)	Zeus threatens to hurl any god who inter- feres in the war (8)
Zeus wished to hurl Hypnos (14)	
Zeus hurls gods loosing Hera (15)	
Zeus hurls *Ate* (19)	
(Hera hurls Hephaestus [16])	

Except in the case of Hera's hurling, the action is taken or
threatened as a punishment, but each of the inherited cases
has its own rationale and outcome. That is, the hurling motif is not simply repeated in the various tales; rather its

possibilities are explored. If indeed the accounts in Books
15 and 1 refer to the same occasion, they still emphasize almost completely different aspects of the hurling. In 15 the
emphasis is on the crime that is punished; in 1 the crime is
passed over and it is the suffering and results that are emphasized. The threatened hurling of Hypnos in 14 shows a
different twist: it is aborted by Zeus' respect for Night,
to whom Hypnos flees. Still more different is the hurling of
Ate in 19, since this is not only a punishment but also an
explanation of the goddess' presence among men. It seems
fair to say that the hurling motif has been worked for all it
is worth in the inherited cases; so too in the *Iliad* narrative, where Zeus' threat is like the Book 14 version in not
being fulfilled, and like the Book 19 version in using ex-
clusion from Olympus. It nevertheless has its own differences too, in that the destination is neither land (as in
Books 1 and 14) nor sea (as in 16) nor the heads of men (as
in 19), but Tartarus. And whether Hera's hurling in 16 is an
Iliadic innovation or an inherited variant, it exhibits still
another way of handling the motif, as an unemphatic prelude
to the Thetis-rescue motif. Thus two old motifs make a new
combination to serve a specific purpose, to motivate
Hephaestus' work on Achilles' armor.

One oddity concerning the hurling-motif has not been noted:
that despite Hypnos' original worry in 14 that Zeus would
again seek to punish him (forgotten when the bribe proves ir-
resistible), Zeus completely ignores Hypnos' role in his de-
ception and accurately zeroes in on Hera as the instigator.
It is in this kind of omission that the *Iliad* poet shows true
mastery of his craft. By having Hypnos cite Zeus' previous
threat as a precedent he not only shows Hypnos successfully
angling for a greater reward and foreshadows Zeus' coming

anger, but also disposes of any need later to slow down the
narrative with an account of Zeus' treatment of Hypnos. The
paradeigma thus serves to prefigure the present situation,
which can then be developed in its own way because the ground-
work has already been laid in the precedent. We know that
Hypnos will flee to Night and that Zeus will not touch him.
Thus the poet uses the inherited motif both as a pattern or
inspiration of an episode (the distraction of Zeus' attention
so that Hector, like Heracles, can be persecuted) and as a
precedent to prepare the ground. So the Hephaestus doublet
of this episode in Book 1 serves a similar purpose: again it
is a matter of 1) hurling from heaven, 2) Zeus, and 3) a
helper of Hera. This time, however, the helper Hephaestus
was actually hurled, and tells the story to persuade Hera not
to pit herself against Zeus. He thereby provides a heavenly
parallel and precedent for Achilles, who was similarly dis-
suaded from attacking Agamemnon. Achilles' withdrawal from
battle is paralleled by Hera's withdrawal in Book 4, and in
the divine arguments in both 1 and 4 Hera's resentment of
Zeus' authority and privileges echoes almost every point made
by Achilles in 1 and 9 against Agamemnon: she toils in vain;
he pulls rank on her, has no regard for her honor and the
people she loves, but does as he pleases; and his decision to
support the Trojans means that she is deprived of Greek victory just as Achilles is deprived of *his* symbol of victory,
Briseis. This kind of reverberation between past and present,
heaven and earth, love and war, with mutual attraction and
like calling to like, exemplifies the organic unity of the
Iliad's complex structure. Such a complex whole could not
have resulted from any single act of composition, but must be
the result of repeated re-creations.

Lack of space prevents a similarly detailed examination of
the other divine *paradeigmata* for evidence of reverberation.
We may, however, point up the possibilities in this kind of
speculation by a quick review of Iliadic themes and episodes
which seem to echo these *paradeigmata*, but may also have influenced them in return:

the rivalry and hostility of Zeus and Hera, for which
  the ground is laid by the two *paradeigmata* in Book 1;
Hector as Zeus' protégé and Hera's victim, like
  Heracles, with Hypnos as Hera's helper and Athena as
  active agent;
Paris' refusal to honor a commitment, echoing
  Laomedon's double-dealing and used as justification
  (once again) for the sack of Troy;
the comparatively unmotivated wounding of Aphrodite and
  Ares, copying the understandable hostility to the
  gods on the part of Heracles and Otus and Ephialtes;
Athena as guardian angel for various heroes as for
  Tydeus and Heracles;
Zeus' sexual susceptibility, for which ground is laid
  by the list of former conquests.

Whether the "mothering" role which Thetis assumes in three
different *paradeigmata* (for Zeus, Dionysus, and Hephaestus)
is inspired by her relationship with Achilles in the *Iliad* or
whether her care for her son there is an extension of an old
role may be uncertain. Nevertheless, the interaction between
the two shows once again the kind of two-way innovation to
which only repeated reworkings and re-creations of a narrative would give rise. That is, whether an *Iliad* theme attracted old tales as *exempla* or an old tale inspired an *Iliad*
episode for which the old tale was used as support, each
would be liable over time to infiltration of details from the

other. For if like attracts like in epic narrative, as the
use of both similes and mythological *paradeigmata* suggests,
it is probable that in a situation of ongoing, non-static
composition this kind of attraction, like that between
charged particles in the physical world, would be a force
acting mutually between stories.

NOTES

1. Johannes Kakridis, *Homeric Researches = Skrifter utg. av
   Hum. Vetenskapssamf. i Lund* 15 (Lund: Gleerup, 1949),
   p. 99.
2. M. M. Willcock, "Mythological Paradeigma in the *Iliad*,"
   CQ 14 (1964), 141-154.
3. Ben E. Perry, "The Early Greek Capacity for Viewing Things
   Separately," *TAPhA* 68 (1937), 403-427.

Homer in Byzantium: John Tzetzes

Gareth Morgan

It is rare for a classical scholar to become rich.[1] If it could have happened anywhere, surely it must have been in twelfth-century Byzantium. Not only was there that general efflorescence of literature and the arts that we have learnt to call the Comnenan Renaissance, but the members of the royal house itself were active writers in the classical style and even concerned themselves specifically with topics of classical scholarship. Alexius Comnenus, at the beginning of the century, had written classical iambics of *Advice to a Son*. His daughter Anna Comnena's great work, the *Alexias*-- more a historical novel than a history--is in an atticizing style. She even turns her folk songs into the antique, and only with regret handles such barbarian names as "Hugo" and "Saint-Gilles." Her quotations from Homer are almost as frequent as her quotations from the Bible, and they are more accurate. Her husband, Nicephorus Bryennius, writes a more sober, and still atticizing, history. Her brother, Isaac, actually writes essays on Homer, as well as original poetry in classical and Byzantine meters.

But still, John Tzetzes found difficulty in making a living. He was the leading interpreter of Homer, and he still could not make a living. The leading commentator on Homer, that prodigious compiler Eustathius, certainly did make a living, but he made it by virtue of his office as Archbishop of Salonica: Byzantine archbishops looked after themselves pretty comfortably. One of the most learned poets of the time, Theodore Prodromus, had even achieved a position as teacher to the Emperor's sister-in-law, and wrote many poems

in her honor; but in another persona, as Ptochoprodromus, the
"Pauper Prodromus," he complains of his miserable poverty,
his existence on black bread, onions, and anchovies, while
the churchmen all around him eat their roast lamb and rolls
of white flour.

Tzetzes is forced to turn to the two resources of classical scholarship through the ages: teaching, and the getting
of grants. The first comes easily to him. He is a born
teacher, as naturally pedagogic as any man in this pedagogic
age. In the second, the begging of grants (not from institutions, of course, but from individual patrons), he is only
partly successful. He applies to one patron for the gift of
a mule and gets back a pick-axe, and blunt at that. Sometimes, presents that are spontaneously sent him are not to
his taste. In a very nineteenth-century fashion, the
Surgeon-General Michael sends him some partridges from the
countryside, and other friends send him lambs and hens: but
Tzetzes eats no fresh meat, only salt or pickled. In fact,
his real pleasure of the senses is not in food at all, but in
the enjoyment of incenses and perfumes. He asks one patron
for Assyrian xylaloe, and another is asked to send seedlings
of a particular frankincense that grows near Amastris.[2]

This mild eccentricity in its turn fits into the stereo-
type of the classical scholar. One more trait is regrettably
familiar: the tactlessness that can lead to long-lasting enmity. When Tzetzes wrote a rude epigram about the tasteless-
ness of a certain seal, it would have been better for him to
realize that the seal belonged to an influential ecclesiastic;
when he inveighed against certain vulgar and heretical
priests, it was a pity that the priests enjoyed the favor of
personages near the imperial court.

So Tzetzes lives poor, and ends poor, selling his books
one by one, granted lodging in a monastery where the flour
was sweepings, and the wine opaque.

The world of classical learning thinks of him first as a
commentator: it thinks of his commentaries on Aristophanes,
and, rather less frequently, of his scholia and commentaries
on Hesiod, Pindar, Homer, and other writers. He is a mine, a
quarry to be dug and sifted for nuggets of antiquarian information on mythological variants and authors not extant.
Tzetzes would not have concurred in this assessment of his
work. He was proud of his commentaries, and especially of
his work on Lycophron's *Alexandra*. This was the Everest of
classical scholarship--to explain the most obscure and
oblique of ancient authors. But if anyone had asked him what
was the greatest work of his career, the answer, I think,
would have been the *Epistulae*--the collection of 107 careful-
ly-wrought and richly elaborated letters. From the first
they are intended for publication. Most are addressed to the
nobility and officialdom of Byzantium, even to the Emperor
himself and to his Empress. Others go to prelates and monks.
They are not artificial in the sense that the unfortunate
letters of the late Pope, John Paul I, for example, are artificial. They grow out of occasions--the receipt of a gift,
the interpretation of a dream, the death of a friend; and
sometimes these occasions can be intimate and touching. But
they are artificial in the other sense, that their language
is elaborately designed at a level above that of the recipi-
ent. To a fellow-scholar Tzetzes can write at a level of er-
udite allusiveness near complete unintelligibility; to a
simple monk, he uses a style pure and almost plain, until the
odd word or phrase makes you realize that his very plainness
is forced with an antique precision. His letters are meant

to be models; and in an age that treasured obscurity and an-
tiquarianism, an age when the ceremonies of the Great Palace
could contain whole songs in Gothic, a language that had not
been spoken, nor yet understood, in Constantinople for five
hundred years--in such an age, models of style are necessarily hard to comprehend.

But Tzetzes is a teacher; and so, in this his masterwork,
he takes care that his letters are understood, by writing a
running commentary upon them for public consumption. He does
not write it in prose, of course, because Tzetzes' prose is
what caused the trouble in the first place. So he uses
verse--rhythmic Byzantine fifteen-syllabled political verse--
to write explanations of the allusions in his personal letters. This is the origin of the *Chiliads*, another mine of
antiquarian information for the classical scholar: the scholar who will be appalled by the general sense of mindless accumulation (the very title, *Thousands*, though not Tzetzes' own,
accurately suggests the feeling that the author is accumulat-
ing mileage rather than shaping form). The same scholar may
speculate wildly on the sequence of topics, how apparent
groups of Homeric subjects will suddenly get interspersed
with Herodotus, or even Cosmas Indicopleustes, until he real-
izes that they merely reflect what Tzetzes has been reading
recently, what is at the top of his mind as he pens an epistle
to one of his friends or enemies.

Even this is not the end of his explanatory mania. Take
an example from his Letter 82, written to his old friend, the
Most Holy Metropolitan of Dristra on the Danube, on the very
edge of Scythian territory. He'd sent Tzetzes some very fine
presents, including an inkwell carved of fishbone, and a
Russian boy-slave (who was more trouble than he was worth,
and turned out on investigation to be only Serbian after all).

But recently, the Metropolitan has not written. Is it because the mails are bad? Or is he perchance using Meton's
calendar?

   This, of course, is incomprehensible to the common reader:
so Tzetzes, in the *Chiliads*, jumps into an account of ancient
astronomy, starting from Atlas, Heracles, Orpheus, and
Homer.[3] But suddenly we are transferred to yet another level
of discourse: there is a violent attack on people who don't
understand the subtleties of what Tzetzes is trying to explain

>   Ignorant abominations, babble-twisters,
>
>   men who have barbarized the art of letters
>
>   by not minding books, where all wealth lies.
>
>   Their nectar is the stink of the dunghill
>
>   --pigs do not want to eat the bread of angels.

And so on and so on, an invective which culminates in a highly corrupt line that contains a modern Greek obscenity previously unrecorded. It appears that an adversary had had the
temerity to criticize Tzetzes on this very topic, and also
has committed several metrical solecisms. As an example of
real learning, Tzetzes now proceeds to write on Meton and
astronomy in quantitative iambics. The process which began
with a one-line joke in a letter addressed to the far north
has become a three- or four-decker pedagogic parade for the
admiring students of the Byzantine world.

   Above all, a teacher. And necessarily a teacher of Homer,
for Homer was still the basis of education. Tzetzes knows
teaching, literally from the bottom up. On explaining the
word *scutále* (the ancient Spartan message-stick) he associ-
ates it (rather dubiously) with *scũtos*, which, as he says, is
"the tawse for whipping schoolboys' rumps." One of his
shortest letters neatly puts what many a teacher has wanted
to say to a complaining parent. I quote it in its entirety:

I don't like a father to be sad because of the uselessness
of his son. Why not put some sense into him yourself, if
you really are his father?[4]

To the guardian of another weak student he uses a quite different technique, which again might be recommended to the
modern teacher. Instead of complaining about the boy's idleness, he adopts the pose of commiserating with the guardian
and sending his condolences:

I feel it a wound in *my own* heart; I am deeply sorry for
you . . . his fellow-students construed five whole books,
and he was left completely behind, as I said to you per-
sonally. Since he made a second start, the other students
have been working on another three books; some have got to
the end, some to the middle, and some at least well away
from the beginning, but *he* has not construed anything at
all.[5]

By "books," of course, are meant books of Homer. Perhaps we
see a hint of what is now fashionably called self-paced or
individual-study methods.

We can get a glimpse of Byzantine teaching-methods in a
set of Homeric scholia from a Rome manuscript that contains,
as well as the *Iliad*, some of Tzetzes' own Homeric writings.
They may even reflect Tzetzes' own teaching.[6]

It's often forgotten that the word "scholia" covers a
range of information intended for a range of audiences. The
bulk of the set we are discussing is very close to that of
the Geneva manuscript (Erbse's group "h"), but the first few
pages are completely different. They represent a teacher's
guide, a working technique for teaching at a learning level
even lower than the simplest scholia (the "Didymi" scholia)
that festoon the margins of so many Byzantine texts. Here is
the opening, on the first few words of the *Iliad*.

Mēnis means five things: *mēnis*, *orgḗ*, *thūmós*, *chólos*, and
kótos. *Mēnis* is that which persists and does not diminish
[a false etymology connects *mēnis* with *men-*, 'to remain'].
Orgḗ is the raising of hands [*órexis*, a correct etymology,
but semantically dubious]. *Chólos*, 'one's whole being
pouring out' [*cheómenos hólos*, a wildly incorrect etymol-
ogy] or from the pouring of the *thūmós*. *Kótos* is that
which always lies in the soul [connecting the word with
kei-, 'lie'--again wrong].

   Thūmós means five things.
1. 'the soul' as in "great-souled Achaeans" [*megáthūmoi*].
2. 'anger' as in "great is the *thūmós* of Zeus-born kings."
3. 'concord' as in "having one *thūmós*, mind, and cautious
    counsel."
4. 'afterthought' as in "another *thūmós* arose unto me."
5. 'desire' as in "yielding to his *thūmós*, he went to bed
    with her."

   How do you decline *mēnis*? Answer: *tês mḗnidos*, and it
should be declined *mḗnithos*, like *órnīs*, *órnīthos*, 'hen';
but nouns in *is* sometimes are declined in *dos* and sometimes in pure *os*. When a noun has two consonants before
the iota, it has *thos*, like *mérmīs*, *mérmīthos*, 'a fine
thread', or *órnīs*, *órnīthos*, 'a hen'; when it has one con-
sonant before the *is*, it has *dos*, like *Krãthis*, *Krãthidos*,
'the River Crathis'; but appellatives have the plain *os*,
like *óphis*, *óphios*, 'a snake', and *mántis*, *mántios*, 'a
prophet'.

   Why did he say *theã*, and not *theḗ*? We say: "When the
nominative masculine singular ends in *os* . . . "
And the simple explanation familiar to all first-semester
students follows.

In other words, in these comments on the very opening of
the *Iliad*, we have seen one very simple point of declension
(on the word *theá*) which can only have been included to provide a teaching-base for a future discussion of Ionic forms;
we have seen a much more complicated and dubiously useful
point of declension, on *mēnis*. We have seen a series of syn-
onyms for *mēnis*, supported by etymologies; and a series of
shades of meaning, supported by Homeric quotations, of an al-
lied word (*thūmós*) that is not even in the text. Again, a
teaching-base is being provided for future work. The whole
is united by a colloquial style, but the purpose may be described as saturation-teaching. This is the same technique
which prevailed in the West at this time for the teaching of
Vergil. On the first day, the pupil went into the classroom
and heard "arma virumque cano, Troiae qui primus ab oris,"
and would, in catechetic style, learn the morphology, meanings, connotations, of *arma* before he went on to the next
word. The Western material is simpler, but the Eastern
material can afford to be richer because so much of the language of Homer is still alive in Byzantine mouths.

But this is elementary teaching; this is the first level
of understanding, the construe that some of Tzetzes' pupils
had found so hard to understand and learn by heart. Higher
techniques of teaching are demonstrated in Tzetzes' two major
Homeric works, the *Allegories* to the *Iliad* and *Odyssey*.

It seemed that he had struck lucky at last. How he must
have dreamed of the perfect pupil--the pupil who was intelli-
gent and well motivated, with a good home background and fam-
ily-support; the pupil who could start from the beginning,
not spoiled by previous teachers' ineptitudes; above all, the
pupil who was *very very rich*. And now, he found her.

In 1146, Manuel Comnenus, relentlessly pursuing his pro-Western policy, had married Bertha von Sulzbach, an Austrian princess, sister-in-law of Conrad III of Germany. The new Empress had been given the Greek name Irene, and, to help in her education, Tzetzes was commissioned to write an authoritative *Allegories of the Iliad*; commissioned at a truly royal rate--twelve nomismata for every quaternion that he produced. (Twelve nomismata would have been about seven months' wages for a common laborer.)

We have to confess that Tzetzes bungled even this opportunity. The *Allegories* of both *Iliad* and *Odyssey* were finished, it is true. But about half way along in the *Iliad*, he had the idea that, since he was being paid by area, it would do no harm to (shall we say) use double-spacing. Or even triple-spacing. Soon, the secretaries of the Imperial Treasury tumbled to the fact that there was more white than black in the latest installment. The money was cut off, the contract rescinded. Tzetzes tried to argue his way out of the situation, but it was no use. The officials of the Treasury might not know much about literature, but, by God, they knew how many lines went to the page; and though Tzetzes produces an extremely bitter letter about the oppression of the poor in Byzantium, the goose that laid the golden eggs has been killed.[7] The *Odyssey* is done on a smaller scale, and for smaller rewards, for a less eminent patron.

The intent of the work is, from the beginning, teaching. Allegory is conceived as a method of making things easy. This may not have been exactly its original motivation, as we shall see later; but it is clearly in the forefront of Tzetzes' mind, and made explicit in the prologue to the *Odyssey Allegories*, where he looks back at the earlier work.

This prelude is so explicit, and so illustrative of the
faults, and the virtues, of Tzetzes' style, that it's worth
looking at in some detail.

He takes Herodotus' story of how King Cyrus was provoked
by the fact that a favorite white stallion of his had been
drowned in the deep and treacherous River Gyndes. He tamed
the river by having it diverted into many tiny and innocuous
channels that anyone could cross. This is the metaphor for
Tzetzes' achievement with the *Iliad*: by simplifying and ana-
lyzing, he has made it possible for everyone to traverse the
difficulties of Homer.

In the translation that I am about to give, and in which I
have tried to make English line equivalent to Greek line,
cling to one fact: that Tzetzes uses the order "Subject-
Object-Verb." In the first sentence, the subject is "Cyrus,"
the object is "the River Gyndes," and the verb (a mere five
lines away) is "made passable." In the second half of the comparison, the subject is "I," the object is "Calliope" (the
Muse), and the verb, twenty-three lines astern, is again
"made passable."

> *Cyrus* once, *the River Gyndes* of Babylon
> (a navigable stream, that had drowned a white horse of
>   his)
> with three hundred and sixty channels
> (digging one hundred and eighty on one side,
> and on the other again an equal number)
> *made passable* for old women and for toddlers.
> That's what good old Cyrus did in years gone past.
> And *I* now, Homer's soprano *Calliope*
> who brilliantly sings the catalogues of heroes,
> the war of the Greeks and the battles of Troy
> that have a yawning gulf of allegories

--not like River Gyndes, but like great Ocean,

from which flow river, sea, and well of words;

not having drowned a white horse, but about to drown

the skipping of illustrious desire (for literature, I

    mean)

of my Empress, who was the ornament of women,

by her august command and bounties worthy of her,

and also by the pleas and gifts of other friends,

bridging in some places like Mandrocles

(who was a Samian engineer in Darius' time)

and like Apollodorus (Apollodorus of Damascus)

who lived in the time of Emperor Trajan:

so, bridging in some places like these men,

and in some places making the Ocean dry land like

    Dexiphanes

(who boasted Cnidus as his home in Cleopatra's days)

and in some places, as old Thales of Miletus

passed Cyrus over the impassable River Halys,

so now I with art diverting the bed

and elsewhere in a myriad channels slicing thin the

    depths

have *made permanently passable* for a dry-foot crossing,

writing in transparent language, understandable to any-

    one at all.

In the proemium to his *Iliad Allegories*, Tzetzes begins
from the marriage of Peleus and Thetis, and the casting of
the Apple of Discord, which he equips with a line of political verse that could come from a modern folk-dance:

Λάβε καλὴ τῶν θεαινῶν, λάβε καλὴ τὸ μῆλον

(Take, O fairest of the goddesses, fair one take the
    apple).

The Judgment of Paris follows, then a flashback to Hecuba's

dream when she was pregnant with Paris, that she would give birth to a flaming torch; and the further prophecy, that when the newborn child became thirty he would destroy his father-land. (It may be noted that the name "Paris" is capable in Byzantine, and Modern, Greek of being interpreted as "you would take": and this ill-omened word serves as an explana-tion for the change of name to Alexandros.)

Two versions are then provided of Paris' exile from Troy. In the first, he was exposed on Mount Ida and suckled by a she-bear (Romulus-style) and then pitied and rescued by the officer who had been told to expose him, and brought up as his own (Cyrus-style); in the second version, he was more peaceably sent to the town of Amandros, which later, from the *aítion*, was known as Parios.

So far, I suppose, so good: a familiar sort of story, not so different from the kind of thing that Rex Warner, for in-stance, produced in his *Men and Gods*. But already there have been hints of Tzetzes' impatience with such naiveties. His authorities have been described as "rather simpleminded" (my charitable translation of *agroikóteron*). Now, jumping on the chronological inconsistencies involved in the relations of Achilles and Paris, he begins a quite different story.

Paris was brought up in Amandros, and given a royal educa-tion: horsemanship, archery, ball-games (*sphaírās paízein*); above all, a rhetorical training. So equipped, he proceeded to allegorize a cosmogony. Peleus, the primeval matter (for *pēlós* means 'mud' in Greek) is wedded to Thetis (whose name means 'arrangement' or 'placing'). Present at the rites are such entities as Athena (Prudence), Hera (Courage), Aphrodite (Temperament, balance of elements), and Hephaestus (Fire, from whom come all the heavenly bodies). Only Eris (Discord, disarrangement) was not invited. When she turns up, like the Evil Godmother, all else follows.

Already, Tzetzes has used all the three recognized methods
of allegory. He regards some gods as elements (Hephaestus as
Fire) and so is using "elemental" allegory (*stoicheiakē*).
Other gods he names as psychological factors (Athena as
Prudence) and so he uses "psychic" or "spiritual" allegory
(*psychikē*). Finally, in turning so many of the preliminaries
of the *Iliad* from supernatural into natural or rational
events, he is using "historical" allegory (*historikē*). These
three forms are familiar through the history of allegory, and
are more than once programmatically named by Tzetzes. For
instance, he says:

> All is allegorized in triple wise,
>
> elementally, spiritually, and (the third)
>
> as is the nature of things physical.

Even a compressed account of classical and medieval allegory would unbalance this paper.[8]   It was already in existence in the sixth century B.C., and the motivation then was
the same as it was later, when Pseudo-Heraclitus summed it up
in the words "Homer would have been utterly without piety, if
he had not been allegorizing": in other words, Olympian im-
morality is unacceptable if we believe it literally. Later,
Eustathius was to say "Allegory cured the inherent *atopiā*--
senselessness, inappropriateness, grotesqueness--of the
story.[9]   Tzetzes is very conscious of this tradition, and
specifies his obligations. He owes much to the Stoic allegorists: Cornutus in the first century, with his handbook of
allegorical identifications, and Palaephatus in the fourth
century, who specializes in the historical method--Scylla is
a pirate ship, Pasiphae had an affair with a man called
Taurus. He rejects, also specifically, the mysterious sixth-
century lady allegorist, Demo, whom he rather unchivalrously
calls a "braggart baboon"; more significantly, he rejects

Michael Psellus, whom he ridicules for introducing Cherubim
and Seraphim into Olympus. Tzetzes may live in a monastery,
but he's far from being a monk. He does not mix Christianity
in his Homer.

There are other oddities of allegoresis that he also
avoids. He does not, for instance, make his Greeks and
Trojans into elements like the gods; nor does he make his
gods into parts of the body, like Metrodorus, for whom
Demeter means the liver, and Apollo means the spleen. But he
does make one advance, that you may already have seen. From
a literary point of view, his incorporation of all the earlier legend into the imagination of Paris, a participant in the
legend, is a tautening and potentially exciting rearrangement.
Unfortunately, he does not persist in it. This is one of the
characteristics that most alienates the modern reader--the
freedom with which allegorists move from one interpretation
to another.

The story goes on with a richness of detail and character.
Tzetzes knows how old Paris was and how old Helen was; he
knows how much he paid her maid for her cooperation. Inci-
dentals from the body of the *Iliad* are filled out and given
context. Agamemnon is said by Homer to have received a horse
from Echepolus, and a breastplate from Cinyres the Cypriot.
Tzetzes expands this to show that Echepolus and Cinyres were
cowards, buying their way out of the Greek expedition.
Homer's mention of the raids on the coastal towns of Asia
Minor is filled out with details of participants and booty.
A whole section is given to the physiognomies of the heroes.
Aeneas is "short, plump, with reddish hair, fair skin, grey
eyes, a fine nose, good beard, broad face; prudent; and his
hair is thinning on his forehead." Pandarus is "slim, pleas-
ant-faced, agile, middle-aged, dark-complexioned, and

black-haired." The same method, incidentally, is used in
Byzantine icon-painting: each saint has his own precise
physiognomy, according to a system that was already being
developed in Tzetzes' time, and reached its fullest written
form in the *Painter's Manual* of Demetrius of Phourna, in the
early years of the eighteenth century.[10]

Much of Tzetzes' material comes from his predecessors (the
physiognomies apparently from John of Antioch). It's often
hard to tell how much. Much of it, I'm sure, comes from
Tzetzes himself. Originality of invention is not the chief
point here. What we have to see is that anyone who thinks
like this, any students who are trained in this way of looking at Homer, are likely to regard the poem with a vividness
and immediacy that more modern readers may not have. If you
see Aeneas in your mind's eye, and recognize him by his nose
and his high forehead, you are within the story--or at least
within *a* story.

After these preliminaries (and the pattern is substantially the same as that of his archaizing poem *Antehomerica*)
Tzetzes reaches the *Iliad* itself.

> Homer the all-wise questions his own intellect,
>
> introducing it as Calliope, the goddess and the muse,
>
> about the reason for Achilles' wrath . . .

The answer given is, in effect, the whole of the book.
Immediately Chryses, the old priest of Apollo, is introduced
as "wizard, astrologer, and magus." Details are given of his
wand--is it *lítyon* or *litouon* (Plutarch says one, and
Coccianus Cassius the other). His raiment is described, and
his stactomantic methods. Wizards, to Tzetzes, are not prae-
ternatural, and require no excuse, but the effect of their
art must be explained. The sun is under Chryses' control:
so he makes it burn very hot, and bring heavy rains. The

humidity, combining with the sewage of so close-packed an en-
campment, produces plague--a plague that comes from the
ground, and so infects animals first, since they are nearer
the ground, and men thereafter.

The assembly of the Greeks, the first quarrel of Achilles
and Agamemnon, bring no surprises. When Achilles is tempted
to draw his sword, Athena is sent by Hera from the sky--that
is to say, Prudence is sent by the Soul from the head. (The
head is naturally represented by the sky, since both are
spherical). Nestor gives his advice, and Achilles retires
to sit weeping upon the seashore.

Now comes the supreme challenge for Tzetzes or for any
other allegorist. Achilles' mother Thetis arises from the
sea, hears her son's sad story, and undertakes to intercede
with Zeus. The Father of the Gods is away among the
Ethiopians. When he returns, after twelve days, Thetis goes
to him, and takes the posture of a suppliant, laying her left
hand upon his knees, and her right upon his beard. Zeus
hears her, and is silent for a while; then he nods his irrev-
ocable assent. Thetis leaps back into the sea, and the
Olympian gods rise as Zeus takes his throne.

Now comes the moment of tension when Hera confronts Zeus
over Thetis' visit. But she is cowed, and Hephaestus breaks
the tension by puffing through the hall. holding out a double-
handled drinking-cup to his mother, and reminding her jocu-
larly of how Zeus had taken him and hurled him down upon
Lemnos. Hera smiles, and takes the cup. Apollo and the
Muses sing to entertain the feasting gods, and Zeus retires
to bed with Hera.

I have to say that to me this scene in Olympus is one of
the really exciting parts of the *Iliad*, combining delicacy
with a sense of power and awe: but of course, to an

allegorist it is utterly unacceptable. What does Tzetzes do
with this? In his own words:
> This is the mythical way as it lies in the text.
> Now learn the truth and allegory.

Thetis is the daughter of Chiron the Philosopher. "Philosopher," of course, implies "seer" and "astrologer."
Chiron's specialty is lecanomancy--the seeing of the future
by gazing into bowls of water, and it is by this method that
Achilles learns of his short-lived destiny, whereas most children learn from their mothers what they are to become in this
world. Achilles, too, was born under Aquarius. Many years
later, when he was killed, and his body lay in state upon the
Sigean beach, there was a sudden swelling tide, and a flood
that came so high as to lap the corpse where it lay; and
there was a soughing of the sea which some said was the
mourning of Thetis and the Nereids.

However this may be (and of course the reader is conscious
of the circular, or even interlocking nature of these explana-
tions--Thetis is seen as the sea, and the sea is seen as
Thetis, and all the interpretations shimmer in and out of
each other), water was Achilles' natal element, with which he
felt a special affinity. As he sat by the seashore solilo-
quizing on the sorrows of the day, he saw an evening sea-mist
arising from the waves, and felt moved to pray for the defeat
of the Greeks, so that they might come begging to him.

All this happened on September the eighteenth. Before
laughing this to scorn, consider again the vividness and immediacy of the *Iliad* to students who have learnt all this.
We have become cavalier in our treatment of dates. George
Washington has lost his birthday, and the Queen of England
has two, but we still get extra significance from certain
days--many of them personal (birthdays and anniversaries),

some of them public. Occasionally this specialness spills
over into the world of the arts--Bloomsday, or Beethoven's
birthday. There was an extra reality for Byzantine students
who knew that Paris came back to Troy from Ida on April 22,
and left on his embassy for Sparta on June 18.

The day of the quarrel was September 18--the beginning of
that particular season that melts the snows of Ethiopia and
causes the rise of the Nile. However unscientific that may
be, a modern geography textbook will tell you that in Lower
Egypt the peak of the Nile flood occurs in early October;
specifically, in Cairo about October 1. October 1 is the
date when a clear cold spell in the latitude of the Northern
Aegean ushers in the formal beginning of winter. So, on the
thirteenth day after the quarrel, Achilles, sitting on the
beach near his ships, sees another sea-cloud rising. Part of
it moves over the foothills (and the word *gónata*, 'knees',
is still used in Greece for the foothills of a range), while
part of it rises up the side of the mountain to linger close
under the crest.

There is a sudden flurry of wind at the top of the mountain, a quivering of the clouds (as Zeus sighs and nods, and
the other elements--heat, ether, and so on--rise in confusion). For a while, as Achilles gazes into the distance, a
storm seems in the offing; but warm air rises (Hephaestus)
and the sky becomes red. This is Hephaestus' double cup,
for redness of the sky can be good or bad:

> Red sky at night, shepherds' delight,
>
> red sky at morning, shepherds' warning.

But this time it is good, and the harmony of sun and breezes
(Apollo and the Muses) brings fair weather and good hope.

So we come to our great question. What are we to make of
all this? The facile answer is to declare it to be rubbish,

reject it, and forget it; but there must be considerable danger in such a response to a framework of thought that had lasted for many centuries, and certainly been the dominant critical method of the Middle Ages. At the lowest level, we can say that allegoresis deserves our attention as the parent of allegory.

In fact, Tzetzes has achieved a lot more than this. We can regret the loss of the dialogue between Thetis and her son, we can regret the loss of the scene on Olympus, but we have to admit that Tzetzes has created something significant in their place. His verbal techniques are defective (and how he would have hated to hear that comment), but his perception of the psychological flow gives us much to think about. Perhaps we are meant to think of Achilles through the last part of Book 1; perhaps we should read it and listen to it with Achilles at the center of our perception. Tzetzes, using a technique of allegoresis that seems to me far more sensitive than that of other practitioners of the same methods, has made available to us this sequence of scenes--mists, storms, brilliance, and ether--seen through and happening in the mind of the hero. At a much higher level, he is doing the same with Achilles as he did with Paris--concentrating external events into the mind of his protagonist.

Tzetzes does not reach this level often. Much of his interpretation is pedestrian, and he is often forced to fall back on what seems to me to be a system of shotgun astrology, in which anything seems capable of signifying anything, provided a planet intervenes.

Even if we put aside this meditation of Achilles as a flash in the pan, it surely makes us think a little more deeply about how much of allegory is already inherent in Homer. Suppose we take the first form, elemental allegory.

We find that obviously Iris is there in divine and elemental
qualities, as goddess and rainbow. The specialized case of
Xanthus (and of his brother Simois) is even clearer. He
functions as a god: "in likeness of a man, he spoke from the
deep river-eddy,"[11] and warned Achilles. Then, as Achilles
defies him, he functions as a river, driving the hero away:

> every time, the rushing river
>
> hurled a wave at his back . . .
>
> the water's torrent tore and pressed at his knees,
>
> and washed the sand from under his feet.[12]

And if this is but a minor god, soon a major god, Hephaestus,
comes to meet him. I cite Whitman's famous essay on "Fire
and Other Elements":

> Xanthus threatens to quench the fire of Achilles, and fire
> itself must answer the challenge. Hephaestus "aims the
> divine fire" like a spear, burning first the plain with
> the bodies on it, and begins to restrain the water. Trees
> and shrubs are consumed. The fish are tormented, and at
> last the water itself burns, or boils, and cries out in
> surrender.[13]

While this is the center of Whitman's argument, he goes on
cogently on a second theme:

> . . . the sea is always there as the vast backdrop of the
> poem. When Thetis on occasion comes from it wrapped in
> mist, her presence is primarily felt as that of goddess
> and mother; yet she is also the sea goddess, and there is
> even some hint of the *Urmutterschaft* of the ocean in
> Patroclus' accusation to Achilles: "Not Thetis, but the
> grey sea bore you," as also in the quasi-funeral of Book
> XVIII, when the Nereids form a lamenting chorus. Yet on
> one occasion the sea distinctly enters the action . . .
> at the moment when Zeus finally dozes and Poseidon overtly

leads on the Greeks in renewed strength, Homer suddenly
injects this line: "And the sea crashed among the tents
and ships of the Argives." This is the decisive moment.
Not only in his personal form, but also in his elemental
form, Poseidon assists the Achaeans, and the confusion between god and element is the same as in the case of
Xanthus and Hephaestus in the *Theomachia*.[14]
We can see that inherent and even explicit in Homer there is
ample material to make elemental allegory easy.

The other categories are less obvious. There are the
simple abstractions of Eris, Hypnos, and such minor deities
as Phobos, Deimos, and Kudoimos. Historical allegory is almost completely impossible. We still have to ask ourselves
how far the methods of allegoresis which we tend to despise
en masse have been absorbed in detail into our perception of
the Homeric poems.

Let me be very personal. I have taught the first book of
the *Iliad* (the one we have tried to see through Tzetzes'
eyes) a number of times, both in Greek and in translation.
At the critical moment of the quarrel, I feel that I may well
have said something like "Achilles is on the point of drawing
his sword to kill Agamemnon, but he controls his anger." I
suspect that others may have said something very similar. In
fact it is not true. It is not true even if you go on to say
"he controls his anger on the command of the goddess." At no
point does Achilles control his anger. All he does is comply
with Athena's command, and let his anger run in other channels. Is it the unconscious influence of the allegorical
tradition that leads us automatically to formulate the divine
intervention in psychological terms?

Again, certain "realisms" or "naturalisms" have established
themselves close to our common acceptance. In what sense can

we say that Charybdis *is* a whirlpool? Is it in the same
sense that we can say Scylla *is* a rock? Can we go further and
say, in a similar sense, that the island in the harbor of
Corfu *is* the Phaeacians' galley? To be yet more provocative,
may we regard the whole course of Homeric archaeology as a
continuing effort towards the historic allegoresis of the
epics?

But this encroaches on other discussions, and I would prefer to leave you with some feeling of Tzetzes. Vasilievsky
said that the *Allegories* lacked "not only good taste, but
sound sense."[15] I wonder what Vasilievsky would have said
about the later Greek allegorist, Christopher Contoleon, who,
writing at considerable length about the arming of Agamemnon,
concluded that Agamemnon's greaves were "the necessary mobile
power" assumed by the intellectual soul as it passed from the
uniform and the incorporeal into number and body.[16] But no,
it was of Tzetzes' *Allegories* that the words were used; and
of course Vasilievsky was quite right. They lack any *modern*
good taste, and they lack any *modern* good sense. But if we
can separate ourselves from our modern prejudices, they reveal a man soaked in Homer, a man revelling in Homer, a man
who had occasional curious insights into Homer that can instruct us even today in this cleverer century of ours.

NOTES

1. The style of this paper is that in which it was first delivered. Apologies may be due to readers for occasional
   colloquialisms. Or perhaps not: should a speaker on oral
   literature be diffident about an oral style?

   A list of forty-odd works by Tzetzes, some still

unpublished, is given by C. Wendel in *RE* (1948). The ones
that chiefly concern this essay are as follows.

    Odyssey Allegories, ed. H. Hunger: Books 13-24 in *ByzZ*
       48 (1955), 4-48; and Books 1-12 in *ByzZ* 49 (1956),
       249-310.

    Iliad Allegories in *Anecdota Graeca*, ed. P. Matranga
       (1850; repr. Hildesheim: Olms, 1971), pp. 43-223.

    Epistulae, ed. P. A. M. Leone (Leipzig: Teubner, 1972);
       superseding Th. Pressel's edition (1851; repr.
       Amsterdam: Hakkert, 1964).

    Histories, or "*Chiliads*," ed. P. A. M. Leone,
       Pubblicazioni dell'Istituto di Filologia Classica,
       Università degli Studi di Napoli, I (Naples: Libreria
       Scientifica Editrice, 1968).

    Antehomerica, Homerica, et Posthomerica, ed. F. Iacobs
       (1793; rpt. Osnabrück: Biblio Verlag, 1972).

2. Tzetzes' biography remains to be written, and will be
   based upon his letters. Episodes in this and the following paragraph will be found in *Epistulae* 26 (mule and
   pickaxe); 29 (xylaloe); 39, 93 (pickled meat); 48 (partridges); 51 (perfumes); 93 (lamb and hens); 98 (salt
   fish); 100 (frankincense seeds); 103 (quality of monastery
   food); 55 etc. (picking the wrong adversaries); 89 (the
   tasteless seal).

3. *Histories* 12.119-291. The lines translated are 223-227.

4. *Epistulae* 62.

5. *Epistulae* 22.

6. *Anecdota Graeca*, ed. Matranga, pp. 372ff.

7. *Epistulae* 57.

8. A first-class introduction to the history of allegoresis,
   which identifies many of the elements of Tzetzes' method,
   will be found in H. Hunger, "Allegorische Mythendeutung

in der Antike und bei Johannes Tzetzes," *Jahrbuch der Oesterreichischen Byzantinischen Gesellschaft* 3 (1954), 35-54. See also the following articles of J. Tate: "The Beginnings of Greek Allegory," *CR* 41 (1927), 214-215; "Plato and Allegorical Interpretation," *CQ* 23 (1929), 124-154 and (especially) "On the History of Allegorism," *CQ* 28 (1934), 105-114.

9. *Commentary on the Iliad* ad 1.3 (ed. J. G. Stallbaum, Leipzig, 1825-30 [repr. Hildesheim: Olms, 1960]), p. 17, line 25.

10. Homeric physiognomies mentioned in R. Foerster's *Scriptores Physiognomonici* (Leipzig: Teubner, 1893) are those of Ajax, Paris, and Thersites; a list which would be much expanded if Tzetzes had been taken into account.

11. *Il.* 21.212f.

12. *Il.* 21.268-271.

13. C. H. Whitman, *Homer and the Heroic Tradition* (Cambridge, Mass.: Harvard University Press, 1958), pp. 128-153; repr. in *Homer: A Collection of Critical Essays*, ed. G. Steiner and R. Fagles (Englewood Cliffs, N. J.: Prentice-Hall, 1962), pp. 40-61. The passage cited is on p. 140 of the original and on p. 50 of Steiner and Fagles.

14. Whitman, p. 146; Steiner and Fagles, p. 55.

15. Cited in A. A. Vasiliev, *History of the Byzantine Empire*, 2nd ed. (Madison: University of Wisconsin Press, 1968), p. 499.

16. *Anecdota Graeca*, ed. Matranga, pp. 510ff.

On the Death of Sarpedon

Gregory Nagy

This presentation owes its momentum to three general principles established in three distinct fields, each of which
has a direct bearing on Homeric studies. The fields are:
(1) archaeology, (2) comparative linguistics, and (3) study
of "oral poetry." I propose to outline the three principles
field by field, and then to correlate them with the Iliadic
passage describing the death and funeral of Sarpedon, *Il.*
16.419-683.

First, we consider archaeology. A 1971 book by Anthony
Snodgrass, *The Dark Age of Greece*, has made it plain that the
eighth century B.C.--the era in which the *Iliad* and *Odyssey*
were reaching their ultimate form--is as important for our
understanding of Homeric poetry as is the late second millennium B.C.--the era which provides the actual subject-matter
for both of these epics. Granted, Homeric poetry draws upon
details that archaeologists can indeed assign to the late
second millennium.[1] But the point is that it also reflects
the overall orientation of the eighth century, which is a
watershed for the evolution of Hellenic civilization as we
know it: in this era, alongside the emergence of the *pólis*,
'city-state', as a general institution with a strong trend of
localized traditions (cult, law, etc.), there emerged a com-
mensurately strong trend of Panhellenism.[2] Homeric poetry,
which is a product of the same era, reflects both these
trends: it synthesizes the diverse local traditions of each
major city-state into a unified Panhellenic model that suits
the ideology of the *pólis* in general[3]--but without being restricted to the ideology of any one *pólis* in particular.[4]

Perhaps the clearest example is the Homeric concept of the Olympian gods, which incorporates yet goes beyond the localized religious traditions of each *pólis*; the Panhellenic perspective of Homeric poetry has transcended local phenomena such as the cult of gods, which is functional only on the level of the *pólis*.[5]

The present focus of interest, however, is not the cult of gods but the cult of heroes. Erwin Rohde's monumental book *Psyche* remains one of the most eloquent sources for our understanding the *hḗrōs*, 'hero', as a very old and distinct concept of traditional Greek religion, requiring cult-practices that were distinct from those of the gods.[6] What archaeology now tells us is that this Hellenic institution of hero-cults, in much the same form that we see in the classical period, is a product of the eighth century B.C.--the same era that produced the *Iliad* and *Odyssey*.[7] It is of course tempting to explain the upsurge of hero-cults throughout the city-states as a phenomenon motivated by the contemporaneous proliferation of Homeric poetry,[8] but it would be better to follow the cautious approach of Snodgrass in looking for a more comprehensive explanation.[9] Again the key is the twin eighth-century phenomena of the *pólis* on one hand and Panhellenism on the other. I cite Rohde's thesis that the *cult of heroes* was a highly-evolved transformation of the *worship of ancestors*--a transformation that took place within the social context of the *pólis*.[10] This thesis, which is perhaps most appealing from the anthropological point of view,[11] allows room for considering the constituent elements of hero-cults to be far older than the eighth century.[12] In other words, we can posit a lengthy prehistory for not only the epics of heroes but also the cults of heroes, with this qualification: the ultimate forms of the epics and of the

cults were shaped in the eighth century. The strong eighth-
century upsurge in the local cults of heroes can thus be
viewed as a phenomenon parallel to--rather than derivative
from--the Panhellenic epics of heroes, namely the *Iliad* and
Odyssey.

It is worth stressing that the hero as a figure of cult
must be local because it is a fundamental principle in Greek
religion that his power is local.[13] On the other hand, the
hero as a figure of epic is Panhellenic and consequently cannot have an overtly religious dimension in the narrative.
Such a restriction on the self-expression of Homeric poetry
led Rohde to misunderstand the elusive evidence of the *Iliad*
and *Odyssey* on heroes as cult-figures. His thesis was that
the general Homeric silence on the subject of hero-cults implies an absence of even the ideological background.[14] And
yet, even Rohde had to admit that a central scene like the
funeral of Patroclus in *Iliad* 23 preserves unmistakable and
pervasive signs of cult.[15]

In fact, a general argument can be made that Homeric poetry is permeated with references--direct as well as oblique--
to heroes in their religious dimension as figures of cult.
Since I have already offered such an arguemnt in a 1979
book,[16] I confine myself here to citing *en passant* the one
central scene that Rohde himself acknowledged as just such a
reference.

This same scene, the funeral of Patroclus in *Iliad* 23,
happens to be an ideal point of transition to the second of
the three principles to be surveyed before we finally consider the death and funeral of Sarpedon in *Iliad* 16. This time
the field is comparative linguistics, but the focus is still
the funeral of Patroclus. As for the principle in question,
the briefest of summaries will suffice: not only is the

Greek *language* cognate with other Indo-European languages
such as Hittite and Indic, but also countless Greek *institu-*
tions are cognate with the corresponding institutions of
other Indo-European-speaking peoples. In other words, such
diverse groups as the ancient Greek, Hittite, and Indic peoples have a common Indo-European heritage not only on the
level of *language* but also on the level of *society*. To ap-
preciate the breadth and depth of this Indo-European heritage
in Greek institutions, one has only to read through the prodigious collection of detailed evidence assembled by Emile
Benveniste in his 1969 book *Le Vocabulaire des institutions*
indo-européennes. For now, however, I wish simply to single
out one particular instance where the manifestation of a
Greek institution can be matched with corresponding evidence
attested in other societies with an Indo-European heritage.
I refer to the funeral of Patroclus in *Iliad* 23, as compared
with the royal funerary rituals that are recorded in official
Hittite documents.[17] The convergences in detail between the
Iliadic scene and the standard ritual procedures prescribed
in the Hittite records are so strikingly close that the only
plausible explanation available is the positing of a common
Indo-European heritage.[18] When we add the comparative evidence of funerary rituals and ancestor-worship in the Indic
traditions, the thesis of a common Indo-European heritage is
further reinforced.[19] The relevance of the Hittite and Indic
comparative evidence to the archaeologist's perspective cannot be emphasized enough: for instance, the evidence of cognate Hittite and Indic procedures in cremation makes instant-
ly obsolete the archaeological controversy over the cremation
of Patroclus. Since inhumation seems to have been the standard procedure for the Hellenic people in the second millennium B.C., with cremation becoming common only in the first

millennium, the cremation of Patroclus and other heroes in
Homeric poetry has been interpreted as a phenomenon characteristic of the first millennium from the archaeological
point of view.[20]   The evidence of comparative linguistics,
however, suggests that the procedures of cremation as attested in Homeric poetry are in fact so archaic as to reflect a
period of Indo-European civilization that predates the Indo-
European penetration of Greece in the beginning of the second
millennium.   To put it another way: the literary testimony
of Homeric poetry is in this case far more archaic than the
archaeological testimony of Mycenaean civilization.

This is not to say, however, that the evidence of comparative linguistics on matters of ritual simply bypasses the
second millennium B.C.   I cite a 1959 article by Nadia Van
Brock, in which she shows that the Greek word *therápōn* is a
borrowing, sometime in the second millennium, from one of the
Indo-European languages spoken at that time in the area of
Anatolia.   The given language may have been Hittite, Luvian,
or some unattested near-relative, but in any case the evidence that we have for the word which was borrowed as
therápōn comes primarily from Hittite: there the word appears as *tarpan(alli)-* or *tarpašša-*, corresponding to Greek
therápōn and its by-form *théraps* respectively.   In Hittite
the word means 'ritual substitute'.   The entity requiring
substitution is as a rule the king himself, and *tarpan(alli)-*
/*tarpašša-* designates his *alter ego* ("un autre soi-même"),
a projection upon whom the impurities of the king and his
community may be transferred in ritual.[21]   Here again, the
evidence is applicable to the death and funeral of Patroclus:
as Van Brock points out,[22] there is a Greek reflex of the
Hittite semantics in the Iliadic application of the title
therápōn to Patroclus (*Il.* 16.244, etc.), the hero who dies

while wearing the armor of Achilles and who functions in the
Iliad as the actual surrogate of Achilles.[23]

Mention of the Greek word *therápōn* brings us finally to
the main subject of this presentation, the death and funeral
of Sarpedon in *Iliad* 16. Again we will have occasion to see
the deployment of a key word with Anatolian origins, and
again this word conveys the ritual dimension of the hero in
epic. Before we can examine the word in question, however,
the actual tradition of the Sarpedon story in the *Iliad* has
to be defended. Such influential Homerists as Wolfgang
Schadewaldt have cast doubt upon the authenticity of this
tradition, arguing that the death of Sarpedon in *Iliad* 16 is
a derivative story modeled on the death of Memnon as reflected
in the *Aithiopis*.[24] This point of view has been seconded on
an iconographical as well as literary basis in a 1978 article
claiming that the theme of the dead Memnon's removal by Eos
is a basic and pervasive tradition among the Hellenes, and
that the parallel theme of the dead Sarpedon's removal by
Apollo seems by comparison marginal and flawed by artistic
inadequacies.[25]

Such a line of argumentation, however, misses one of the
most basic principles to be learned from the fieldwork of
Milman Parry and Albert Lord in the realm of "oral poetry."[26]
This principle is also the third and last of the three principles to be considered and then applied to the Iliadic passage describing the death and funeral of Sarpedon. To put it
briefly: in oral poetry, a given theme may have more than
one version or variant, but such multiplicity of thematic
variants does not mean that any one of them is somehow basic
while the others are derivative. Each thematic variant is
but a multiform, and not one of them may be treated as a sort
of *Ur*-form. The same principle applies also to the study of

myths in general. In the case of the Sarpedon story, to
prove that it has artistic inadequacies that do not exist in
the Memnon story is not the same thing as proving that one
was modeled on the other. Each multiform can be expected to
have its own inadequacies, and all we can say is that some
may have more inadequacies than others. But even this value-
judgement may be a matter of cultural bias: it is possible
that the very criteria of adequacy and inadequacy are in this
and other instances too narrowly based on the vantage-point
of one particular multiform that has for whatever reason become canonical.

The kind of reasoning that leads to the discounting of one
variant as an invention based on another variant is but a
symptom of a more general oversight that commonly afflicts us
Homerists: in our struggle to come to terms with the concept
"oral poetry," we tend to forget something more fundamental,
that oral poetry is traditional poetry. An oral poet does
not make up stories: rather, he retells stories that his
audience has heard before and expects to hear again. As
Albert Lord observes, "the picture that emerges is not really
one of conflict between preserver of tradition and creative
artist; it is rather one of the preservation of tradition by
the constant re-creation of it. The ideal is a true story
well and truly retold.[27]

With these thoughts in mind, we are ready to consider the
Greek word of Anatolian origin that occurs in the Iliadic
passage telling of the death and funeral of Sarpedon, son of
Zeus himself. After this prominent Lycian prince dies at the
hands of Patroclus, the plan of Zeus is that Apollo should
remove his body by having the twins *Húpnos*, 'Sleep', and
Thánatos, 'Death', convey it to his homeland of Lycia (16.454-
455, 671-673). At this point, the following will happen:

ἔνθα ἑ <u>ταρχύσουσι</u> κασίγνητοί τε ἔται τε

τύμβῳ τε στήλῃ τε· τὸ γὰρ γέρας ἐστὶ θανόντων.

. . . and there his relatives and comrades *will give*
  him a funeral

with a tomb and a stele, for that is the privilege of
  the dead.

16.456–457=674–675

The conventional translation, 'give a funeral to', for *tarkhúō*
is inadequate, as we shall presently see. If indeed this
story of Sarpedon--as also all other Homeric stories--is a
faithful retelling of a genuine tradition, then its Lycian
setting assumes added significance. As it happens, the Lycian
language is Indo-European in origin and closely related to
Hittite and Luvian. In Lycian, there is a word *trqqas*, which
designates a god described as one who smashes the wicked;[28]
this form is directly related to Luvian *Tarḫunt-*, which is
the name of the storm-god who is head of the Luvian pantheon.[29] There is also a Hittite by-form, attested as *Tarḫu-*
in theophoric names; it is also attested as the adjective
tarḫu-, meaning 'conquering, victorious'.[30] This whole family of noun-formations stems from the verb *tarḫ-*, 'conquer,
overcome', which can be reconstructed as the Indo-European
root *$ters_2$*.[31] The point of this brief survey is now at hand:
all indications are that the Greek verb *tarkhúō* is a second-
millennium borrowing from an Anatolian language, and that the
form borrowed was something like *tarḫu-*, 'conquering, victorious'. This explanation of *tarkhúō* has been accepted in
Pierre Chantraine's authoritative *Dictionnaire etymologique*
de la langue grecque--a work known for its rigorous avoidance
of uncertain explanations.[32]

We are still left, however, with the problem of translating
Greek *tarkhúō*. Since *tarḫu-* can designate a divinity in the

Anatolian languages, Chantraine follows Paul Kretschmer's example in interpreting the Greek expression ἔνθα ἑ ταρχύσουσι at *Il.* 16.456=674 as 'and there they will treat him like a god.'[33] We may compare the Hittite expression designating the death of a king or queen in the royal funerary ritual: DINGER^{LIM}-*iš kišat*, '[he or she] becomes a god'.[34] The adverb *éntha* in the Greek expression refers to the *dêmos*, 'district', of Lycia (*Il.* 16.455, 673; cf. 683).[35] I draw attention to this word *dêmos* not only in view of the aforementioned fact that cult is a localized phenomenon in archaic Greek religion but also because of the following Homeric formula:

θεὸς δ' ὣς τίετο δήμῳ.

. . . and he got *tīmḗ* [= honor] in the *dêmos*, like a

god.

Il. 5.78, 10.33, 11.58, 13.218, 16.605

The verbs *tío/tīmáō*, 'honor', and the corresponding noun *tīmḗ*, 'honor', are crucial, since one of their uses in Greek is to designate the 'honor' that a god or hero gets *in the form of a cult*; this usage is not recognized as a distinct category in the dictionary of Liddell and Scott, although it is richly attested in the language of archaic prose and poetry.[36] If indeed cult is also implied in the Homeric formula presently under consideration, then we could immediately justify Chantraine's interpretation of ἔνθα ἑ ταρχύσουσι at 16.456=674 as "and there they will treat him like a god": in the *dêmos* of Lycia, Sarpedon will get *tīmḗ* just as a god would.[37]

What still stands in the way, however, is that the Homeric formula θεὸς δ' ὣς τίετο δήμῳ, ". . . and he got *tīmḗ* in the *dêmos*, like a god," applies in each attestation to a hero who is still alive, whereas Sarpedon has already died. In fact, the procedure designated by the verb *tarkhúō* at *Il.*

16.456-674 is equated at *Il*. 16.457=675 with the procedure of
providing Sarpedon "with a tomb and a stele, for that is the
privilege of the dead." We should also keep in mind the archaeological evidence of the second millennium B.C. and thereafter, which suggests that a tomb and a stele are indeed
standard features that mark the burial of the dead.[38] The
problem is, how to reconcile this perspective of the hero as
an apparent figure of cult with that of the hero as a figure
of epic?

The solution to this problem, I suggest, lies in the actual
contexts of the formula announcing that a given hero "got
tīmḗ in the *dēmos*, like a god" (*Il*. 5.78, 10.33, 11.58,
13.218, 16.605). In each of these contexts, the hero appears
in the function of either priest or king.

5.77-78	Dolopion as priest of Scamandrus
10.32-33	Agamemnon as king of all the Argives
11.58-60	Aeneas as grouped with the Antenoridae; at 2.819-823, he and the Antenoridae are described as joint leaders of the Dardanians
13.216-218	Thoas as king of the Aetolians
16.604-605	Onetor as priest of Zeus Idaius

The sacral aspect of priests is in these cases overt, but not
of kings. As we turn from Homeric to Hesiodic poetry, however, we find an overt attestation showing that kingship is
not only sacral but also intrinsic to the hero as a cult-figure who gets his due *tīmḗ*.

The passage in question is the Hesiodic description of the
Gold and Silver Generations of mankind, *Works and Days* 109-
142. As Rohde has shown, the essence of the Gold and Silver
Generations is that together they form a complete picture of
the generic cult-hero.[39] A review of the manifold details
would go far beyond the scope of this presentation,[40] and I

confine myself here to the themes of kingship and *tīmḗ*.
After the death of the Gold Generation is narrated (116, 121),
they are described as having what is called the γέρας
βασιλήιον, 'honorific portion of kings' (126). We have already seen the word *géras*, 'honorific portion, privilege', in
the context of designating the funerary honors accorded to
the corpse of Sarpedon--honors which included the procedure
designated by the verb *tarkhúō*:

ἔνθα ἑ <u>ταρχύσουσι</u> κασίγνητοί τε ἔται τε

τύμβῳ τε στήλῃ τε· τὸ γὰρ γέρας ἐστὶ θανόντων.

. . . and there his relatives and comrades will

   [ταρχύσουσι] him

with a tomb and a stele, for that is the privilege of

   the dead.

Il. 16.456-457=674-675

It is worth noting in this connection that the Gold Generation
"died as if overcome by sleep" (θνῇσκον . . . ὥσθ' ὕπνῳ
δεδμημένοι: *Works and Days* 116), whereas the corpse of
Sarpedon was flown to Lycia by *Hupnos*, 'Sleep', and *Thanatos*,
'Death', who are described as "twins" (*Il*. 16.672). Since the
word *géras*, 'honorific portion, privilege', in Hesiodic diction and elsewhere represents a specific manifestation of
tīmḗ (as in *Theogony* 392-396),[41] we can correlate what is
said at *Works and Days* 126 about the Gold Generation's royal
géras with what is said later about the Silver Generation:
after the death of this next generation is narrated, they are
described as

δεύτεροι, ἀλλ' ἔμπης τιμὴ καὶ τοῖσιν ὀπηδεῖ.

. . . second in rank--but nevertheless they too get

   tīmḗ.

Works and Days 142

The irony here is that the Silver Generation, which represents

the negative and latent side of the cult-hero, earned an untimely death from Zeus for the following reason:

οὔνεκα τιμὰς

οὐκ ἔδιδον μακάρεσσι θεοῖς οἳ Ὄλυμπον ἔχουσιν.

. . . because they did not give *timḗ* [plural] to the
blessed gods who control Olympus.

Works and Days 138-139

This theme, that a hero gets *timḗ* even though he failed to
give *timḗ* to the gods, is a key to understanding the religious ideology of god-hero antagonism, but a proper treatment
of this subject would again go far beyond the scope of this
presentation.[42] It will suffice for now to observe that the
Silver Generation's failure to give *timḗ* to the gods is in
part equated with their failure to make sacrifice to them:

ὕβριν γὰρ ἀτάσθαλον οὐκ ἐδύναντο

ἀλλήλων ἀπέχειν, οὐδ' ἀθανάτους θεραπεύειν

ἤθελον οὐδ' ἔρδειν μακάρων ἱεροῖς ἐπὶ βωμοῖς,

ᾗ θέμις ἀνθρώποισι κατ' ἤθεα.

. . . for they could not keep wanton *húbris* from each
other,

and they were unwilling either to be ministers to the
immortals[43]

or to sacrifice on the altars of the blessed ones,
which is the socially right thing for men, in accord-
ance with their local customs.

Works and Days 134-137

In other words, the factor of *timḗ* is here expressed directly
in terms of ritual sacrifice.

Our survey of formulas involving the concepts of *timḗ* and
dḗmos leads to the following conclusion: the hero who gets
timḗ from the *dḗmos* is said to be "like a god" *because he is*
thereby being treated as a cult-figure. In Homeric poetry,

of course, the generic hero is predominantly a figure of epic, and his dimension as figure of cult has to be latent--
basically because he is still alive. Once he is dead, however, the perspective may change, as in the case of Sarpedon:
the verb *tarkhúō*, designating what his relatives and comrades
do to the dead hero, conveys the notion that he is being
treated like a god--which is the epic way of saying that he
is being treated like a cult-figure.

It does not follow, however, that we may dismiss as poetic
fancy the traditional notion that a hero is being treated
like a god by virtue of getting *tīmḗ* from the *dḗmos*. The institution of hero-cult is visualized, from the religious
standpoint of the institution itself, as a form of *immortalization after death*. In the *Hymn to Demeter*, for instance,
the young hero who is protégé of the goddess loses his chance
to be exempt from death (lines 260-264) but is offered as
compensation a *tīmḗ* that is everlasting, *áphthitos* (line
263).[44] In the following three lines, the ritual form of
this *tīmḗ* is then actually made explicit: the youths of
Eleusis will hold a festival of mock battles at a given
season every year for all time to come (265-267). In other
words, the cult-hero is being awarded the permanent institution of a yearly ritual in his honor.[45] It is not without
interest that the name of this young protégé of Demeter who
becomes a cult-hero is *Dḗmophóōn* (234, etc.), which seems to
mean 'he who shines for the *dḗmos*'.[46]

If we now contrast Demophon as hero of cult with Achilles
himself as a hero of epic, we can see more clearly the
Homeric perspective on the very nature of being a hero.
Whereas Demophon gets as compensation for his mortality a
tīmḗ that is *áphthitos*, 'everlasting', Achilles says that he
will get as compensation for his own untimely death a *kléos*

that is *áphthiton*, 'everlasting' (*Il*. 9.413). As I have argued at length elsewhere, this word *kléos* designates the
'glory' that a hero gets *specifically by way of poetry*.[47]
The ultimate hero of the *Iliad* is in effect saying that he
will be immortalized by his own epic tradition. We have here
in nuce the essence of the Homeric perspective: the theme of
a hero's immortalization has been shifted from the realm of
cult to the realm of epic itself. Accordingly, Homeric poetry tends not to speak in a direct fashion about immortalization because Homeric poetry presents itself as the very
process of immortalization.

This is not to say, however, that Homeric poetry ignores
the dimension of cult: rather, it places itself above cult.
The *kléos* that the hero earns in Homeric poetry by way of
valor in battle serves to validate and even justify the *tīmḗ*
that he gets at home from his *dḗmos*. While he is still alive
in the *Iliad*, Sarpedon himself says so:

Γλαῦκε, τίη δὴ νῶϊ τετιμήμεσθα μάλιστα
ἕδρῃ τε κρέασίν τε ἰδὲ πλείοις δεπάεσσιν
ἐν Λυκίῃ, πάντες δὲ θεοὺς ὣς εἰσορόωσι,
καὶ τέμενος νεμόμεσθα μέγα Ξάνθοιο παρ᾽ ὄχθας,
καλὸν φυταλιῆς καὶ ἀρούρης πυροφόροιο;
τῶ νῦν χρὴ Λυκίοισι μέτα πρώτοισιν ἐόντας
ἑστάμεν ἠδὲ μάχης καυστείρης ἀντιβολῆσαι,
ὄφρα τις ὧδ᾽ εἴπῃ Λυκίων πύκα θωρηκτάων·
"οὐ μὰν ἀκλεέες Λυκίην κάτα κοιρανέουσιν
ἡμέτεροι βασιλῆες, ἔδουσί τε πίονα μῆλα
οἶνόν τ᾽ ἔξαιτον μελιηδέα· ἀλλ᾽ ἄρα καὶ ἲς
ἐσθλή, ἐπεὶ Λυκίοισι μέτα πρώτοισι μάχονται."

Glaucus, why is it that you and I get the most *tīmḗ* of
    all,
with a special place to sit, with choice meats, and
    with full wine-cups,

in Lycia, *and everyone looks at us as gods,*
and we are allotted a great *témenos* [=piece of land] at
   the banks of Xanthus,
fine land, orchard and wheat-bearing ploughland?
Therefore it is our duty to take our stand in the front
   ranks of the Lycians, and to meet blazing battle
   head-on,
so that one of the close-armored Lycians may say of us:
"Indeed it is not without *kléos* that our kings
are lords of Lycia, who feed upon fat sheep
and drink choice sweet wine, since they have genuine
   strength
and since they fight in the front ranks of the
   Lycians."

                                        12.310-321

On one level, the examples of *tīmé* recounted by Sarpedon to
Glaucus can function as attributes of a living epic hero who
happens to be a king; on another level, however, each example
can be matched with a corresponding sacral honor accorded to
a cult-figure. As we know from Greek religious practices attested in the classical era, cult-heroes receive libations,[48]
choice cuts of meat placed on a special table,[49] and the allotment of a *témenos*, 'sacred precinct'.[50]

   From the standpoint of the *Iliad*, then, Sarpedon's goal is
to get a *kléos* that matches the *tīmé* that he already has at
home in Lycia. From the standpoint of cult, however, this
tīmé would be possible only after he dies, so that the epic
perspective has the logical sequence reversed: by placing
epic above cult, Homeric poetry allows the hero to have the
kind of *tīmé* that befits a cult hero even before he dies.
What he still has to earn by dying is *kléos* itself.

Sarpedon then goes on to say that he and Glaucus should be prepared to die in battle at Troy (12.326-328), and that he would choose to escape from battle only if escaping entailed immortality (322-325). The implication seems to be that the welcoming of death may succeed in bringing immortality where the avoidance of death has failed: after all, both *tīmḗ* and *kléos*, which are in store respectively for the hero of cult and the hero of epic after death, are *áphthito-*, 'everlasting'.

The same sort of implication can be found in the words of Hera at *Il.* 16.440-457, where she tells Zeus that he must not permit Sarpedon to escape death in battle and thus send him back home to Lycia alive (see especially line 445). Implicitly, Sarpedon would then have *tīmḗ* without having had to experience death. The exemption of Sarpedon from death in battle, Hera says to Zeus, would be without precedent: in her words, "beware lest some other divinity may wish to send his or her son back home, away from the battle" (16.446-447). Instead, Hera suggests, Zeus should let his own dear son die at the hands of Patroclus, after which *Thánatos* and *Húpnos* will take Sarpedon's body back home to the *dḗmos* of Lycia (450-455). Immediately after these verses, we come upon the verse that describes the ritual performed on Sarpedon's corpse, as designated by the verb *tarkhúō* (456, repeated at 674). From the context of Hera's words, we now see that the action conveyed by this verb is presented as a compensation for the death that Sarpedon must experience. From the other contexts that concern the theme of compensation for mortality, we also see that the verb *tarkhúō* entails the theme of immortalization after death--in a way that is yet to be defined. That is to say, the verb *tarkhúō* indicates not only that the relatives and comrades of Sarpedon will treat him like a cult-figure but also that he will thereby attain some form of immortalization after death.[51]

The explanation of *tarkhúō* that I have just offered is corroborated by the evidence of comparative linguistics. The Indo-European root **tera₂-* which survives as Hittite *tarḫ-*, 'conquer, overcome' also survives as Indic *tar(i)*, 'overcome', which takes the shape *-tur-* in compounds (e.g., *ap-túr*, 'overcoming the water'). As Paul Thieme has shown, the latter formation corresponds to the *-tar-* of Greek *nék-tar*, the substance that sustains the immortality of the Olympian gods; furthermore, the root *nek-* in *néktar* is the same as in Latin *nex*, 'death', and Greek *nék-ūs* / *nek-rós*, 'corpse'.[52] Thus the word *nék-tar* must once have meant something like 'overcoming death'; in fact, Rüdiger Schmitt has found a kindred combination in archaic sacral Indic poetry, where the verb *tar(i)-*, 'overcome', is actually attested in a context where *mr̥tyú-*, 'death', is its direct object (*Atharva-Veda* 4.35.1d-6d).[53]

This evidence not only provides one more argument for the existence of an Indo-European poetic language.[54] More immediately, it also gives us a broader perspective on the semantics of Greek *tarkhúō*. To put it another way: the meaning of Greek *-tar-* in *néktar*, where the root is directly inherited from Indo-European, may help us comprehend the meaning of Greek *tarkhúō*, where the stem *tarkhu-* is indirectly inherited from Indo-European by way of a Greek borrowing from the Anatolian language-family.[55] I draw special attention to the corresponding Anatolian form *tarḫu-* as it appears in Hittite *tarḫu-*, 'victorious', and in Luvian *Tarḫunt-*, the name of the storm-god who is head of the Luvian pantheon—and who wields the thunderbolt as his attribute.[56] Perhaps these formations convey the theme of overcoming not just evil-doers or other

such immediate obstacles, but also the ultimate obstacle of
death itself.[57]

Let us look for a parallel in the figure of Zeus himself,
head of the Greek pantheon and wielder of the thunderbolt in
his own right. With his thunderbolt, Zeus can cause both the
death and the immortalization of heroes. Consider the poetic
tradition that tells how Semele became immortalized as a direct result of dying from the god's thunderbolt (Pindar *Ol.*
2.25, in conjunction with Hesiod *Th.* 942).[58] Then there is
the case of Heracles, son of Zeus, who is struck by the thunderbolt of his divine father and thereby elevated to Olympus
as an immortal god (Diodorus Siculus 4.38.4-4.39.1).[59] Finally, we may consider yet another son of Zeus, the Lycian
king Sarpedon, whose dead body undergoes a process designated
by the verb *tarkhúō*. I submit that this process entails immortalization of the hero after death.

The fundamental difference, however, between the explicit
immortalization of Heracles and the implicit immortalization
of Sarpedon is that the first is narrated as an event on the
level of myth while the second is narrated as an event on the
level of ritual. Still, the myth and the ritual are complementary aspects of one ideology. The rituals of cult are a
code which can convey the same message as that conveyed by
the code of the myth. On a formal level, we can see most
clearly the complementary function of myth and ritual in expressing the theme of immortality by considering the name
Ēlúsion. We are all familiar with the famous passage in *Od.*
4.561-569 where this name designates a special place of immortalization for heroes, and indeed the concept of Eylsium
has become a permanent fixture of Western Civilization. But
we seldom hear of what ancient commentators on Greek religion
have to say about *ēlúsion* as a plain noun. In the

Alexandrian lexicographical tradition (Hesychius s.v.
'Ηλύσιον), the word is glossed as κεκεραυνωμένον χωρίον ἤ
πεδίον, "a place or field that has been struck by the thunderbolt," with this added remark: καλεῖται δὲ καὶ ἐνηλύσια,
"and it is also called *enēlúsia*." As Walter Burkert points
out,[60] this definition is confirmed by the testimony of
Polemon (*fr.* 5 Tresp), who explains that *enēlúsion* is a place
made sacred by virtue of having been struck by the thunderbolt; also, the adjective *enēlúsios* is attested in Aeschylus
fr. 17 N (=263 M) as an epithet of the hero Capaneus, who was
struck dead by the thunderbolt of Zeus. We may compare the
semantic relationship of *enēlúsios/enēlúsion* with that of
hierós/hierón, 'sacred'/'sacred place'. Moreover, the body
of the thunderstruck Capaneus is described as *hieró-*, 'sacred', in Euripides, *Suppliants* 935.[61]

Besides *Ēlúsion*, there is also another example of a form
which serves to designate both a place of immortalization on
the level of myth and a cult-site on the level of ritual. In
Hesiod, *Works and Days* 171, we hear of a place called *Makárōn
nêsoi*, 'Isles of the Blessed', where heroes who fought in the
Theban and Trojan wars are immortalized after death (167ff.).
But there is also a tradition that the name *Makárōn nêsos*,
'Isle of the Blessed', was actually applied to the old acrop-
olis of Thebes, the Cadmeion; specifically, the name desig-
nated the sacred precinct where Semele, the mother of
Dionysus, had been struck dead by the thunderbolt of Zeus
(Parmenides ap. Suda and ap. Photius, s.v. Μακάρων νῆσος;
Tzetzes ad Lycophron 1194, 1204).[62]

As we return to take one last look at the corpse of
Sarpedon, it is appropriate to note that the *Iliad* contains
other indications of his impending immortalization besides
the verb *tarkhúō* at 16.456=674. Each of these indications

would require a discussion that goes beyond the scope of this presentation, and I will content myself with merely listing them as signposts for future elaboration:

¶ Apollo bathes the body of Sarpedon in a river (16.669 and 679).[63]

¶ Apollo anoints the body of Sarpedon with *ambrosíē*, 'ambrosia'[64] (16.670 and 680) and clothes it with vestments that are *ámbrota*, 'immortalizing' (ibid.).[65]

¶ The name *Sarpedon* applies not only to the hero but also to various places associated with the mythological theme of abduction by winds or by bird-like harpies.[66] This theme is expressed by way of various forms containing the verb-root *harp-*, 'snatch' (as in *hárpuia*, 'harpy', and *harpázō*, 'snatch'), which may be formally connected with the *sarp-* of *Sarpēdōn*.[67] Emily Vermeule remarks: "It is not too surprising that Homer makes Sarpedon the subject of the only big snatch in the *Iliad*, though he transformed the carriers from lady birds to Sleep and Death, to match more familiar configurations of epic mortality.[68]

¶ The snatching of Sarpedon's body by *Húpnos*, 'Sleep', and *Thánatos*, 'Death' (16.454, 672, 682), can be correlated with the manner in which the hero faints and dies. As in the case of other Homeric heroes, Sarpedon loses his *psūkhḗ* when he dies (16.453) as also earlier when he falls into a swoon from a terrible wound (5.696). Nowhere in Homeric poetry, however, is a hero ever described as regaining his *psūkhḗ* when he is revived from a swoon. This rigorous stricture in Homeric diction implies that the reintegration of the *psūkhḗ* with the body is understood as immortalization, the overt expression of which is programmatically avoided in the *Iliad* and *Odyssey*. Still, the manner in which Sarpedon recovers from his swoon seems to be a latent expression of this hero's

destiny of immortalization: Sarpedon is revived by a blast
from Boreas the North Wind (5.697). We note that it was to a
rock named Sarpedon that Boreas snatched Oreithuia away
(scholia ad Apollonius of Rhodes 1.211 = Pherecydes, *FGrH*
3.145).[69]

Coming now to the end of my inquiry into the death of
Sarpedon, I feel perhaps even more mystified by this strange
Anatolian Heracles than when I had started. There are so
many ramifications waiting to be explored that this presentation amounts to a set of questions rather than answers. But
this much at least is certain: Homeric Epos is a repository
of secrets about life and death--secrets that it will never
fully reveal. In the case of Sarpedon, his Anatolian heritage helps the *comparatiste* get a glimpse behind the veil of
Homeric restraint--and the secrets are almost given away.

NOTES

1. Cf. D. L. Page, *History and the Homeric Iliad* (Berkeley and
   Los Angeles: University of California Press, 1959).

2. A. M. Snodgrass, *The Dark Age of Greece: An Archaeological
   Survey of the Eleventh to the Eight Centuries* (Edinburgh:
   Edinburgh University Press, 1971), pp. 421, 435.

3. Ibid.

4. Cf. Gregory Nagy, *The Best of the Achaeans: Concepts of
   The Hero in Archaic Greek Poetry* (Baltimore and London:
   The Johns Hopkins University Press), pp. 115-117.

5. Erwin Rohde, *Psyche: Seelencult und Unsterblichkeitsglaube
   der Griechen*, 2nd ed. (Freiburg i. B., Leipzig, and
   Tübingen: J. C. B. Mohr, 1898), vol. 1, pp. 125-127.
   Translated by W. B. Hillis (London and New York: Kegan

Paul and Harcourt, Brace, 1925).   Translation reissued in 1966 (New York: Harper and Row).

6. Rohde, passim.

7. Snodgrass, pp. 190-193.

8. Cf. J. N. Coldstream, "Hero-Cults in the Age of Homer," *JHS* 96 (1976), 8-17.

9. Snodgrass, pp. 398-399.   Cf. also his paper "The Origins of the Greek Hero-Cults," presented at the Convegno internazionale sulla ideologia funeraria nel mondo antico, Naples and Ischia 6-10 December 1977, sponsored by the Istituto Universitario Orientale (Naples) and the Centre de Recherches Comparées sur les sociétés anciennes (Paris).

10. Rohde, vol. 1, pp. 108-110.

11. Cf. A. Brelich, *Gli eroi greci* (Rome: Ed. dell'Ateneo, 1958), p. 144, note 202, and M. Alexiou, *The Ritual Lament in Greek Tradition* (Cambridge: Cambridge University Press, 1974), p. 19.

12. Cf. again Snodgrass, pp. 398-399.

13. Rohde, vol. 1, pp. 184-189.

14. For a sensible critique: R. K. Hack, "Homer and the Cult of Heroes," *TAPhA* 60 (1929), 57-74.

15. Rohde, vol. 1, pp. 14-22.

16. See Nagy, *The Best of the Achaeans*, pp. 69-117.

17. The definitive edition is H. Otten, *Hethitische Totenrituale* (Berlin: Akademie, 1958).

18. See L. Christmann-Franck, "Le Rituel des funérailles royales hittites," *RHA* 29 (1971), 61-111, esp. 61-64.   Cf. also M. Vieyra, "Ciel et enfers hittites," *Revue d'Assyriologie* 59 (1965), 127-130 and Gregory Nagy, "Six Studies of Sacral Vocabulary Relating to the Fireplace" *HSPh* 78 (1974), 71-106.   The article by Christmann-Franck is also valuable for providing a full translation of the

Hittite funerary texts.

19. I merely note here *en passant* one remarkable correspondence between the Indic ideology of death and the Iliadic
references to the death of Patroclus; for a fuller presentation, see G. Nagy, "Patroklos, Concepts of Afterlife, and
the Indic Triple Fire," *Arethusa* 13 (1980), 161-195. In
the *Atharva-Veda*, we see that there are two elements which
are separated from the body after death and which are destined for immortalization: they are called *ásu-* and *mánas-*
(*Atharva-Veda* 1.9.3; 5.30.1; 8.1.1, 7, 15; 8.2.3, 26; see
H. Oldenberg, *Die Religion des Veda*, 2d ed. [Stuttgart and
Berlin: J. G. Cotta, 1917], pp. 523ff., esp. p. 528).
Now *mánas-* is cognate with Greek *ménos* (see further in
Gregory Nagy, *Comparative Studies in Greek and Indic Meter*
[Cambridge, Massachusetts: Harvard University Press,
1974], pp. 266-269), which is used as a synonym of *psūkhḗ*
in Iliadic contexts where the life-force leaves the body
after death (e.g., 5.296). At 24.6, Achilles, is described as longing for what is missing in the dead
Patroclus, the hero's *ménos* *ēΰ*! Also, it may be that the
adjective *ēΰ* here is formally related to the Indic noun
ásu-, but further work is required on the precise morphology of *ásu-*. For an example of a striking correspondence
in detail between the Indic funerary rituals and the actual funeral of Patroclus, see Steven Lowenstam, *The Death
of Patroklos: A Study in Typology = Beiträge zur
Klassischen Philologie* 133 (Meisenheim am Glan: A. Hain,
1981). On Indic funerary rituals and ancestor-worship in
general, see W. Caland, *Die altindischen Todten- und
Bestattungsgebräuche* (Amsterdam: Müller, 1896) and
Altindischer Ahnencult (Leiden: E. J. Brill, 1893) respectively. On the indirect comparative evidence of

Iranian testimony about the practice of cremation, cf. G.
Nagy, "Six Studies," pp. 100-105. A synthesis of all the
comparative evidence from Greek, Hittite, and Indic
sources is presently being prepared by Leonard Muellner.

20. Cf. Manolis Andronikos, *Totenkult* = *Archaeologia Homerica*
    III W, ed. Friedrich Matz and Hans-Gunter Buchholz
    (Göttingen: Vandenhoek and Ruprecht, 1968), esp. p. 76.

21. N. Van Brock, "Substitution rituelle," *RHA* 65 (1959), 119.

22. Van Brock, 125-126.

23. See Fred W. Householder and Gregory Nagy, "Greek,"
    Current Trends in Linguistics, ed. Thomas A. Sebeok, vol.
    9 (The Hague: Mouton, 1972), pp. 774-76; also Dale S.
    Sinos, *Achilles, Patroklos and the Meaning of Philos* =
    Innsbrucker Beiträge zur Sprachwissenschaft 29 (Innsbruck:
    Institut für Sprachwissenschaft der Universität Innsbruck,
    1980) and Lowenstam, *The Death of Patroklos*. More at note
    44 below.

24. Wolfgang Schadewalt, *Von Homers Welt und Werk*, 4th ed.
    (Stuttgart: R. F. Koehler, 1965), pp. 155-202.

25. M. E. Clark and William D. E. Coulsen, "Memnon and
    Sarpedon," *MH* 35 (1978), 65-73.

26. Cf. Adam Parry, ed., *The Making of Homeric Verse: The
    Collected Papers of Milman Parry* (Oxford: Clarendon Press,
    1971) and Albert B. Lord, *The Singer of Tales* (Cambridge,
    Massachusetts: Harvard University Press, 1960).

27. Lord, *Singer*, p. 29.

28. E. Laroche, "Etudes de vocabulaire VII," *RHA* 63 (1958),
    98-99; A. Heubeck, *Lydiaka: Untersuchungen zu Schrift,
    Sprache und Götternamen der Lyder* (Erlangen:
    Universitätsbund Erlangen, 1959), pp. 32-35.

29. Laroche and Heubeck; cf. Calvert Watkins, "God," in
    Gedenkschrift für Hermann Güntert, eds. M. Mayrhofer,

W. Meid, B. Schlerath, and R. Schmitt (Innsbruck, 1974),
p. 107, and Gregory Nagy, "Perkūnas and Perunu," id.,
p. 119.

30. Laroche, pp. 90-96.

31. Laroche, p. 96.

32. Pierre Chantraine, *Dictionnaire étymologique de la langue grecque*, I/II/III/IV.1/IV.2 (Paris: Klincksieck, 1968/ 1970/1974/1977/1980, p. 1095.

33. Chantraine, ibid.; Paul Kretschmer, "Die Stellung der lykischen Sprache," *Glotta* 28 (1940), 103-104.

34. See Otten (above, note 17), pp. 119-120.

35. For the semantics of *dēmos* as 'district', see Chantraine, pp. 273-274. By extension, the word comes to mean 'people from the district' (cf., e.g., *Od.* 7.11).

36. *Prose*: cf. the use of *tīmḗ* in Herodotus 1.118.2 (cult of god) and 1.168 (cult of hero); also the use of *tīmáō* in 1.90.2, 2.50.3, 2.75.4, 5.67.4-5. *Poetry:* cf. the use of *tīmḗ* in the *Hymn to Demeter* 311-312, where the theme of the gods' getting "honors" is explicitly correlated with the observance of their general cults by mortals (also lines 353, 366-369); for commentary, see N. J. Richardson's edition of *The Homeric Hymn to Demeter* (Oxford: Clarendon Press, 1974), pp. 260-261. For more evidence from poetry, see J. Rudhardt, "Les Mythes grecs relatifs à l'instauration du sacrifice," *MH* 27 (1970), 6-7. See also in general Rohde, vol. 1, p. 99, note 1.

37. See Kretschmer, p. 104 on the later literary and epigraphical evidence for the local cult of Sarpedon and Glaucus as heroes in Lycia. In Lycian Xanthus, there is also epigraphical evidence for a *dēmos*, 'deme', named *Sarpēdónios* (Kretschmer, ibid.).

38. Andronikos, pp. 114-121.

214   *Gregory Nagy*

39. Rohde, vol. 1, pp. 91-110.

40. I have attempted such a review in Nagy, *The Best of the Achaeans*, pp. 151-173.

41. Cf. Emile Benveniste, *Le Vocabulaire des institutions in-do-européennes*, I. *Economie, parenté, société*. II. *Pouvoir, droit, religion* (Paris: Les Editions de Minuit, 1969), vol. 2, pp. 43-50 (= *Indo-European Language and Society*, trans. E. Palmer [London and Coral Gables, Florida: University of Miami Press, 1973]).

42. Again I cite Nagy, *The Best of the Achaeans*, pp. 118-150.

43. The use of *therapeuein*, 'be a *therápōn* [=minister]', may have deeper significance. As my former student Dale Sinos has shown (see above, note 23), the *therápōn* in Homeric narrative is an inferior look-alike who can function as an equal of his superior look-alike and thus be invulnerable-- *so long as he serves him*. Once he leaves his superior counterpart and acts on his own, however, the *therápōn* loses his invulnerability and dies, thus fulfilling his function as ritual substitute.

44. On the semantics of *áphthito-*, 'unfailing, everlasting', see Nagy, *Comparative Studies*, pp. 229ff.

45. Cf. the commentary by Richardson, pp. 245-248.

46. I offer a fuller discussion in Nagy, *The Best of the Achaeans*, pp. 181-182. In Greek vase-inscriptions, the form ΔΕΜΟΦΑΟΝ is actually attested: for documentation and other variant forms, see Richardson, pp. 236-237.

47. Nagy, *Comparative Studies*, pp. 244-261.

48. See Walter Burkert, *Griechische Religion der archäischen und Klassischen Epoche* (Stuttgart: W. Kahlhammer, 1977), pp. 299, 315.

49. On the practice of *trapezṓmata*, see D. Gill, "Trapezomata, A Neglected Aspect of Greek Sacrifice," *HThR* 67 (1974),

117-137. Sarpedon's royal diet of mutton (12.319) may be correlated with recent archaeological discoveries at Eretria showing that sheep are the usual victims sacrificed to heroes (see Theodora Hadzisteliou Price, "Hero-Cult and Homer," *Historia* 22 (1973), 136).

50. On the *témenos* as a sacred precinct, see Burkert, *Griechische Religion*, pp. 142-146; on the precincts of Pelops and Pyrrhus, see Burkert, *Homo Necans: Interpretationen altgriechischer Opferriten* (Berlin: de Gruyter, 1972), pp. 111-117 and 134-137 respectively.

51. This interpretation can be extended to the only other Homeric attestation of *tarkhúō* besides *Il.* 16.456-674, at *Il.* 8.85. The dead body in this case is that of the hypothetical hero who answer Hector's challenge to fight "the best of the Achaeans" (see 7.50) in one-to-one combat (7.67-91). Elsewhere I argue that the words of Hector ironically apply to Achilles himself (Nagy, *The Best of the Achaeans*, pp. 26-41), and that Achilles himself is destined for personal immortalization in alternative epic traditions that are implicitly recognized by the *Iliad* (*The Best of the Achaeans*, pp. 174-210 and 317-347).

52. P. Thieme, *Nektar/Ambrosia/Hades: Studien zur indogermanischen Wortkunde und Religionsgeschichte = Berichte über die Verhandlungen der Sächsischen Akademie der Wissenschaften zu Leipzig, Philologisch-historische Klasse* (Berlin: Akad. Verl., 1952). Reprinted in R. Schmitt, ed., *Indogermanische Dichtersprache* (Darmstadt: Wiss. Buchges., 1968), pp. 102-153; see also R. Schmitt, *Dichtung und Dichtersprache in indogermanischer Zeit* (Wiesbaden: Otto Harrassowitz, 1967), pp. 186-192. The objections raised against this etymology have been convincingly refuted by Schmitt, "Nektar--und kein Ende,"

Gedenkschrift für Hermann Güntert, eds. M. Mayrhofer, W.
Meid, B. Schlerath, and R. Schmitt (Innsbruck, 1974), pp.
155–163.

53. Schmitt, *Dichtung*, p. 190.

54. See Schmitt, *Dichtung*, pp. 190–191; cf. Householder and
Nagy, "Greek" (above, note 23), pp. 771–772. On Indo-
European *Dichtersprache* in general, I cite the entirety
of Schmitt, *Dichtung*.

55. Chantraine, *Dictionnaire*, p. 1094, allows for the possibility that the Greek word *tárikhos*, 'smoked fish', is a
related borrowing. In Herodotus 9.120, the word is applied to the corpse of the hero Protesilaus, endowed with
supernatural powers!

56. On *Tarḫunt-* and the thunderbolt, see Laroche, p. 95; cf.
Nagy, "Perkūnas," p. 119.

57. Cf. the contexts assembled by Laroche, pp. 90–91.

58. In the Pindaric narrative, Semele's abode of immortality
is Olympus itself. See also Diodorus Siculus 5.52,
Charax, *FGrH* 103.14, etc.

59. Cf. Rohde, vol. 1, pp. 320–322.

60. Burkert, "Elysion," *Glotta* 39 (1961), 208–213.

61. Cf. also the testimony of the Thurian gold leaves at
A1.4, A2.5, A3.5 (Günter Zuntz, *Persephone: Three Essays
on Religion and Thought in Magna Graecia* [Oxford:
Clarendon Press, 1971], pp. 301–305), where the persona
of the dead man declares in each instance that his immortalization was preceded by death from the thunderbolt!

62. Cf. Burkert, "Elysion," p. 212., note 2.

63. Cf. the "baths of Oceanus" at *Il.* 18.489 = *Od.* 5.275 as
discussed in G. Nagy, "Phaethon, Sappho's Phaon, and the
White Rock of Leukas," *HSPh* 77 (1973), 148–172, esp. 169.
In the case of *Il.* 16.669 and 679 it is possible that

these verses referred originally to the local waters of
the Lycian river Xanthus (cf. *Il*. 2.877, 5.479, 6.172).

64. Note that *ambrosíē* is used in Homeric diction as a synonym of *néktar*; in other words, they do not seem to be
specialized always as food and drink respectively (see
Schmitt, "Nektar" [above, note 52], p. 158).

65. On the use of *ámbroto-* and its derivatives to designate
the notion of 'immortalizing' as well as 'immortal', see
Thieme, *Ambrosia* (above, note 52).

66. See Emily D. T. Vermeule, *Aspects of Death in Early Greek
Art and Poetry* (Berkeley and Los Angeles: University of
California Press, 1979), p. 242, note 36, and p. 248, note
36, on the Harpy Tomb of Xanthus. On the theme of death/im-
mortalization in the form of abduction by winds, see Nagy,
The Best of the Achaeans, pp. 190-203.

67. On the Morphology of *-édōn*, see Ernst Risch, *Wortbildung
der homerischen Sprache*, 2d ed. (Berlin: de Gruyter,
1974), p. 61.

68. Vermeule, p. 169.

69. Cf. Vermeule, p. 242, note 36.

The Economic Man

James M. Redfield

I. ON INTERPRETATION

Those who have written on Homer and History have usually tak-
en the epic at its word, and have discussed the reality of
the heroes. Had we been present, however, at the first performances of these monumental compositions we would have been
made aware of their presence in history in a different sense.
A poem is a communication, and a successful communication engages and thus characterizes its audience; it is something
the audience wants to hear, understands, and finds significant. In this sense the *Odyssey* is evidence for life in the
late eighth century B.C.

Stories are about better and worse, values are in play,
and the story-teller's communication is founded on a shared
normative culture, an ethical complicity with his audience.
We can respond to Homer only if Odysseus is to us admirable,
while Antinous is not; we must find the death of Dolon ig-
noble, while pathetic. A story is meaningful because it
tests comprehensible motivations against relevant consequences; the characters make choices, and enjoy or suffer the
result. Our response is an evaluation; a story need not have
a moral, but it must be shaped by a morality. If we come un-
instructed to culturally alien narrative--to Sanskrit drama,
for instance, or the Noh--we may well find the story opaque.
Conversely, to understand any story is to participate imagi-
natively in the culture of its intended audience.

If values were unambiguous, our lives would be as undra-
matic as those of the social insects, and culture would find
room for at most one story. In fact life is interesting and

drama is possible because culture presents us, not with a coherent set of instructions, but with a structured problematic, a set of dilemmas and hard choices. We cannot be all at once successful men of affairs, creatures of romantic spontaneity, and utterly committed saints, yet all of these are admired. When they appear together in a story we can see that each in his own way acts well. Stories are not so much about good against evil as about good against good, and about intelligible disputes concerning the location of the lesser evil. It is often appropriate to take sides with the hero, but even the most perfect villain is one whose motives we reject, and therefore recognize, and therefore find at some level within ourselves.

Stories, in other words, dramatize values; each story is a kind of thought-experiment which explores the problematic of a culture. As the culture is complex it gives rise to many heroes and many stories. From this point of view the *Iliad* and the *Odyssey*--and for that matter the *Works and Days*--can be thought of as essentially contemporary. These poems elaborate contrasting perspectives on a common set of problems. Odysseus refuses an immortality for which Achilles has a tragic longing. Eumaeus (as it were) takes center stage in the *Works and Days* and makes a virtue of his limited aspirations. Everywhere we find dramatized in different forms the conflicting claims of household and community, a contradictory longing for security and pride in the taking of risk, a tension between the need for functioning authority and the assertion by the individual of his equal dignity. These conflicts characterize the culture which nourished the epics.[1]

The Homeric world, the world inhabited by the heroes, is not and has not been anywhere. It is an amalgam of elements from various periods and is to some extent purely imaginary.

Nevertheless as an imaginary history it places its audience
in history. Everywhere in epic we are told that the heroic
age was earlier, and different. Yet even this point has different meanings in different poems. The *Iliad* is a retro-
spective poem; it tells of the death of heroes and the fall
of cities, and ends in funerals and continuing war. The
Odyssey looks back on an heroic age already ended, and also
looks forward; its hero survives and leaves an heir, and it
ends with a kind of wedding and a patched-up peace. The
Iliad looks at the heroic world *per se*; the *Odyssey* links
that world with the post-heroic.

A sign of the differences between these worlds may be
found in the relations of men and gods. Long ago or far
away, we are told, men and gods are or were on equal terms.
At the ends of the earth, among the Ethiopians, gods feast
publicly with men (*Od.* 1.26; cf. *Il.* 1.423); in previous
times, says Alcinous, the gods came in this way to the feasts
of the Phaeacians (*Od.* 7.199-206) as they came to the wedding
of Peleus and Thetis (*Il.* 24.62-63). Within the world of the
Iliad proper, however, the gods are less open. They appear
to only one hero at a time, and when they appear in public
they are invisible or disguised to all but one. When they
speak to the crowd on the battlefield it is as disembodied
voices or disguised presences.

In the *Odyssey* the gods are still farther away. Athena
appears to mankind, but in dreams or in disguise; she reveals
her identity to Nestor only by the manner of her departure
(*Od.* 3.371-379). In another case Athena's intervention is a
matter of deduction (4.655-656). Only to Odysseus (and in a
modified sense to Telemachus, since her appearance to him
[15.6-42], while like a dream, is not a dream) does she appear in her own person. Odysseus is thus marked as a hero in
a world growing unheroic.

In the *Iliad* the gods help the heroes with their own hands;
they strike a man from behind (*Il.* 16.790-793), shift the
path of an arrow (4.127-140), pick up their favorites and
move them out of danger (3.380-382, 5.311-317). In the
Odyssey the gods work through the means of nature, as when
Poseidon sends a storm, or through the minds of men, by implanting an idea or changing a character's appearance to
others. (An exception is Athena's final epiphany--24.531-32.)
When Athena comes to the slaying disguised as Mentor she
promises to fight, but does no fighting; she turns herself into
a bird and sits in the rafters, not giving victory, but testing the valor of the combatants (22.236-240). Odysseus has
Athena's help on Ithaca, as he had it at Troy, but it seems
less sure, less direct.

As Odysseus moves from Troy to Ithaca, in fact, he moves
into a world much like that of the poet's audience. In that
world the gods were surely always invisible, their interven-
tions always uncertainly recognized, screened behind the
means of nature. Odysseus enters a world grown demystified.
If he survives as a hero in this world it is because his own
kind of heroism is peculiarly suited to it. He can dispense
with magic armor, immortal horses, and a titan-mother to whom
even Zeus is obligated; he can carry out his action with ordinary human means. His adversaries on Ithaca are dangerous,
not because of their heroic stature, but for the banal reason
that they are numerous (16.241-255). Odysseus speaks of the
help of the gods (16.259-265) but he finds his really useful
allies within his own household.

The difference between the *Iliad* and the *Odyssey* can also
be seen in the differences of the killings. In the *Iliad*
killing takes place in the open, in the space between communities, a marginal environment often compared in the similes

to the wild country where hunters meet wild beasts. In the *Odyssey* killing takes place within the community, and indoors. Several times in the poem we hear of the unheroic death of Agamemnon, killed by his wife's lover at a dinner party "like an ox at the manger" (4.535=11.411). Similarly (and conversely) Odysseus kills his wife's suitors at a dinner party, and they rush about like cattle stung by the gad-fly (22.299-301). The hunter has become a butcher.

We need not, as I say, ascribe the differences between the poems to cultural change between the moments of their composition; it is in fact impossible to place them far enough apart in time to allow for so massive a change. Rather the two poems give us, in the mirror of heroic story, two different integrations drawn from a common stock of cultural themes, which continued. Heroic values did not end with the *Iliad*; when Socrates wants to explain why he is helpless before the imperatives of his own ethic he can do no better than to compare himself to Achilles (*Apology* 28c-d). The post-heroic Odysseus, paradoxically, was less well received by later tradition; by the fifth century his special virtues of craft and patient indirection were often reconceived as vices, and he appears, most notably in the *Philoctetes*, as an unprincipled manipulator. As civil society grew more settled, Odysseus' talents perhaps seemed less necessary, and more dangerous. The Odysseus of the *Odyssey* justifies himself by his success as the refounder of his own house; he is ruthless, practical, inventive, self-seeking, and utterly committed to a few close loyalties. Such a man would surely have found ample play for his talents in the first great age of Greek entrepreneurial expansion, which was also the moment of the composition of the *Odyssey*.

In the last third of the eighth century the Greeks took
effective if still tentative control of the east coast of
Sicily and of Italy as far north as Taras, and of the bay of
Naples. This explosive event, which was the foundation of
later Greek development, must also be evidence of earlier
development, of new material resources, a new cultural morale
and social effectiveness in the Greek homeland. Such development will have been uneven; the most progressive states
were evidently the Corinthian and Euboean oligarchies, with
Miletus and some of the islands close behind. But as the
transformation of Greece proved itself by its success it
gradually became pervasive.

The textbook label for this transformation is "The Rise of
the City-State." As the city-state was an inclusive form of
life its rise implies correlative changes on many levels. On
the political level it involves the shift from a hierarchy
centered on the king to oligarchic institutions relying on
the rotation of office among a plurality of full citizens.
On the social level it involves the creation of a free peas-
antry and the simultaneous spread of chattel slavery, with
the sharpening of older class stratifications into class conflict. On the level of juridical and economic institutions
it involves the emergence of private alienable property in
land, of enforceable contracts, and an international market
in agricultural commodities. Furthermore, this was an age of
economic development, of capital accumulation and public in-
vestment, what Thucydides calls *periousia*. The rapid development of the western colonies can itself be seen as an effective deployment of capital by individuals and states.

To the culture-historian economic development appears as
an aspect of a general transformation; it happens not of itself, but as persons come to see new kinds of behavior as

possible, desirable, and admirable. Implicit in every organization of economic life is a specific economic ethic. I
here propose to discuss the *Odyssey* as a document dramatizing
the progressive economic ethic of late eighth-century Greece.

II. THE ECONOMIC ETHIC

The economy, from one point of view, is the sphere of material
life, of our interaction with nature. Our struggle to survive, however, gives rise to specifically economic activity
only when it becomes problematic to ourselves. Breathing and
dreaming both have survival value, but as they take place un-
reflectingly, neither is economized. If all activity were
similarly instinctual or effortless, as in Eden or the Reign
of Cronos, mankind would have no economic life. Thus many
traditions see economic activity as the mark of our fallen
condition, between god and beast.

It follows that the economic sphere comes into existence
because we both are and are not part of nature, and therefore
contend with nature as an adversary. Economic goods are
those we wring from nature at the cost of our labor. Labor,
then, is activity negatively evaluated as the necessary means
to a desired end. Any activity--thinking, prayer, making
love--may at certain moments become laborious in this sense.
On the other hand, any activity may be undertaken for its own
sake, for fun, for therapy, as an act of devotion. Tolstoy
reaping with the peasants does what the peasants do, but for
him the work has a different meaning--although the peasants
also feel pride in their strength and skill, and the satis-
faction of doing what is proper. Economic motives are always
mixed with non-economic. The economic measure of labor, furthermore, is not the effort expended, but the negative evaluation of the activity as a necessary means. The economy,

from this point of view, is not the sphere of material life
(with which it certainly overlaps) but rather the sphere of
economic motives, of this kind of evaluation.

Labor thus becomes a measure of value. We judge the value
of the thing to us by what we are willing to undergo to obtain it. This way of thinking gives rise to others--for instance, to thought about efficiency. We seek to minimize
labor--by skill, for instance. We also try to get others to
do our labor for us; thus the idea of labor gives rise to the
idea of dominion, and the economy generates a class structure.

Here again economic and non-economic motives are mixed.
Skill may be valued for its own sake, so that production becomes a display of virtuosity, and shades into fine art. Dominion may be prized for the honor it confers, so that the
labor of others, instead of being a means of production, becomes for us a kind of consumer good. The division of labor
may be related to status, so that certain tasks are beneath
the dignity of certain persons. In all these ways efficiency
is restricted by other kinds of evaluation.

Yet it remains true that labor is the primary measure of
value, for only in labor, where the activity is acceptable
but negatively evaluated, can the means and the end be measured against one another. Thus it happens that while labor
is negative, the capacity to labor is positively evaluated.
There is an ethic of labor; it is a mark of seriousness, maturity, and discipline that a man is willing to undertake the
necessary means.

The ethic of labor is complemented by the ethic of saving.
The economic stock exists because we have held ourselves back
from consuming all commodities immediately. Thus consumption,
like production, enters the economic sphere only to the degree that it is negatively evaluated and minimized. A man who

is willing to save receives (conversely) a positive evaluation; he has subjected his appetites to reason. By labor we overcome the nature outside us; by saving we overcome the nature within us.

"Economic" thus names a specific type of deliberation, which concerns itself with the problem of the necessary means. Because these means are always to be minimized—in the sense that we labor and save as little as possible—economic problems are problems of allocation. Allocation implies scarcity, and also the ethical neutrality of the means; we shall feel free to allocate them freely only if they are not of value in themselves, but only as means. The economic ethic is thus not an ethic of ultimate commitments, but of managerial rationality; this is not a sphere in which the purpose or meaning of life can be determined, but rather where the trade-offs between various options are rather cooly assessed. Economic thinking does not inquire into values; it estimates the cost of achieving values which it receives as a given, labeled as "demand."

Nor are these values found in nature, even though economic activity copes with nature. The song says: "Since man is only human, he must eat before he can think." However, it is also true that being human he must think before he can eat, think not only how to eat but what to eat; he will eat only what he thinks he ought to eat. Thus, although we confront nature, our economics is in the service of culture, and is itself cultural.[2] Each culture has its own view of basic human needs, and each has its own list of those means which are sufficiently neutral to be rationally allocated.

Nevertheless it is in the nature of mankind to be rational and to strive, at least some of the time, for an efficient allocation of some of the means available. While the economy

is a different problem in every culture, it is always some
kind of a problem. Therefore every culture has its own kind
of economic thought, and in its own way institutionalizes economic life. In very simple societies the institutionaliza-
tion may not go beyond the contrast between working day and
a restful evening; in more complex societies more complex
patterns emerge.

Different kinds of people are at home in different set-
tings. Some will be happier collecting grubs, others telling
stories. Some find happiness in thinking about money, others
in ignoring it. It is with economics as with religion--for
Clifford Geertz has reminded us that, while religion is a
"culture universal," it is by no means true that religion is
of equal interest to all.[3] On the contrary: in any culture
there will be some primarily concerned with religious questions, and many profoundly uninterested. Similarly with economics; a disregard of such questions may actually be one of
the characteristics of a specific social role: the devoted
scholar, the childlike wife, the soldier in combat, the fool
of God. All these require others to look after them. If any
society is to function, there must be some who, as we say, are
"minding the store." Thus society generates some for whom
economic questions are the most interesting questions. Such
a one may well be called the "economic man."

III. ODYSSEUS' LABORS
If we could pass through some Alice's Looking Glass into the
imaginary world of the epics and begin an ethnographic study
of their economics, we would surely make Odysseus our chief
informant. He seems the person in Homer most at home with
this aspect of life. Already in the *Iliad* he is notable for
his cool rationality, as in the passage (11.401-410) where he

considers becoming a coward, but decides that on the whole it is not for him. Odysseus does a kind of cost-benefit analysis of everything, weighing present expenditure against hoped-for utilities. It is miserable to spend even one month from home, he tells the troops, and for them it is already the ninth year, "but all the same it is disgraceful to stay long and come home empty" (2.297-298). Similarly in the *Odyssey* he tells Alcinous that however eager he may be to get home, he would stay another year to come home rich (11.355-361). We may also think of his false but plausible tale of himself lingering among the Thesprotians, collecting gifts that would "feed the tenth generation" (14.325=19.294).

Cedric Whitman says that Odysseus is a master of the delayed response, the long way round.[4] Much of his well-known craft is a matter of taking thought for the necessary means and the claims of material life. Thus in the *Iliad* he reads Achilles two lectures on the necessity of eating before battle (19.155-170, 216-232). He strikes a related note in the *Odyssey* when asked if he is a god:

Alcinous, that is the wrong question. I'm not
Like to the immortals, those that keep the heavens,
In frame or stature, but like to mortals who die.
Whomsoever you know most heavily burdened with grief
Among men, to theirs I would compare my pains,
And greater still the evils I could tell you--
So many I've struggled through by the will of the gods.
Just let me take my meal, although I've had troubles.
There is nothing more like a dog than the hateful
    belly;
By force it calls me to remember it
Worn though I am, for all my sorrow at heart.
So I keep sorrow at heart, but always it

Calls me to eat and drink; it puts out of my mind
All my sorrows, and orders me to fill it.

7.208-221

This is materialism of the Brechtian sort: "Erst kommt
das Fressen, dann kommt die Moral." Odysseus' version is:
"First feeding, then grieving." As so often, economic
thought is a matter of setting priorities. Odysseus speaks
of his own organic nature as an adversary whose overriding
claims must be respected. (See also 17.281-289.)

For Odysseus an essential element of nobility is the willingness to measure up to the demands of reality. Nobody
promised him a rose garden; μετὰ καὶ τόδε τοῖσι γενέσθω, as
he says to Calypso and Eumaios (5.224=17.285). His action is
not so much achieved as endured; it is a matter of *aethloi*.

An *aethlos*, of course, is properly an event in the games.
The word is used once by Nestor in the *Odyssey* (3.262) and
once by the narrator of the *Iliad*--in the description of
Helen's web (3.126)--for the struggle around Troy. (Helen is
the prize of that contest.) Otherwise the word is used for
the labors of two heroes: Odysseus and Heracles. Both do
what must be done, and both have their eye on the prize.

There are other parallels: both are bowmen, both descend
into the underworld (*Od*. 11.623-624). But they also contrast.
Heracles labors in the service of another, and his prize is to
marry a goddess and live forever (*Od*. 11.602-604). Odysseus
labors for himself; he refuses immortal marriage with Calypso
and wins as his prize a quiet old age and peaceful death (*Od*.
23.281-284). He never tries to say why these things are
worth having; he says only ἀλλὰ καὶ ὣς ἐθέλω, "yet even so I
wish it" (*Od*. 5.219). Odysseus' house is a "second-rate palace," as Alan Wace says, "where the geese waddle about the
court littered with dung-heaps."[5] Odysseus wants what most

men already have: a family, a house, a city where he is at
home. We measure the value of these things by the extraordinary price he is willing to pay for them. The *Odyssey* displays to us in this way the extraordinary value of ordinary
things. In this sense the *Odyssey* is a poem about the labor
theory of value.

Odysseus' labors throughout are in the service of his
household, and this makes him an economic hero in another,
specifically Greek, sense. Within the *Odyssey* the secure
possession of an *oîkos* is the working definition of happi-
ness--as in Odysseus' prayers for the Phaeacians (7.146-52,
13.44-46). Odysseus' aim throughout is to recover and reconstruct his own *oîkos*. If he must reestablish himself as king
of Ithaca, this is because he can only in this way securely
regain his property. Odysseus' drive for possession--rather
than honor, fame, or power as primary aims--marks his engage-
ment in the problem of the necessary means, and his commitment to the economy as institutionalized by his society.

The *oîkos* is in Odysseus' (as in later Greek) society the
only functioning economic unit. It administers consumption,
and also production (of food and textiles), and also saving;
the surplus is held in household stores. The household joins
the material means with the social preconditions of livelihood; the household loyalties of husband and wife, parent and
child, master and servant, are seen as a mutual support system against a hostile world. The implicit ideal is that of
household autarky and autonomy; possession and inheritance
secure the honor of men and the sexual purity of women.

Yet Odysseus is also interested in public honor, fame and
power; he is no Hesiod, to live by the proverb: "Home is
best, since harm is out of doors" (*Works and Days* 365 = *Hymn
to Hermes* 36). The sort of household which is proper to an

Odysseus is necessarily involved in a complex fabric of relationships, both redistributive and reciprocal. The wealth of
the king's household is in a sense held on behalf of the community at large, and involves sacred and secular obligations
of entertainment and sacrifice. The king holds a *temenos* as
the gift of the *dēmos*; he has private relations with certain
clients and a public standing, a *geras*, enacted and adjudi-
cated in the *agorē*. Household self-sufficiency is modified
by the positive reciprocities involved in relations with
xenoi--and, at a deeper level, by marriage-exchange--and by
the negative reciprocities of the vendetta. At least one
human good--*kleos*, enduring fame--is absolutely unavailable
within the household. Thus the very proper stress placed by
M. I. Finley and others on the primacy of the household
should not lead us to ignore this other aspect.[6] There is, in
fact, in the *Odyssey* a persistent tension between the aspiration to household self-sufficiency and the recognition that
security and happiness are only possible in the context of a
wider community. This tension is finally enacted at the conclusion of the poem, where Odysseus' purification of his
household, while righteous, leads to an explosion of vendetta
made harmless only by divine intervention. We find already
in the *Odyssey*, in other words, a version of that tension between private and public which structures so much of later
Greek discourse--a tension which, as J.-P. Vernant has seen,
can be talked about in terms of Hestia and Hermes, or in
terms of a private sphere centering on women and marriage and
a public sphere centering on male solidarity and warfare.[7]
And this tension, like so many other aspects of the poem, must
have had its correlate in the early colonies, since they were
from the beginning founded on the distribution of property
and attracted settlers by offering private *klēroi*, while at

the same time they must have required an extraordinary solidarity to survive on a hostile frontier.

To this tension corresponds an ambiguous attitude toward labor in the literal sense of agricultural work. Insofar as labor involves servitude it is low; the lowest position of all is to be day-laborer to a man without a *klēros* (*Od.* 11.489-90).[8] But in itself agricultural labor can be admirable. When Odysseus, disguised as a beggar, is ironically offered a job hedging and ditching (or terracing, the Mediterranean equivalent) he reacts with an angry challenge: if only there could be a contest in reaping or plowing, so that he could outwork them all, or a war, so that he could outfight them all (18.356-386). He responds much as when challenged to the games in Phaeacia. Agricultural labor, like games and warfare, is a proper test of manhood, and as such is classless.[9]

In the *Odyssey*, in fact, culture is often quite literally gardening, and a master-symbol of the poem--of equal standing with Odysseus' scar and Penelope's bed--is Dolius' garden, where the old Laertes retires to solace himself by working the land. Odysseus finds that everything in this garden bears the marks of *komidē*, "close care and attention," except the old man himself (24.244-255). The implicit contrast is with Alcinous' garden, where the same fruits grow by magic; here, in the real world, the garden is maintained only by constant labor. And such labor is a form of heroism. We can here, I think, glimpse the ethical basis of Greek colonization, which from the beginning involved the agricultural exploitation of the *chōra*, most often by Greek smallholders, and was thus in contrast to Phoenician colonization, which until the fifth century was a matter of outposts and emporia, focused on the search for metals. So when Odysseus describes

the island offshore from the Cyclops (this island could well
be Pitheccousa, the earliest of the western colonies) he describes it with a farmer's eye: its meadows, possible vine-
yards, and arable land with deep topsoil (9.116-151).

Exchange of commodities, by contrast, is not in the poem
a source of livelihood. It is rather a form of social interaction, and takes the positive and negative forms of gift-
giving and stealing, whereby we enact and reinforce our relations with friends and enemies. The commodities exchanged
as gifts are usually not intended for consumption; they are
keimēlia, intended for display and future gift-giving. Commodities stolen include cattle and slaves, and these are in a
sense consumed, but raiding is itself a form of display, not
of rational accumulation. In his story of himself as a
Cretan bastard Odysseus says that he was a raider, unconcerned
for *oikōpheliē*, "the increase of the household. which nourishes lovely children" (14.223).

Trade, in fact, is deleted from the Homeric picture of the
heroic world; like fish-eating and iron weapons it is something Homer (and his audience) knew all about, but thought
unsuitable for heroes. This deletion is itself important evidence for late eighth-century values. Odysseus bristles to
be called a master of *prēktēres*, traders (8.162). Only the
Phoenicians trade; they are like gypsies, selling gee-gaws
and stealing babies.

However it is also true that Odysseus has a trader's mind.
In the Cretan lie already quoted there is an odd contradiction; after saying that raiding does nothing for *oikōpheliē*,
he then says that his spoil made his house increase, οἶκος
ὀφέλλετο, and he became impressive and respected among the
Cretans (14.233-234). Odysseus known that those who acquire
wealth can buy social status with it; this is the basic
bourgeois insight (cf. also 11.60-61).

Sometimes we see Odysseus inspecting the gift-giving system with the cool eye of the narrator of the *Iliad*, whose
comment on "bronze for gold" (*Il.* 6.234-236) caused Marcel
Mauss to assert that Homer did not understand heroes.[10]
Odysseus exploits the system by taking gifts from Phaeacia,
where he will never have to reciprocate. Furthermore, he
makes it clear that it is the value of the gift, not the
thought that counts. No wonder Odysseus takes so readily to
the role of beggar. Such unreciprocated reception of gifts
is really a form of begging, but on a heroic scale. The
clash of scale is represented on the language level by a
clash of formulae in Odysseus' story of himself among the
Thesprotians, where he says he will come home rich, κειμήλια
πολλὰ καὶ ἐσθλὰ / αἰτίζων ἀνὰ δῆμον (*Od.* 19.272-273). Here
the objects obtained are heroic riches, like those obtained
from the sack of a city (cf. *Il.* 9.330 with *Od.* 19.272), but
the phrase for the mode of acquisition is proper to begging
(cf. *Od.* 17.558 with *Od.* 19.273).

A man who can find peaceful entertainment and come home
rich is most of the time a trader; Odysseus' voyage is not a
trading voyage, but it works like one. In this sense trade
is a latent theme in the *Odyssey*, and this latency is suggested in a number of places, as when the disguised Athena
twice describes her own voyaging in language appropriate to
trade (*Od.* 1.183-184, 3.366-368). In Odysseus' description
of the island near the Cyclopes there is great praise of the
harbor; Odysseus clearly imagines living there as the Greeks
lived everywhere--as a seafaring farmer. The economic aspect
of this seafaring is not, however, discussed.

Here again we find in the *Odyssey* an ambiguity which continues in the later Greek economic ethic: there is a tenden-
cy to undervalue trade at the expense of agriculture, and yet

to trade far more than one admits. The later version is the oligarch or Athenian bourgeois who presents himself as a landed gentleman, although the greater part of his fortune might be invested in the carrying trade in agricultural commodities. So also Odysseus, although his journey is involuntary and he says he wants no more than to recover what is already his, does not fail to grasp his opportunities. As the sort of man he is, we think all the better of him for that.

IV. ODYSSEUS' ADVENTURES

The plot of the *Odyssey* is in its second half; the first part of the poem is all prelude. The scenes on Ithaca are an exposition of the problem which the plot of the poem will resolve. Otherwise the first half consists of two journeys. Odysseus begins on the far periphery; he makes his way back and on the way tells the story of where he has been. Telemachus makes his way to the center of Greek life and hears the stories of where others have been. Through these journeys and stories the poet gives us an extended account of the world; it is as if the first half of the poem tells us all we need to know in order to understand the second half.

Among these adventures the narrative of Odysseus has a privileged place, not only because it is the hero's own, and thus defines him twice, in the doing and in the telling,[11] but also because it sets against the human world another world. The world of the adventures, as Vidal-Naquet noticed, lacks agriculture and sacrifice, the cultural bonds between man and nature, man and god.[12] The gods never go there; while he is there Athena leaves Odysseus strictly alone (*Od.* 13.316-321). Helius is traditionally the god who sees everything (*Il.* 14.344-345), but when his cattle are killed he does not know it; a nymph has to go with a message (*Od.* 12.374-375).

Zeus is present, but only in the form of the weather (*Od.*
12.403-417). Only Hermes, crosser of boundaries, can visit
in his own person (as at *Od.* 10.275-308), but even he is a
rare and unexpected visitor; there are here no cities of men
"who would make sacrifice and choice hecatombs" (*Od.* 5.102).
Similarly there is no proper economics here; life is largely
or entirely without labor. Even the Laestrygonians, who appear to occupy a city with an *agorē* (*Od.* 10.114) have no
plowed fields, "works of men and oxen" (*Od.* 10.98)--and turn
out to be murderous cannibals.

The world of the adventures is a void populated by monsters. *Alkē*, the prowess of the warrior, is of no value here
(*Od.* 12.116-120), and those who perish receive neither funeral
nor *kleos*. They simply disappear, snatched by the *harpuiai*
(*Od.* 1.234-243, 5.306-312, 14.365-371).

Nevertheless this world has a structure, represented by
the variety of the adventures; no place here is fit for man
or god, but this does not mean they are all the same. I see
two patterns in the adventures. They are, first, grouped and
proportioned to form a satisfying whole; this pattern is a
little like sonata form. Two brief adventures are followed
by a long one, this last being introduced by an elaborated
description of landscape and incidents of hunting. The whole
is then repeated, two more short adventures again followed by
a long one, again introduced by elaborated landscape and
hunting. There is then a sort of free development, the
nekuia--which has a pattern of its own: three encounters,
catalogue, narrative break, three encounters, catalogue.
This unit is framed by the two visits to Circe. Finally
there is a sort of recapitulation consisting of adventures
foretold by Circe; this section concludes with an internal
repetition or coda. The very first adventure concludes, as
the last is introduced, with a storm.

Across this pattern runs another, based on strict alterna-
tion. Odysseus faces two kinds of dangers; he may be killed
before he gets home, or he may be induced to stop on the way.
He faces violence and temptation. The interplay of these two
patterns may be represented by the following diagram:

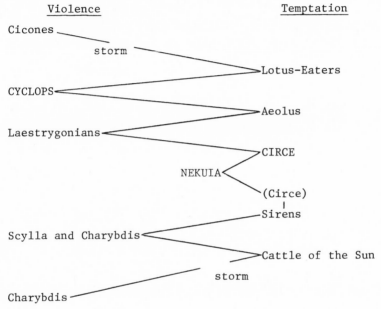

       Violence   Temptation

Cicones

         storm

                              Lotus-Eaters

CYCLOPS

                          Aeolus

Laestrygonians

                      CIRCE

             NEKUIA

                    (Circe)
                       |
                   Sirens

Scylla and Charybdis

                      Cattle of the Sun

              storm

Charybdis

On his travels Odysseus seeks the status of guest; he is
the victim, alternately, of hypo-entertainment and hyper-entertainment. In hypo-entertainment the stranger is treated
as a creature of another species, a beast or fish (cf. 10.124)
usable for food. This theme is introduced among the Cicones
(for combat, as we learn from the *Iliad*, is a modified form of
cannibalism), continues with the Cyclops and the Laestrygonian
cannibals, and concludes with Scylla, a carnivore whose proper diet is the traveller, and Charybdis, a whirlpool which
simply swallows everything.

To be eaten is to be incorporated into the nature of another. Hyper-entertainment, by contrast, threatens cultural

incorporation; the traveller is to be transformed by his host and so perfectly socialized that he can never leave. The transformation is accomplished by drugs--the lotus, the drugs of Circe (who is *polypharmakos*--10.276), the song of the sirens (the sirens do not eat their victims, but allow them to rot--12.46). In the case of the Cattle of the Sun and Aeolus, improper consumption prevents the travellers from leaving; while Aeolus tries to send them home Odysseus' men treat his winds as a consumable commodity, and their attempts to "consume" them bind them to their source.

The contrast between hypo- and hyper-entertainment is an aspect of the broader contrast between hypo-culture and hyper-culture. At one extreme stand the purely natural monsters, and next to them the Cyclopes, primitives who lack agriculture (9.108) and seafaring (9.126) and whose social organization consists of isolated families "unconcerned with one another" (9.115, cf. 188-189). The Cyclops' vessels are baskets and he sleeps on withes (9.219, 247, 427-428). He lives in a cave surrounded by a rough stone wall (9.184-185). He seems not to have the use of metal tools. At the opposite extreme is Aeolus, whose palace walls are made, not *with* bronze, but *of* bronze (10.3-4). The little society here is excessively intimate, and is in fact incestuous (10.5-7).

Both hypo-culture and hyper-culture are abundant, but differently. For the Cyclops abundance comes unlaboriously from a fertile nature (9.109-111); the Laestrygonians are similarly blessed (10.82-86). Goods here are simple but plentiful. The Cyclops is a milk-drinker, and while he has some kind of primitive wine (9.357-358), the civilized product of Ismarus tastes to him like nectar and ambrosia (9.359) and acts on him like a drug.

Aeolus, on the other hand, feasts endlessly without any territory at all; his floating island is a city in the sea. His abundant roast meats (10.10) must be supplied by magic. Circe (like Calypso) also lives in a magic household; both live in utter social isolation, yet both have servants (5.199, 10.348-351); both live in utterly wild territory, yet are supplied with human food.

I have written elsewhere of the *Iliad* as a poem which dramatizes the contradiction of nature and culture, a contradiction which is there seen to be tragic, which can be mediated only in thought and in poetry.[13] In the *Odyssey*, I think, culture is seen in contrast to the primitive and the decadent; in contrast to these two kinds of abundance, spontaneous or magical, stands a sober culture founded on a respect for the realities of scarcity. Culture is thus itself the mediating term, defined by contrast to the two negations of excess and defect. The cultural order is seen, not as a given, parallel with nature, but as a human construct, something man has made, could spoil, and might reconstruct.

This brings us back to the economic ethic. If we look at the contrast between violence and temptation from the point of view of Odysseus we shall not, I think, be utterly fanciful to see in it the contrast between labor and saving. Faced with temptation Odysseus must husband his resources, not consume, or not too much, or too soon. He must not go to bed with Circe until she has sworn an oath; otherwise he would have been castrated (cf. 10.296-301). Twice, with Aeolus and the Cattle of the Sun, disaster comes because he falls asleep, and because his men are greedy. The precondition of ultimate enjoyment, it seems, is the capacity to endure deprivation.

On the other side of the chart Odysseus is threatened by a violence to which mere counter-violence is an inappropriate response. He confronts overwhelming forces, and counter-force must be supplemented by agile planning and technique. With the Cicones the time comes to retreat (9.43-44). With Scylla he can only minimize his losses; similarly with the Laestrygonians Odysseus, when he hears his companions screaming for help, unhesitatingly cuts his cable and runs (10.121-132). Odysseus resists the temptation to kill the Cyclops (9.299-302). He survives because he knows the limits of his powers and is clever enough to use such forces as he has where they will be most useful. Uncultivated nature is a realm of forces which can be overcome only if they are respected.

If we now apply our diagram to the poem as a whole, we are immediately struck by an asymmetry. Except within the rigid frame of the adventures, the balance is not maintained; the *Odyssey* as a whole is mostly about the threat of hyper-culture. Telemachus journeys into hyper-cultural territory; Nestor suffers from hyper-piety and looks faintly ridiculous making Athena sacrifice to her adversary Poseidon (3.36-62); when we last see him he is trying to repair the confusion by making another massive sacrifice, this time to Athena. Nestor also hyper-entertains; it is dangerous to call on him, in case he makes you stay too long (15.199-201).

Menelaus elaborately disclaims any such tendencies (15.68-74), but his house is hyper-culturally like that of the gods (4.74-75). Menelaus is almost a god himself. Mortals survive through their sons, but Menelaus has no legitimate son (4.12-14); on the other hand he will not know death, but will go to the Isles of the Blessed (4.561-568). In the meantime he has experienced good and bad fortune, but seems to have achieved no synthesis, only a mixture. When he is tired of grieving, Helen hands about the Lotus-like Nepenthe, imported from hyper-cultural drug-rich Egypt (4.227-232). Menelaus had offered to include Odysseus within his own kingdom (4.169-182), but Odysseus had evidently preferred to attempt a return to Ithaca, "a rough land, but a good nurse of men" (9.27). Telemachus also is eager to get back, even though he knows well that the land is rough (4.594-608).

Odysseus' own travels are asymmetrical, in that the framing adventure, that of Calypso, is hyper-cultural and the leading instance of hyper-entertainment; Calypso's offer to make him immortal would presumably involve transforming him by feeding him nectar and ambrosia (cf. 5.195-199). The Phaeacians also, with their metal palace, extraordinary fabrics, magic servants, ships, and garden, are hyper-cultural. They also threaten to keep Odysseus, by transforming him into Nausicaa's husband (7.313-314).

Yet for all the charm and luxury of Phaeacian life--"feasting, the lyre and the chorus, changes of clothing and hot baths and bed" (8.248-249)--there is a latent strain of savagery here. The Phaeacians are hereditary enemies of the Cyclopes (6.4-6), but both peoples are descended from Poseidon (9.529, 13.130), and Periboia, the consort of Poseidon who founded their royal house, was herself descended from the Giants (7.56-59). The Phaeacians are close to the gods "as are the Cyclopes and the savage race of the Giants" (7.206). They are thus like the Laestrygonians, who are like the Giants (10.120), and at first glance Laestrygonia and Phaeacia look very much alike. Travellers to both places meet a little girl carrying water from a spring (7.19-20, 10.105-108), then the queen, last the king. No wonder Odysseus had feared he might again be among savages (6.119-

121); indeed, the disguised Athena warns him that the
Phaeacians are unwelcoming to strangers (7.30-33), and
Nausicaa herself says "there are some pretty overbearing peo-
ple here" (6.274). (*Hyperphialos* is also used of the
Cyclops--*Od*. 9.106).

This is odd, because the Phaeacians boast of their kindness to strangers (8.32-33); certainly they are lavish to
Odysseus. This very lavishness, which Odysseus exploits, is
nevertheless also a problem. Entertainment, properly, involves generalized exchange; the same person is at one time
guest, at another time host (4.33-36). When we entertain we
see ourselves in the other; the host and the guest, the secure man and his vulnerable double, recognize their common
dependence on the will of Zeus. One may fail of this recognition in two ways: in hypo-entertainment the man away from
home is treated as if he were not a man at all; in hyper-entertainment one fails to recognize that his home is not here
but elsewhere. Both failures are somehow the same; the extremes meet. That is why the frivolity of hyper-culture has
latent in it the savagery of hypo-culture.

The Phaeacians feel immune to circumstance, and are thus
somewhat careless of the gods, like the Cyclops (*Od*. 9.275-
276). They live far off (6.8), where no one can attack them
(6.200-205, cf. 6.270-271). So also they form no bonds with
others. Their voyaging does not make them into guests, since
their magic ships can make the longest voyage in a single day
(7.325-326). Their entertainment of others is thus not an
enactment of our common vulnerability, but is rather a sort
of self-indulgence and self-display, like their other amuse-
ments. Zeus says that in entertaining Odysseus they have
"yielded to strength and to force" (13.143). Thus Zeus-of-
the-stranger does not protect them; rather he allows Poseidon
to punish them.

From the Phaeacians Odysseus passes through the hut of Eumaeus, where he is properly entertained, into his own house, where he is entertained by the loathsome suitors. In the case of the suitors the meeting of the extremes is complete; their continuous feast is hyper-cultural and treats Odysseus' resources as if they were magically infinite, while at the same time they are a sort of cannibals, eating Odysseus' house (4.318, 11.116, 13.396=13.428=15.32, 19.159, 19.534). Odysseus feels himself almost back in the Cyclops' cave (20.18-21). The suitors might indeed kill Odysseus—or they might incorporate him in their mad society as a pet beggar (18.48-49).

The suitors' momentary success has utterly deprived them of judgement, as with Odysseus' men among the Cicones; Odysseus nearly makes the comparison explicit (17.419-444). Later he is still more explicit, in the speech in which he tries to get Amphinomus to leave before the massacre begins.[14]

The earth rears nothing more wretched than mankind,

Of all that breathe and creep upon the earth.

He says no trouble will happen to him later

While yet the gods give excellence and maintain him;

But when the blessed gods bring about sorrows,

Unwilling he bears these too with enduring heart.

Such is the mind of men who live on earth

As the day the father of gods and men may bring them.

I once was ready to be prosperous among men;

I did many outrages, yielding to force and strength,

Confident in my father and my brothers.

So let no man be utterly lacking in law;

Let him keep the gods' gifts in silence, whatever they

give.

18.130-142

Odysseus here explains the strand of savagery latent in luxury. When we have everything we want we forget that these things are not ours by right, but are the gift of the gods to whom we owe in return piety and lawfulness. Odysseus, we should note, calls mankind wretched, not because our life is too hard, but because it is sometimes too easy. The *Odyssey* is mostly about hyper-culture because prosperity, not want, sets the most difficult ethical problems. Nature, the external adversary, proposes mostly technical problems, although there is also an ethic of labor. When, however, these problems have been solved, we too easily forget the problematic of life and fall victim to our inner nature. *Koros* begets *atē* and *hubris*.

The economic ethic is always and everywhere an ethic of realism, of the man who measures up to the realities of the world with the skill and discipline to adopt and conserve the necessary means. Among the Greeks the economic ethic is also an ethic of the middle way.

V. CONCLUSION

The *Odyssey* is a poem of economics in that its hero is driven by economic motives and by his commitment to economic institutions. At the beginning of the poem Odysseus' household—his proper economic arena—is in disarray. The householder is absent, and it is not known whether he is alive or dead. Therefore no one else is able to play a proper role. Penelope is neither wife nor widow, Telemachus is neither child nor man, Laertes is neither rich nor poor, the maids are neither obedient nor free, the herdsmen control flocks which belong neither to them nor to anyone else, the suitors are neither guests nor robbers, neither friends nor enemies. On his return Odysseus clarifies these relations and gradually

reconstructs these roles; he puts the whole institution back
together. In the process he displays the virtues proper to
the economic man.

The *Odyssey* thus complements the *Iliad* on the literary
level as the *oikos* complemented the *polis* on the institution-
al level. The *Iliad* is a poem of public life, in which private relations are important for their public consequences.
From the time of Homer onward the *polis* existed for the sake
of war, and to create public space, an *agorē*, in which people
can become visible, *ariprepeeis*, in debate, in games, in rituals and theatrical performances.[15] The *oikos*, on the other
hand, was an enclosure, a sphere of secrets, intimate or con-
spiratorial. Women, children, and slaves were confined to
the *oikos*, but men could have both sorts of lives. Politics
was agonistic; men defined themselves against each other
through display of strength, rhetoric, and wealth. Economics
was cooperative, founded on the division of labor and a cycle
of production and consumption. Political actors were in
principle equal; they came to inequality as they acted on one
another. The economic actors were in principle unequal; economics, as Aristotle saw, was a sphere of asymmetrical relations: between husband and wife, parent and child, master
and slave--and, we may add, host and guest. As these act,
they come, not to equality, but to unity. Odysseus' aim in
the *Odyssey* is to reestablish this unity, and to do this he
must have an idea of it, a vision of its form.

As the Greeks set out to expand their civilization--an enterprise which was, as much as anything else, an enterprise
of economic development--they took with them the *Odyssey* as a
kind of handbook of the economic life--not on the technical
but on the ethical level. I have suggested three aspects of
this Odyssean economic ethic; each is stateable in terms of

a tension.   There is, first, the tension between an aspiration
to household self-sufficiency and the need to maintain a public order.   Second, there is the tension between an aspiration
to agricultural autarky and the need to maintain market exchange.   Third, there is the tension between an aspiration to
affluence and the need to limit the cultural impact of affluence.   All three of these tensions can be documented right
through the classical period down to the time of Aristotle;
they give us the beginnings of a statement of the Greek economic ethic.

The most important, I think, is the third.   The Greeks always considered economics, not as concerned with problems of
maximization, but with problems of adequacy, of the mean.
The ethical problem was that of developing a *noos* to some degree independent of the day Zeus brings us, able to confront
scarcity and plenty without despair or insolence.   Such a
noos would be capable of economic thought.

NOTES

1. See P. Vidal-Naquet, "Homère et le monde mycénien,"
   Annales ESC 18 (1963), 703-719.

2. See Marshall Sahlins, *Culture and Practical Reason* (Chicago
   and London: University of Chicago Press, 1976).

3. Clifford Geertz, "Religion as a Cultural System," in
   Anthropological Approaches to the Study of Religion, ed.
   M. Banton (London: Tavistock, 1966), pp. 1-46; also in
   Clifford Geertz, *The Interpretation of Cultures* (New York:
   Basic Books, 1973), pp. 87-125.

4. Cedric H. Whitman, *Homer and the Heroic Tradition* (Cambridge, Mass.:   Harvard University Press, 1958).

5. A. J. B. Wace, "Houses and Palaces," in *A Companion to Homer*, ed. A. J. B. Wace and F. H. Stubbings (New York: Macmillan, 1963), p. 489.

6. M. I. Finley, *The World of Odysseus*, 2nd ed., rev. (New York: Penguin, 1979).

7. J.-P. Vernant, "Hestia-Hermes," in *Mythe et pensée chez le Grecs*, 2nd ed. (Paris: Maspero, 1969), pp. 97–143.

8. See Alfonso Mele, *Società e lavoro nei poemi omerici* (Naples: Università di Napoli, Istituto di Storia e Antichità greca e romana, 1968).

9. Cf. H. Strasburger, "Der soziologische Aspect der homerischen Epen," *Gymnasium* 60 (1953), 97–114.

10. Marcel Mauss, "Une Forme ancienne de contrat chez les Thraces," in *Oeuvres*, vol. 3 (Paris: Les Editions de Minuit, 1969), pp. 35–57. This article first appeared in 1921.

11. Cf. J. M. Redfield, "The Making of the Odyssey," in *Parnassus Revisited*, ed. A. C. Yu (Chicago: American Library Association, 1973), pp. 141–154. First published in *Essays in Western Civilization in Honor of Christian W. MacKauer*, ed. L. Botstein and E. Karnovsky (Chicago: The College of the University of Chicago, 1967), pp. 1–17.

12. Vidal-Naquet, "Valeurs religieuses et mythiques de la terre et du sacrifice dans l'*Odysée*," in *Problèmes de la terre en Grèce ancienne*, ed. M. I. Finley (Paris and the Hague: Mouton, 1973), pp. 269–292.

13. Redfield, *Nature and Culture in the Iliad: The Tragedy of Hector* (Chicago: University of Chicago Press, 1975).

14. Cf. G. Bona, *Il νόος e i νόοι nell'Odissea = Università di Torino, Pubblicazioni della Facoltà di Lettere e Filosofia* 11.1 (Torino: 1959).

15. Cf. Hannah Arendt, *The Human Condition* (Chicago: University of Chicago Press, 1958).

The Nature of Homeric Morality[1]

C. J. Rowe

The purpose of this paper is to attempt to reach a proper assessment of the views advanced by Professor A. W. H. Adkins
on the nature of the morality presupposed by the language and
action of the Homeric poems, especially in the first five
chapters of his book *Merit and Responsibility*.[2] Though many
aspects of Adkins' treatment have met with heavy criticism,[3]
there has appeared no other systematic account of Homeric
morality to replace it;[4] over twenty years later, the book remains one with which any serious student of the subject must
come to terms.[5] I propose here to try to evaluate some of
the criticisms which have been made of Adkins' position, in
order to see how well it has in fact survived. The exercise
has special point because Adkins has himself, since 1960,
continued to defend his position virtually *in toto*; in a long
series of articles he has elaborated and amplified the views
stated in *Merit and Responsibility* without apparently making
any major concessions to his critics.[6]

The bulk of the present paper will be built around the
substantial review article by A. A. Long, which appeared in
the *Journal of Hellenic Studies* for 1970.[7] This is the most
complete and detailed critique which has appeared, and it
raises many of the most important points, though I shall suggest that it misses the mark in some crucial respects. I
shall begin by summarizing briefly the treatment of Homeric
morality in E. R. Dodds's classic book, *The Greeks and the
Irrational*,[8] which evidently provided the starting-point for
Adkins' analysis,[9] and which introduces some of its basic
terms; I shall then attempt a broad outline of Adkins' own

fundamental theses, drawing chiefly on *MR*. Long's article
will then be taken in tandem with the riposte published by
Adkins in the following issue of the same journal,[10] and I
shall attempt to adjudicate on the issues between them,
raising further points, some those of others, some my own, as
occasion demands. The net result will be to confirm some
central parts of Adkins' analysis, but to suggest that some
others need to be qualified, and some parts withdrawn
altogether.

     As is well known, Dodds characterizes Homeric society--
"the society described by Homer"--as a "shame-culture."
     Homeric man's highest good is not the enjoyment of a quiet
     conscience, but the enjoyment of *tīmē*, public esteem:
     "Why should I fight," asks Achilles, "if the good fighter
     receives no more τιμή than the bad?" And the strongest
     moral force which Homeric man knows is not the fear of
     god, but respect for public opinion, *aidōs*: αἰδέομαι
     Τρῶας, says Hector at the crisis of his fate, and goes
     with open eyes to his death.[11]
The gods, according to Dodds, at least in the *Iliad*, are not
interested in "justice as such"; for the most part they, like
men, are "primarily concerned with their own honor (τιμή).
To speak lightly of a god, to neglect his cult, to maltreat
his priest, all these understandably make him angry; in a
shame-culture gods, like men, are quick to resent a
slight"[12]--although there are hints, now and then, of a wider
concern, for example in the case of offenses against parents.
In the *Odyssey*, on the other hand, Dodds holds that Zeus *is*
interested in justice; indeed the action of the poem is on
his analysis precisely a working out of divine justice: "the
suitors by their own wicked acts incur destruction, while

Odysseus, heedful of divine monitions, triumphs against the
odds: divine justice is vindicated."[13] This is seen as a
step towards the development of a "guilt-culture"; for the
sense of guilt, according to J. K. Campbell's definition, is
"the consequence of acts which defy the commandments of
God."[14] (That guilt necessarily involved reference to the
commandments of God or gods is doubtful; but it is certainly
one way in which it can find expression.[15]) Dodds goes on to
talk about the idea of pollution, developed essentially in
the post-epic age, and about how this archaic "sense of
guilt" became a "sense of sin," as a result of

> the "internalizing" of conscience--a phenomenon which ap-
> pears late and uncertainly in the Hellenic world, and does
> not become common until long after secular law had begun
> to recognize the importance of motive. The transference
> of the notion of purity from the magical to the moral
> sphere was a similarly late development: not until the
> closing years of the fifth century do we encounter explic-
> it statements that clean hands are not enough--the heart
> must be clean also.[16]

We have here most of the essential ingredients of Adkins'
central thesis in *MR*; although Adkins differs from Dodds in
making even fifth-century Athens fundamentally a shame-culture, and in seeing the *Odyssey* as based essentially on the
same set of values as the *Iliad*. These values are as follows.
The most important social grouping is the *oîkos*, widely conceived as including not only the hero and his family, but his
dependents and followers, and also those only temporarily under his protection: guests, suppliants, beggars. Homeric
society is insecure, with war and depredation ever-present
possibilities; and what it therefore values above all else is
the ability of the chieftain to protect it:

we discover a society whose highest commendation is be-
stowed upon men who must successfully exhibit the qualities
of a warrior . . . men, too, who must display their valour
both in war and in peace to protect their dependents: a
function in which they must succeed, for the most powerful
words in the language are used to denigrate those who
fail.[17]

Success is all-important; *results* are what matter, and intentions matter little—good intentions alone will not be enough:
". . . intentions are of much less importance than results.
The Homeric hero cannot fall back upon his own opinion of himself, for his self only has the value which other people put
upon it."[18] The hero feels *aidōs*, shame, if he fails, and
incurs *elencheiē*; people reproach him. Homeric culture is
thus both a "shame-culture" and a "results-culture." (Dodds
does not separate the concept of a "results-culture" from
that of a "shame-culture" in *GI*; but perhaps he implicitly
uses both concepts.[19])

    Adkins develops his position in terms of the by now noto-
rious distinction between two types of "excellences" in Homer:
the "competitive" excellences, on the one hand, and the "cooperative," or "quiet," excellences on the other. The need
of the society for effective protection against a hostile
world leads to the predominance of the former over the latter;
for "it is not evident at this time that the security of the
group depends to any large extent upon [the co-operative] excellences,"[20] in the way it plainly does upon the competitive.

    The highest word of commendation, *agathos*, is reserved for
men who are "well-armed, strong, fleet of foot and skilled in
war, counsel and strategy . . . . it is unnecessary for men to
possess any of the quiet virtues in order to be *agathos*: the
agathos need not be *pinutos*, *pepnūmenos*, *saophrōn*, or

dikaios"[21]--though he may well need to be these things for
prudential reasons. In this competitive scheme of values,
"*moral* responsibility has no place . . . and the quieter virtues, in which such responsibility has its place, neither
have sufficient attraction to gain a hearing nor are backed
by sufficient force to compel one."[22] There is certainly
room for cooperative action within the Homeric ethos; there
are strong ties between *philoi*; but even here, it is "actions
and results" that matter.

In order to be an Homeric ἀγαθός, or to display Homeric
ἀρετή, actions and results were necessary, not emotions or
intentions. The reason lay in the nature of Homeric society; and this is so also in the case of Homeric φιλότης.
The essence of the φίλος-relationship is cooperation, not
competition, so that we might expect intentions to be relevant; but it is cooperation to meet the harsh demands of
Homeric life.[23]

As Adkins remarks elsewhere, "if the *agathos* had to use his
strong right arm actively to protect his *philos* he would
think of it as an exercise of *aretē*, though he would of
course be exercising it because the person had been drawn by
him within the *philos*-group."[24] The requirements of *philotēs*
are seen generally by Adkins as falling within the sphere of
aretē, i.e., of the competitive excellences, insofar as they
arise within the context of the relationship between the
agathos and his dependents. There are contexts, he freely
admits, in which cooperative excellences come into play in
and by themselves, in the case of women, for example, of whom
the competitive excellences are not expected; but Homeric society is predominantly a male society, and predominantly competitive; and "as soon as a crisis forces the essential
framework of values into view, the competitive values are so

much more powerful than the co-operative that the situation
is not treated in terms of the quiet values at all."[25]
"Wrong-doing is not admired by those who suffer from it; but
right-doing, 'quiet' virtue, is less highly admired by society as a whole than skill and courage, for the latter are
more evidently needed."[26]   The support of the gods for justice, even in the *Odyssey*, is doubtful; Adkins suggests--un-
less I misunderstand him--that on the whole the idea that the
gods guarantee moral relationships belongs to later sections
of the poems, and is not representative of their general con-
ception of morality.[27]   He claims that if right triumphs in
both poems, "it does not do so *because* it is right. Achilles
obtains divine aid because he has, through Thetis his mother,
the ear of Zeus himself; and Odysseus is assisted by Athena
because she is, for reasons never made clear by Homer, his
patron-goddess."[28]   In any case, if the gods do in some sense
and in some contexts guarantee morality, their sanctions are
observably ineffective, because the unjust man frequently--as
a matter of common experience--escapes any penalty; thus,
Adkins concludes, "this attempt to link the quieter virtues
with *arete* fails in its purpose."[29]   The gods, like men, are
predominantly concerned with their own *timē*, in the *Odyssey*
as well as in the *Iliad*.

Long's first serious criticism is aimed at Adkins' attempts to derive Homeric values from the needs of Homeric society. These attempts are suspect, he suggests, because we
have no independent access to the "facts of Homeric life" on
which Adkins claims to draw. The items of epic moral language are presented to us in an exclusively literary context;
and the consequence is, Long claims, that "we should interpret Homer's ethics primarily by means of the internal logic

of the poems."[30] Long's attack here is misdirected. As
Adkins says in his riposte, it does not in fact matter to his
case whether or not "Homeric society," or anything like it,
ever existed in fact; if Homeric values could be shown to derive from the conditions of some particular type of society,
then whether or not that society existed would be irrele-
vant.[31] The real issue is whether Adkins can in fact establish the connection he wants between Homeric values and the
supposed conditions of Homeric society. I myself doubt
whether he can. To suggest, as he does, that the *agathos*
acts primarily in the interests of his group (and of himself)
because of the need to defend them against threats from outside begs the question why those interests are so central to
him. What comes first is the value-system; one based in the
twin concepts of honor and shame, and centering on a concern
with assurance of one's standing and power.[32] It is not
clear in any case that insecurity about the *oikos* is as basic
as Adkins supposes to the motivation of the hero. After all,
much stress is laid on the fact that the Greeks have been
away from home for ten long years; and in some cases with
disastrous results. Defense of one's interests is only one
side of the coin; positive action is also required to maintain
and increase one's honor. This presumably explains the presence of the mass of the Greeks at Troy--those that died, as
Odysseus ironically remarks, merely "brought favor to the
Atreidae."[33] So too on the Trojan side Pandarus complains,
in fear of his death, that he led his contingent to Troy merely to "bring favor to Hector"; he himself will get nothing
from it.[34]

One aspect of Adkins' thesis that has received particularly
heavy criticism is his distinction between the "competitive"

and the "cooperative," or "quiet," excellences. J. L. Creed,
for example, points out that the two terms "cooperative" and
"quiet," used for the second half of the opposition, suggest
rather different things. The expression "quiet virtues" suggests the qualities of men at peace, contrasted with the ag-
gressive qualities of men in times of war; on the other hand,
the contrast between "cooperative" and "competitive" suggests
the distinction between those who pursue their own interests
and those who put the community's interests before their own.
But now, Creed goes on, military prowess and courage, which
are far from "quiet" qualities, are, or may be, eminently cooperative; both "may depend as much on a willingness to co-
operate as on a capacity to fight." On the other hand,
sōphrosunē, which is treated as a "quiet" virtue, need not be
a "cooperative" one; and "justice," which is "cooperative,"
may not be quiet--insofar as it involves harming one's enemies as well as helping one's friends. Creed ends by con-
cluding that "it is no doubt the conflict between the 'co-operative' and the 'competitive' virtues which is at the heart
of the distinction Adkins is drawing," i.e., in Creed's terms,
between self-regarding excellences, on the one hand, and oth-
er-regarding excellences on the other.[35] This view certainly
has some substance: it is borne out, for example, by the suggestion, made in *MR*, that the exercise of the "competitive"
excellences may lead to "wrong-doing,"[36] and more generally
by the natural inclusion among the cooperative virtues of excellences like justice and fairness. But it is clear that if
this were indeed the basis of Adkins' distinction, then he
would be unable to say without heavy qualification that competitive excellences outweigh cooperative ones; for the competitive excellences themselves contain a strong other-re-
garding element, insofar as they involve the defense not only

of one's own property, status, and kin, but also that of others who in some way fall within one's group and whose interests are not straightforwardly identifiable with one's own:
friends, strangers, beggars, suppliants.

"Competitive" and "cooperative" ("quiet") cannot then be
taken as simply equivalent to "self-regarding" and "other-re-
garding." Long sees the distinction differently: competitive excellences are those that involve judgement by results,
while cooperative excellences involve "some different crite-
rion like fairness." If that is Adkins' point, Long argues,
one difficulty will be that even a virtue like justice, which
is treated as a preeminently "cooperative" excellence, now
appears also to fall under the heading of "competitive," because it too involved actually *doing* something; and other
"quiet" terms, like *pinutos* and *saophrōn*, have no connection
with fairness. Words like *ēpios*, *aganos*, and *prophrōn*,
again, have nothing to do either with fairness or with results, or with intentions. Then too,

> if ἀρετή/ἀγαθός describe and evaluate the hero's success
> in war and peace, as they often do, then the majority of
> actions which might ordinarily be called "co-operative,"
> though not necessarily "quiet," prove also to belong to
> the competitive category, as Adkins defines it. Showing
> hospitality to ξένοι, sacrificing to the gods, assisting
> one's fellow heroes in war, feasting--these are perhaps
> the most obvious examples in Homer of men 'co-operating
> for a common end.'[37]

Adkins takes contracts and partnerships as typical examples
of cooperative behavior; of these, Long rightly says, Homer
has little to say, but "this does not mean that 'fair dealing'
is not sometimes valued in the epics. It is highly valued in
certain specific situations, so much so that heroes are

expected to be successful at it. To put it in a more Homeric
way, τιμή is involved in some joint enterprises as well as in
individual acts of prowess and the hero's personal status."[38]
Long gives as examples Glaucus' reproach against Hector for
not rescuing Sarpedon's corpse in *Il*. 17, Sarpedon's similar
reproach against Hector in *Il*. 5, and Deiphobus' appeal to
Aeneas on grounds of kinship in *Il*. 13. The behavior being
urged on Hector and Aeneas is in each case behavior which (so
Long claims), though it is seen in terms of *timē*, is nevertheless essentially cooperative: "certain types of co-operation are required by a man's personal status and situation."[39] Long sums up this part of his case as follows:

> for Homer Adkins' distinction between competitive and co-
> operative values proves to be not a categorical distinc-
> tion between two kinds of judgement, but a distinction be-
> tween powerful words for commending success or denigrating
> failure and allegedly weaker words for evaluating results,
> not intentions, of a different kind. How much weaker re-
> mains to be seen. But in both cases the failure or suc-
> cess adjudged may concern inter-personal or co-operative
> activities.[40]

There seem to be two main points here: 1) that the "cooperative" virtues too, as much as the competitive excellences, are judged in terms of results; and 2) that competitive and cooperative behavior are often indissolubly linked.
Neither point upsets Adkins; he repeats that it is actually
part of his case that the demands of society upon the *agathos*
frequently require cooperative behavior; it is *part of*
aretē, thought of in terms of the competitive excellences,
because it is for a competitive end, and is itself judged exclusively in terms of results. On the other hand, Adkins
says, there *are* contexts where intentions are taken into

account, namely those in which the "safety of the group" is
not concerned. "The difference between competitive and cooperative activities lies not in the demand that one should
perform the action if possible (and if its performance is the
most powerful claim upon one in the circumstances), but *in
the willingness to accept excuses if it is not possible.*"[41]
In other words, if I interpret this reply correctly, "cooperative" in its opposition to "competitive" is strictly to mean
"involving co-operation with those outside the group."

The fundamental sense of the competitive/cooperative distinction, then, appears to be that the competitive excellences, those required for the defense of the group, are judged
by results alone, not by intentions; whereas the cooperative
excellences do allow for intentions to be taken into account,
since these are involved in one's interaction with those outside one's group, to whom any obligations are only weakly
felt. In these terms, the distinction is perhaps coherent
enough, though, as Adkins himself admits, the terms "competitive" and "cooperative" do not seem particularly apt to express it: "as technical terms," he says, "they have defects."[42] The crucial question then is whether there is in
fact the crucial difference that he claims between the two
types of activity: that involving members of one's "group,"
as he conceives this, and that involving those outside it.
The behavior of Aeneas in *Il.* 13 becomes a prize exhibit for
his case, rather than against it: Aeneas is moved by
Deiphobus' appeal to the obligations of kinship, but is apparently unmoved by the plight of the Trojan army in general,
who are outside his *philos*-group. But we may reply that
Aeneas' behavior here is not typical of the heroes in the
Iliad as a whole, who frequently put themselves at risk for
the sake of those with whom they have no stated ties other

than that they belong to the same side, to protect them, to prevent their armor and their bodies from falling into the enemy's hands, or to avenge them; and they appear to do what they do with precisely the same fireceness as when they act to defend the interests of their *philoi* or themselves. The idea of loyalty within the larger as well as within the smaller group is of some importance in the *Iliad* generally, as Lloyd-Jones, for example, makes clear in his largely admirable analysis of the plot of the poem. A central strand in the plot is Achilles' unwillingness to bend, and to put the ties of friendship and loyalty before the insult done to him by Agamemnon. It is expected of Achilles that he should put aside his anger, at least once proper--and indeed more than proper--compensation has been offered, and fight along with the rest, "pitying" the other Greeks. The language of Odysseus, Phoenix, and Ajax on their embassy to Achilles cannot simply be regarded as deriving from the urgency of the crisis in which the Greeks now find themselves. They use arguments which they hope will persuade him, certainly; but they also think they *ought* to persuade him. What is more, as Lloyd-Jones points out, Achilles seems to agree; but his anger is too great to allow him to listen. Finally,

when Achilles learns of Patroclus' death, he has no wish to survive unless he can avenge it upon the killer. This attitude has often been considered to be that of a savage. Hector has killed Patroclus not in a private quarrel, but in the course of a war. Achilles feels a strong desire to appease his own feeling of guilt. He has been of no use, he says, to Patroclus nor to any of those friends of his whom Hector has slain--here at last he admits feeling pity for the Achaeans--but supreme as he is in battle he sits here a useless burden on the earth. Not that this emotion

is his only reason for wanting to kill Hector. If vengeance is taken upon his killer, Patroclus will receive
great *time* . . . Achilles [also] speaks of glory, for the
time to win it has arrived; but the glory is only inciden-
tal. He finally sacrifices his life not for glory, but
out of remorse for his responsibility for the death of
Patroclus. In Homer's world loyalty to an individual
friend, like loyalty to the group, is not insignificant;
I suppose loyalty to one's friends counts as a co-operative virtue.[43]

The *agathos* then exercises his *aretē* not merely as head of
an *oîkos*, and as a member of a *philos*-group, but also as a
member of wider groupings, like an army or a raiding-party.[44]
This seems to me to be fatal to the competitive/cooperative
distinction. The *agathos* here too will in a sense act for
the "safety of the group"; but the safety of this wider group
is certainly not "paramount," in the sense that it always, or
normally, overrides all other considerations (or is expected
to, which is a different question). The general picture that
emerges is not of a simple distinction between two sets of
imperatives, the one strong and overriding, the other weak
and generally subordinate, but rather of a complex range of
different pressures operating on the hero, among which it
will sometimes be difficult for him to choose. He is at the
center of a nest of social relationships, whose demands on
him may conflict. Adkins is right to the extent that there
is in general some kind of pecking-order between these relationships: he correctly emphasizes the central importance of
the *oîkos* within the Homeric scale of values; again, the ties
of kinship and friendship will naturally be felt more strong-
ly than those deriving from membership in larger and looser
associations (as is borne out by the case of Aeneas, or by

the similar case of Achilles, who returns to the fighting only after the death of Patroclus, or by the famous incident
between Diomedes and Glaucus). But if some of the demands on
the individual are more weakly felt, they are felt nonetheless. It is wrong, and does Homer--I mean especially the poet of the *Iliad*--a disservice, to suggest that the choice for
the hero is, as it were, already given; the tensions surrounding such choices are central to the plot of the *Iliad* as a
whole.

The conclusion must, I think, be that the competitive/co-
operative distinction is in the end unworkable. But at the
same time there remains a point of considerable substance underlying it. As we saw at the beginning, the distinction
arises from the perception of Homeric society as being, in
essence, a "shame-culture." His fundamental concern with his
"competence, potency, or power" does indeed set the Homeric
hero in competition with others, even when he is involved in
joint activities with them;[45] and all the more, insofar as his
primary impulse is towards the defense of his own interests as
narrowly conceived--honor, property, family. Joint activity
may offer a means of increasing his share of honor, and of
property, which is its material expression; as soon as it
ceases to do that, he is liable to withdraw.

Whether, on the other hand, "society" approves of him for
so acting, as Adkins suggests, is another matter. The issue
here depends on how we understand "society." If it is understood in terms of the *oikos*, as Adkins seems generally to understand it,[46] then "society" will indeed approve (insofar as
on Adkins' analysis the hero acts in response to its demands).
But the attitude of society in a wider sense, as a collection
of similar individuals, will be rather more complex. Since
each will tend to act in the same way in defense of his

interests, such behavior is the norm; but that is not the end of the story. Homeric morality also takes cognizance of the fact that the maintenance by one individual of his *timē* will often vitally affect the interests of others (for example by threatening someone else's share of the same commodity). Conflicts of this kind may be resolved by violence, but there are also peaceful means available, in the formal procedure of arbitration which undoubtedly existed, and which allows clear room for some idea of *justice* between individuals.[47] But there is also (pace Adkins) a general belief that the *agathos* will take account in his behavior of the rights and interests of others as well as of his own, however rarely such a belief may be reflected in the actions of the great figures who people the poems.[48] It is this point which I hope to substantiate in what follows.

I shall begin this section by raising a criticism implicitly made by Terence Irwin, in his book *Plato's Moral Theory*.[49] Adkins tends to suggest that the application to a hero of the term *agathos* without qualification implies that he possesses *all* the qualities which are from time to time associated with it. So, for example, at *MR*, p. 31: "Being the most powerful words of commendation used of a man," *agathos, aretē*, and related words "imply the possession by anyone to whom they are applied of all the qualities most highly valued at any time by Greek society." But it is clear that this must be wrong. Agamemnon acts unwisely in dishonoring Achilles, as events show, but is still *agathos*, presumably in virtue of his general position and his military prowess, which Homer goes out of his way to stress several times; Paris, too, is *agathos*, despite the fact that he recognizes his own limitations as a fighter; Nestor is a great counsellor, but past his best in

hand-to-hand combat. And this is indeed what we would expect.
If all *agathoi* were identical, then there would be no color
to the *Iliad*, and indeed no plot. In Book 1, as Adkins says,
Achilles cannot yield to Agamemnon, because he would thereby
be called (which, Adkins tells us, "in a shame-culture is
equivalent to 'be'") *deilos* and *outidanos*.[50] But by the
stage reached in Book 9, the situation is radically altered:
compensation has been offered, and there would be no more
dishonor attached to Achilles' giving in--or, to use a less
emotive expression, agreeing to a reconciliation--than there
is to Poseidon's bowing to Zeus in Book 15: he would, then,
implicitly be admitting Agamemnon's superior status, insofar
as he would again be placing his fighting qualities at
Agamemnon's disposal; but after all, Agamemnon *has* superior
status--he is, as he says at *Il.* 9.160-161, "more of a king"
and older, though Odysseus diplomatically suppresses this
point in the embassy scene. If Achilles too has status on
the grounds both of his power as a fighter and of his divine
origins, Agamemnon is still *pherteros*, "superior" or "better"
(so at least Nestor argues at 1.280-281), "because he rules
over more people." Similarly, Zeus is superior to Poseidon
in being the elder brother, which Poseidon finally recognizes.
The *Iliad*, certainly from Book 9 on, centers on the different
pressures on Achilles, as a hero fiercely concerned with his
own *timē*, but in the end over-concerned with it. If indeed
στρεπταὶ θρένες ἐσθλῶν,[51] then to the extent that he proves
unbending, he ceases to be *esthlos*, *agathos*, though he could
not *unqualifiedly* be denied the title of *agathos*, because he
fulfills other criteria of *aretē*. The working-out of the
plot of the *Odyssey* involves a similar situation in respect
of the suitors: they are *agathoi* in some respects, and less
than *agathoi* in others.

Long approaches these questions in a rather different way.
He asserts that generally *agathos* (or *aristos*) can have a descriptive as well as an evaluative force; in its descriptive
role, it refers essentially to social status. This, he
claims, is the way *aristos* is used of the suitors; similarly
when Nestor says to Agamemnon in *Il*. 1, "don't take the girl
from Achilles, *agathos* though you are," and when Apollo suggests in Book 24 that the gods will be angry with Achilles,
"*agathos* though he is," for abusing Hector's corpse. In the
two latter cases, Long argues, the suggestion is that there
are limits placed on the actions which the *agathos* can perform in virtue of his preeminence; *agathos* in these contexts
has little *moral* sense or content.[52] Now Long may well be
right in criticizing Adkins for reading these passages as
simply asserting the claims of the *agathos*; they also imply a
judgement of Agamemnon's and Achilles' behavior as excessive
(to use Long's term), and there are no grounds that I can see
in either context for supposing, as Adkins does, that the
judgement is ineffective, has no force. True, Agamemnon and
Achilles may not be moved; but the suggestion is that they
should be moved. But we do not need to go as far as Long
goes, and read the term *agathos* in these contexts, or in the
context of the suitors, in a predominantly descriptive sense.
What Nestor and Apollo are saying, surely, is that under normal circumstances, you might as well have a perfect right to
do what you are doing--because you are what you are; but not
in *these* circumstances. In *Il*. 15.185-186 Poseidon says of
Zeus that "though he is *agathos*, he has gone too far in saying what he says to me now--because in fact our shares are
equal." Similarly, Nestor is saying to Agamemnon that he cannot treat *Achilles* as he proposes to do, because the army
gave Briseis to him as a prize, and also because Achilles,

though inferior on some grounds, is the better fighter; and
Apollo says that Achilles cannot treat *Hector* like that.
There are examples enough in the general fighting of the
Iliad of heroes treating their enemies in what we might think
of as a despicable fashion; Ajax, son of Oileus, for example,
cuts off Imbrius' head and bowls it over the ground like a
ball, a piece of singular barbarity which goes unremarked by
the poet.[53] But Hector cannot be treated like that, because
he has his own *timē*, even though it is not equal to that of
Achilles.[54] Hector is an enemy who has done him great personal injury, and so Achilles cannot be expected to recognize
this; the gods do. These passages, then, suggest the view
that the *agathos* should not assert himself without qualification in all circumstances; and we may justifiably infer that
if he insists on doing so, this will to some degree affect
his claims to *aretē*. This is, I take it, the clear implication of Apollo's suggestion that it will be οὐ κάλλιον for
Achilles to go on behaving as he is.[55] Agamemnon, threatened
as he feels his position to be, does not give in, or gives in
only belatedly; Achilles in Book 24 does desist.

Whether or not the "observance of limits" actually becomes
"part of the meaning" of *agathos*, I should not like to say,
and it is probably a question that cannot profitably be discussed. We must, I think, allow for the possibility that the
content of *aretē* might itself be a matter of dispute in a
given context (Adkins allows for this possibility in the
post-epic age; why not in the epic age itself?). One such
type of context is the one we have just been discussing,
where an individual's view of what he should do is different
from what he may be expected by others to do. It is here, if
anywhere, that Adkins can legitimately be accused of employ-
ing a too rigidly "lexical" approach.[56] It is the function

of a lexicon to define terms; and definitions involve delim-
iting precisely the area they cover. In just this way,
Adkins assumes that there is a fixed meaning for a word like
agathos in Homer; and this entails writing off passages that
seem to extend or modify this supposedly basic meaning as
"persuasive," that is, as attempts by a speaker "to alter the
normal usage of Homeric terms of value in his own interest."[57]
But how are we to decide what is and what is not to count as
"basic," when the speakers of the language are themselves in
dispute about it? Moral language generally is perhaps inca-
pable of being pinned down in the way Adkins suggests. (This
is not to say, however, that we cannot still identify a central core of meaning around which uses by individual speakers
will tend to revolve; and Adkins has in general correctly
identified this core in the case of *agathos* and *aretē* in
Homer.)

The final direct criticisms in Long's article follow up
this line of attack, and generally with success. Adkins argues that *aeikēs*, along with *aidōs*, "spans both co-operative
and competitive excellences,"[58] unlike other terms, like
aischros. Long, however, establishes a close connection between *aeikēs* and the terms *aischos* and *aischros*, and shows
convincingly that they too (and other value-terms besides)
can be used to decry *both* failures in competition *and* actions
by heroes which exceed acceptable behavior. This was the implication of the passage just considered, in which Apollo described Achilles' dishonoring of Hector's corpse as *ou
kallion*--that is, if we may suppose, pace Adkins,[59] that *ou
kallion* here functions as the equivalent of *aischron*. We
would naturally *expect* it to function generally in that way;
and since, as Long points out, *aischros* in fact appears only

twice, in similar contexts, in the whole of Homer, Adkins'
grounds for denying it are, to say the least, meager. Another
important passage on which Long's argument turns is *Od*. 1.228-
229, where Athena says of the suitors' behavior that "a serious man who came in among them could well be scandalized
(νεμεσσήσαιτό κεν ἀνὴρ / αἴσχεα πόλλ᾽ ὁρόων, ὅς τις πινυτός
γε μετέλθοι)." Adkins takes *aischea* here as reflecting on
Telemachus, rather than the suitors: "Telemachus, not the
suitors, should feel ashamed, for it is he whose condition is
aischron."[60] But, as Long shows, there is no warrant for
this interpretation beyond the fact that it fits in with
Adkins' general view of the way in which the terms *aischos*
and *aischros* function, as referring exclusively to failures
of the *agathos*; and that view is badly supported. The whole
context suggests that it is the suitors, not Telemachus, who
are being criticized. And this strikes a crucial blow at an
important part of Adkins' case; for it entails that Homer does
recognize the existence of limits on the behavior of the individual, and that there are, in Adkins' own terms, effective
means of decrying breaches of those limits when occasion
arises to do so.

The suitors' behavior towards Odysseus' property and family is consistently condemned in the *Odyssey*, both by gods and
by men.[61] Admittedly, the human characters (Odysseus,
Telemachus, Penelope, Eumaeus) who express such condemnation
are interested parties; but we have it on Athena's authority
that any sensible (and dispassionate) observer would agree
with them. We may similarly take the gods' condemnation of
the suitors at face value; though Adkins suggests that the
idea of divine sanctions for human morality is a late intru-
sion into the poems, he offers no evidence for this. I do
not wish in any way to support the view of the *Odyssey* as a

simple "poem of justice";[62] Homer is not a moralizer, after
the fashion of Hesiod. He may recommend certain values by
implication, but that is not his main purpose. There is no
simple moral polarity in the *Odyssey*. From the beginning, a
comparison is suggested between the suitors and Aegisthus;
but there is this crucial difference, that Aegisthus steals
Agamemnon's wife knowing him to be alive, whereas Odysseus
is presumed dead, in which case the suitors are apparently
quite justified in pursuing Penelope. What is more, they
have, from their point of view, a legitimate sense of grievance: Penelope has procrastinated, and gone out of her way
to deceive them. In a sense, too, they even have a reason
for being in Odysseus' house, in that she has not gone back
to her father's house, as a prospective bride might have been
expected to do. But at the same time, they are generally
blamed, not merely for their behavior towards beggars and
guests, but also for their encroachment on Odysseus' interests.[63] In the *Iliad*, too, Achilles is clearly thought of as
having a legitimate grievance at Agamemnon's treatment of him.
These central cases suggest that it is expected of the hero
that he should in general show respect for the claims of
others, though there are clearly limitations on the application of this idea, insofar as piracy and sheep-stealing can
at the same time be regarded as perfectly legitimate ways of
increasing one's property.

I conclude, then, that the freedom of the individual in
Homeric society to assert his own interests, narrowly or
broadly conceived, is thought of as being limited by the demand for respect for the claims of others,[64] just as it may
also be limited by the requirements of joint activity. It
remains true, however, and I take this to be the heart of
Adkins' position, that Homeric values center on the demands

of the individual rather than on those of society in the
broad sense, and in particular on the need of the individual
to confirm his "competence, potency, and power." The Homeric
poems are about great individuals whose standing and power
are threatened; their reaction is, and is expected to be,
violent.

NOTES

1. This paper represents an extensively revised version of a
   seminar paper delivered in the University of Texas at
   Austin in March 1979. I am grateful for much helpful
   criticism received on that occasion.
2. A. W. H. Adkins, *Merit and Responsibility: A Study in
   Greek Values* (Oxford: Clarendon Press, 1960), hereafter
   referred to as *MR*.
3. Apart from the criticisms discussed in this paper, see also especially the review by R. Robinson, *Philosophy* 37
   (1962), 277-279.
4. Much has, of course, been written on the subject of
   Homeric morality since 1960; one may single out as examples
   Hugh Lloyd-Jones, *The Justice of Zeus* (Berkeley, Los
   Angeles, and London: University of California Press,
   1971); James M. Redfield, *Nature and Culture in the Iliad:
   The Tragedy of Hector* (Chicago and London: University of
   Chicago Press, 1975); Eric A. Havelock, *The Greek Concept
   of Justice: From Its Shadow in Homer to Its Reality in
   Plato* (Cambridge, Mass. and London: Harvard University
   Press, 1978). But although these add to, qualify, and
   correct Adkins, none attempts quite the same task, of giving a systematic description of the moral assumptions that
   underlie and, in part, determine the actions of the poems.

5. Compare the prediction made by J. R. Bambrough in his review of *MR*, *PhilosQ* 12 (1962), 367.

6. Among these are "'Friendship' and 'Self-Sufficiency' in Homer and Aristotle," *CQ* n.s. 13 (1963), 30-45; "Εὔχομαι, Εὐχώλη, and Εὖχος in Homer," *CQ* n.s. 19 (1969), 20-33; "Threatening, Abusing, and Feeling Angry in the Homeric Poems," *JHS* 89 (1969), 7-21; "Homeric Values and Homeric Society," *JHS* 91 (1971), 1-14; "Truth, Κόσμος, and 'Αρετή in the Homeric Poems," *CQ* n.s. 22 (1972), 5-18; and "Homeric Gods and the Values of Homeric Society," *JHS* 92 (1972), 1-19.

7. A. A. Long, "Morals and Values in Homer," *JHS* 90 (1970), 121-139, hereafter referred to as "Long."

8. E. R. Dodds, *The Greeks and the Irrational* (Berkeley, Los Angeles, and London: University of California Press, 1951), hereafter referred to as *GI*.

9. Adkins himself makes full acknowledgement of his debt to Dodds in his Preface.

10. "Homeric Values and Homeric Society" (above, note 6).

11. *GI*, pp. 17-18.

12. *GI*, p. 32.

13. *GI*, pp. 32-33.

14. J. K. Campbell's definition, cited by Lloyd-Jones, *The Justice of Zeus* (above, note 4), p. 25.

15. A broader, and probably more useful, definition is given in note 44 below.

16. *GI*, p. 37.

17. *MR*, p. 34.

18. *MR*, p. 49.

19. See, e.g., *GI*, p. 37.

20. *MR*, p. 36.

21. *MR*, pp. 36-37.

22. *MR*, p. 52.

23. Adkins, "'Friendship' and 'Self-sufficiency' in Homer and Aristotle," 34.

24. Adkins, "Homeric Values and Homeric Society," 4.

25. *MR*, p. 46.

26. *MR*, p. 55

27. *MR*, p. 65.

28. *MR*, p. 62.

29. *MR*, p. 70.

30. Long, 122.

31. Adkins in fact holds that the institutions and values de-
picted by Homer are indeed those of some real society,
both because of their internal consistency (which he supposes to be too great to have been merely invented by the
poetic tradition), and because of their alleged continuity
with later Greek values. M. I. Finley adds his voice in
support, on the basis of comparative evidence from other
cultures (*The World of Odysseus*, 2nd ed., rev. [New York:
Penguin, 1979], Appendix I). This general view may well
be correct; as Finley himself reminds us, however, the
Iliad and the *Odyssey* are not "sociological documents,"
but poems, and if we are to treat them at all as evidence
for a historical society, we must at the same time take
into account the distorting effect of Homer's aims as a
poet. In particular, it is surely clear that Homer delib-
erately paints his central figures too large; and this is
likely to have consequences for his overall picture of the
society within which their actions take place. The behavior and attitudes of an Achilles and an Odysseus are, at
least in part, a function of the distance that separates
them from ordinary humanity; and we cannot therefore
straightforwardly deduce from such figures what might have

been expected of individuals in a real Mycenaean or Dark
Age society. If so, then to the extent that it centers
around the heroes, "Homeric morality" is, as Long implies,
a construct, even though it may have its roots firmly in
reality.

32. "Shame rests on a concern with one's competence, potency
or power: it is expressive of a desire to avoid an appearance of failure, weakness or dependency" (A. Gouldner,
*Enter Plato: Classical Greece and the Origins of Social
Theory* [New York: Basic Books, 1965], p. 85). As this
definition suggests, the classification of Homeric society
as a "shame-culture" tells us not merely something about
the mechanisms possessed by that society for regulating
behavior, but also about the type of behavior these mechanisms support.

33. *Od*. 5.307.

34. *Il*. 5.211.

35. J. L. Creed, "Moral Values in the Age of Thucydides,"
CQ n.s. 23 (1973), 213-231, especially 214-215 (a partial
and not wholly convincing reply to Creed's points here is
given by Adkins in "Merit, Responsibility, and Thucydides,"
CQ n.s. 25 [1975], 209-220).

36. *MR*, p. 55.

37. Long, 123.

38. Ibid.

39. Long, 125.

40. Long, 126.

41. "Homeric Values and Homeric Society," 4 (emphasis mine).

42. Ibid., 3.

43. *The Justice of Zeus*, pp. 21-22.

44. Another example of such a wider grouping would be whatever forms of political association we should attribute to

Homeric society. The broadest description I find in
Adkins of the "group" whose security the *agathos* defends
is at "Homeric Values and Homeric Society," 5, where he
talks of the primary importance of the "group, *oikos* or
army-contingent" (emphasis mine). But the hero also regularly helps those in other contingents. (If anyone for
whom the *agathos* acts is to be counted as a *philos* in virtue of the fact, then Adkins' position would become empty:
the *agathos* acts [primarily] to defend the interests of
those whose interests he defends.)

45. Here I refer again to Gouldner's definition of the motive
of shame (see note 32 above). Lloyd-Jones insists that no
culture is ever exclusively a shame-culture or exclusively
a guilt-culture; but that is of course recognized by both
Dodds and Adkins. The basic question is whether the attitudes of the Homeric hero have more to do with "a concern
with one's competence, potency or power," or with "a concern with one's rectitude" ("guilt rests on a concern with
one's goodness or rectitude: it is expressive of a desire
to feel right," Gouldner, ibid.). Whether Achilles' feeling at the death of Patroclus is better described as
guilt, as Lloyd-Jones suggests, or rather as shame, is
difficult to say; perhaps it is both. But there can be no
doubt that in general a "quiet conscience" matters less to
the hero than assurance of his standing and power.

46. See, e.g., *MR*, p. 36, where "the security of the group"
and "the security of society" seem to be treated as equivalent terms.

47. Michael Gagarin seems to suggest that arbitration would
typically be based on simple compromise between competing
claims ("*Dikē* in the *Works and Days*," *CP* 68 [1973], 83);

but that is not the case in our best example of the procedure in Homer, the settlement of the dispute over the
chariot race in *Iliad* 23.

48. Adkins claims that the "quieter" virtues are valued only
for prudential reasons: they are valued "because, and insofar as, it is prudent to do so" ("Merit, Responsibility,
and Thucydides," 209). That may often be the case from
the point of view of the individual; but as I shall argue,
"society at large" may expect more of him.

49. Terence Irwin, *Plato's Moral Theory: The Early and
Middle Dialogues* (Oxford: Clarendon Press, 1977), pp. 15-
16.

50. "Homeric Values and Homeric Society," 9.

51. *Il.* 15.203; cf. 9.497, 13.115, 19.67f. and 182f.

52. Long, 126-128.

53. *Il.* 13.204. We might also think here of the slaughter of
the twelve Trojans on Patroclus' pyre; or in the *Odyssey*,
of the treatment meted out to Melanthius.

54. *Il.* 24.56ff.

55. *Il.* 24.52.

56. I take the term from Sir Kenneth Dover's *Greek Popular
Morality in the Time of Plato and Aristotle* (Oxford:
Blackwell, 1974), pp. 46-50. (Adkins replies to Dover's
criticisms of the "lexical approach" in his review article
on Dover's book in *CP* 73 [1978], 153; but he does not meet
the present point.)

57. *MR*, p. 38.

58. *MR*, p. 43.

59. "*Ou kalon*, then, . . . since it is not used to decry failure, is not an equivalent of *aischron* either in usage or
in emotive power," *MR*, p. 45.

60. *MR*, p. 42.

61. Zeus appears in Book 24 to add his voice to Athena's, when he declares (478-486) that it is "proper" (*epeoiken*) that the slaughter of the suitors should end the affair (so too by implication in 1.32-43, when he suggests that Aegisthus brought ruin on himself by his own *atasthaliai*-- if this term includes an idea of moral disapproval).

62. Some, e.g., Michael Gagarin, in his book *Aeschylean Drama* (Berkeley, Los Angeles, and London: University of California Press, 1976) and elsewhere, and Eric A. Havelock, in *The Concept of Justice* (above, note 4), have even claimed that Homer lacked a concept of "moral justice" altogether. I attacked this view at length in a companion paper to the present one, offered in Austin on the same occasion.

63. Nor is this merely a matter of their failing to observe the proprieties of feasting (cf. Finley, *The World of Odysseus* [above, note 31], p. 124); that would scarcely account for the virulence with which they are condemned, or for the comparison of them with Aegisthus.

64. Adkins may be right in saying that in Homer "one has no rights *qua* human being" ("Homeric Values and Homeric Society," 11): if there are clear rules governing behavior within the context of given social relationships, there are in general few which regulate one's behavior towards mankind generally (though one should not forget here the generous emotions that can be felt by the heroes: the kindness of Patroclus, which is heavily contrasted with the fierceness and cruelty of Achilles, or the pity that even Achilles himself feels, finally, towards Priam). But one does have "rights" in some sense *qua* possessor of *timē*, as indeed the very logic of the concept entails.

List of Contributors

Norman Austin is Professor of Classics and Head of the Department of Classics at the University of Arizona.

Ann L. T. Bergren is Associate Professor of Classics at the University of California, Los Angeles.

E. D. Francis is Associate Professor of Classics at The University of Texas at Austin.

Richard Hope Simpson is Professor of Classics at Queen's University, Kingston, Canada.

Mabel L. Lang is Paul Shorey Professor of Greek at Bryn Mawr College, where she is also Chairman of the Department of Greek.

Gareth Morgan is Professor of Classics and Education at The University of Texas at Austin.

Gregory Nagy is Professor of Classics at Harvard University.

James M. Redfield is Professor of Greek and Social Thought at the University of Chicago.

C. J. Rowe is Lecturer in Classics at Bristol University, England.

Carl A. Rubino is Associate Professor of Classics at The University of Texas at Austin.

Cynthia W. Shelmerdine is Assistant Professor of Classics at The University of Texas at Austin.